AF522228

SOCIAL CHANGE IN MODERN INDIA

SOCIAL CHANGE IN MODERN INDIA

Dr. Suresh Chandra

JNANADA PRAKASHAN (P&D)
NEW DELHI

Published by :
JNANADA PRAKASHAN (P&D)
4837/2, 24, Ansari Road, Daryaganj
New Delhi-110002
Phone : 011-23272047
Mobile : 9212137080
Email: jnanadabooksdelhi@yahoo.com
Website: www.jnanadabooks.com; text.ind.in

Assisted by :
TEXT BOOK PROMOTION SOCIETY OF INDIA
4837/2, 24, Ansari Road, Daryaganj
New Delhi-110002
Phone : 011-23272047
Mobile : 9212137080

First Edition : 2018

Social Change in Modern India

ISBN : 978-81-7139-439-5

Typesetting by :
Vardhman Computers
New Delhi-110 017, India

Published by Mrs. S. Chowdhary for M/s. Jnanada Prakashan (P&D) Daryaganj, Ansari Road, New Delhi-110002, India and printed at Balaji Offset, Navin Shahdara, Delhi-110032, India.

PREFACE

Social change is the result of various forces and factors involved in the process of modernization of traditional society. Different theories have been propounded to examine the nature and scope of social change in modern India.

The book entitled "Social Change in Modern India" is a comprehensive and critical analysis of the process of social transformation in India. The very first chapter deals with the various issues associated with the concept of social change. The study of different theories of social change has been made in the second chapter. Social movements play a decisive role in the process of social change. The study of the different social movements like the non-violent approach adopted by Mahatma Gandhi in the form of Satyagraha in India and the Civil Rights Movement led by Martin Luther King in the United States of America has been made in the third chapter.

Socialism had played an important role in social change. A particular focus has been made on the evolution of socialism in the fourth chapter. The study of the relationship between socialism and religion is the part of the fifth chapter. In the wake of globalisation, there has been a phenomenal rise in the number of non-governmental organisations. It has emerged as a major instrument of social change. The study of the role of non-governmental organisation has been the integral part of the sixth chapter.

The study of modernisation in India has been done from various perspectives like the socio-economic, cultural and the economic ones. The seventh chapter makes a thorough investigation of the process of modernisation in India.

Democracy has been an important political method for bringing out social change in India. The study of the role of democracy in the context of social change forms the part of the eighth chapter.

In the process of modernisation, modern Indian family system has encountered enormous challenges. The various challenges faced by the modern Indian family system has been examined in the final chapter. The author in fully convinced that this work would be an important contribution to the literature on social change in modern India.

CONTENTS

1

CONCEPTUAL FRAMEWORK OF SOCIAL CHANGE

Concept of Social Exclusion

It is useful to begin with the recognition that the idea of social exclusion has conceptual connections with well-established notions in the literature on poverty and deprivation, and has antecedents that are far older than the specific history of the terminology might suggest. Indeed, we can appreciate more fully the contribution made by the new literature on social exclusion by placing it in the broader context of the old—very aged—idea of poverty as capability deprivation. That connection with a very general approach will help us to appreciate the particular emphasis and central concerns that the specific idea of social exclusion helps to illuminate.

So let us start far back—in the realm of concepts and ideas. First, consider the characterisation of poverty as simply shortage of income, which is, of course, very ancient and still fairly common in the established literature on deprivation and destitution. This view, which is rather far removed from the relational notion of social exclusion, is not, however, entirely without merit, since income—properly defined—has an enormous influence on the kind of lives we can lead. The impoverishment of our lives results frequently from the inadequacy of income, and in this sense, low income must be an important cause of poor living. And yet—as the last argument itself suggests—ultimately poverty must be seen in terms of poor living, rather than just as lowness of incomes (and "nothing else").

Income may be the most prominent means for a good life without deprivation, but it is not the only influence on the lives we can lead. If our paramount interest is in the lives that people can lead—the freedom they have to lead minimally decent lives—then it cannot but be a mistake to concentrate exclusively only on one or other of the *means* to such freedom. We must look at impoverished lives, and not just at depleted wallets.

Indeed, the Aristotelian account of the richness of human life was explicitly linked to the necessity to "first ascertain the function of man," followed by exploring "life in the sense of activity." In this Aristotelian perspective, an impoverished life is one without the freedom to undertake important activities that a person has reason to choose. Poverty of living received systematic attention also in the early empirical works on the quality of life by such pioneering investigators as William Petty, Gregory King, Francois Quesnay, Antoine Lavoisier, Joseph Louis Lagrange, and others. Adam Smith too felt impelled to define "necessaries" in terms of their effects on the freedom to live non-impoverished lives, such as "the ability to appear in public without shame". Thus, the view of poverty as capability deprivation (that is, poverty seen as the lack of the capability to live a minimally decent life) has a far-reaching analytical history. As it happens, it has also been much explored in the contemporary literature.

The capability perspective on poverty is inescapably multi-dimensional, since there are distinct capabilities and functionings that we have reason to value. It is suggested that it is useful to investigate the literature on "social exclusion" using this broadly Aristotelian approach.

First, we have good reason to value not being excluded from social relations, and in this sense, social exclusion may be directly a part of capability poverty. Indeed, Adam Smith's focus on the deprivation involved in not "being able to appear in public without shame" is a good example of a capability deprivation that takes the form of social exclusion. This relates to the importance of taking part in the life of the community, and ultimately to the Aristotelian understanding that the individual lives an inescapably "social" life. Smith's general point that the inability to interact freely with others is an important deprivation in itself (like being undernourished or homeless), and has the implication that some types of social exclusion must be seen as constitutive components of the idea of poverty—indeed, must be counted among its core components.

Second, being excluded from social relations can lead to other deprivations as well, thereby, further limiting our living opportunities. For example, being excluded from the opportunity to be employed or to receive credit may lead to economic impoverishment that may, in turn, lead to other deprivations such as undernourishment or homelessness. Social exclusion can, thus, be *constitutively a part* of capability deprivation as well as *instrumentally a cause* of diverse capability failures. The case for seeing social exclusion as an approach to poverty is easy enough to establish within the general perspective of poverty as capability failure.

These connections are important to seize, especially since the idea of social exclusion (in the distinctive form of a free-standing concept) has had, as was mentioned earlier, a relatively late entry into the literature of poverty and deprivation. Indeed, its early stirrings—attributed to the writings in the 1970s—were about two hundred years after Adam Smith's (1776) pioneering exposition of deprivation in the form of "inability to appear in public without shame," and more generally, of the difficulty experienced by deprived people in taking part in the life of the community. Once the literature of social exclusion is placed in the general perspective of capability failure, it can be seen as articulating and investigating important issues that have been discussed for hundreds—indeed thousands—of years. We are not dealing with an upstart concept that somehow has escaped notice: a concept that can only be championed by new researchers, to use Else Oyen's crushing phrase, "running all over the place arranging seminars and conferences to find a researchable content in an umbrella concept for which there is limited theoretical underpinning." Rather, we are considering the merits of focusing particularly on relational features that would enrich the broad approach of seeing poverty as the lack of freedom to do certain valuable things—an approach the theoretical underpinning of which has been extensively discussed and scrutinised. By establishing the historical connection, we not only link the literature of social exclusion with earlier ideas, but we also strengthen its conceptual basis and analytical discipline.

Indeed, an advantage of this approach to social exclusion is that it immediately provides a non-ad hoc foundation for the issues involved in this large and somewhat unruly literature. However, we have to be careful that by placing the literature of social exclusion in this conceptually structured approach, we do not end up losing anything valuable in the idea of social exclusion that cannot be adequately captured in the capability framework.

Relational Features in Capability Deprivation

If the analysis presented above is correct, the real importance of the idea of social exclusion lies in emphasising the role of relational features in the deprivation of capability and thus in the experience of poverty. Here too the crucial issue is not the novelty in focusing on relational features (Adam Smith did the same in the eighteenth century, as have others before and after him), but the *focusing* that the social exclusion literature can provide in giving a central role to relational connections.

Adam Smith was much concerned with relational deprivations that would impoverish human lives in an absolute way. The idea of social exclusion fits well into this framework. Indeed, a good part of *The Wealth of Nations* is concerned with the instrumental importance of exclusion, and involves analysis of the effects of particular types of exclusion, for example people being kept out of markets (through legislation) or out of education (through lack of private means and public support). But, in addition, Smith also discussed, with great clarity, constitutively relevant relational deprivations. He investigated the characteristics of social exclusion within a broader concept of deprivation in the form of inability to do things that one has reason to want to do.

Smith placed the ideas of inclusion and exclusion at the centre of poverty analysis when he defined the nature of "necessaries" for leading a decent life:

> By necessaries I understand not only the commodities which are indispensably necessary for the support of life, but what ever the custom of the country renders it indecent for creditable people, even the lowest

> order, to be without....Custom has rendered leather shoes a necessary of life in England. The poorest creditable person of either sex would be ashamed to appear in public without them.

Here Smith is concerned with deprivation in the form of exclusion from social interaction, such as appearing in public freely, or—more generally— taking part in the life of the community.

The relational nature of these capabilities links the two concepts—capability failure and social exclusion. The importance of the new literature lies, thus, in the focusing achieved, and not so much *either* in seeing social exclusion as a free-standing concept of poverty (rather than as its being part and parcel of the more general approach of capability deprivation), *or* even in the newness of the idea of being concerned with relational features.

But, is there something being missed in seeing social exclusion as a part of the general approach of capability deprivation with a particular focus on relational causation? Doubts of this kind may be fed by the belief that the literature of social exclusion transcends altogether the narrow limits of capability analysis. This issue is, indeed, worth considering and scrutinising with care. Take, for example, the important issue raised by Charles Gore in identifying the special merit of the social-exclusion approach:

> Seen as a relational concept, it offers a way of completing the shift away from a welfarist view of social disadvantage which Amartya Sen has begun, but which, in the guise of the concept of capabilities, still remains wedded to an excessively individualist, and insufficiently social view.

Gore is certainly right in seeing the focus on relational features to be a great merit of the approach of social exclusion. But, in what sense is the capability perspective bound to miss these relational connections and doomed to be excessively individualist and insufficiently social? While the individual is seen as the person to whom relational deprivation occurs as it is in the literature on social exclusion, the focus of capability analysis—right from the time of its Smithian formulations—has been very sensitive to the social causes of individual deprivation. For example, both concern with the capability to take part in the life of the community or the more specific capability to appear in public without shame and the causal factors that are seen as influencing such capabilities cannot but be inescapably "social," and have been seen as such. What can more legitimately be seen as a point of departure is not the *acknowledgement* of the idea of relational connections, but the *focusing* on it.

The helpfulness of the social exclusion approach does not lie, in its conceptual newness, but in its practical influence in forcefully emphasising—and focusing attention on—the role of relational features in deprivation. As it happens, many types of exclusionary issues have been integral parts of the development literature for a long time. The issues covered have included deprivations of constitutive importance (whether or not placed in the framework of capability failure), but also instrumentally crucial deprivations. Traditional development analyses have variously addressed such concepts as "exit, voice, and loyalty", "urban bias", the major role of landlessness and credit unavailability the exclusion of women from economic activities of certain types and the lack of opportunity to meet basic needs for substantial sections of the population. To examine these issues in terms of social exclusion can be helpful enough in providing a focused discussion, but it is to investigative advantage rather than to conceptual departure that we have to look to see the major merits of the new literature on social exclusion.

Conceptual novelty is not the real issue in appreciating the creative contribution of the new literature on social exclusion; cogency is. Seen in its proper context, the idea of social exclusion has much to offer, and the new literature has already brought out many important connections that had been neglected in earlier studies of poverty and deprivation.

Language of Exclusion

Social exclusion can, indeed, arise in a variety of ways, and it is important to recognise the versatility of the idea and its reach. However, there is also a need for caution in not using the term too indiscriminately (by skilfully using the language of social exclusion to describe every kind of deprivation—whether or not relational features are important in its genesis). Indeed, the language of exclusion is so versatile and adaptable that there may be a temptation to dress up every deprivation as a case of social exclusion. There is, some evidence in the vast—and rapidly growing—literature on social exclusion that the language has run well ahead of the creative ideas involved.

For reasons of intellectual clarity, there is a strong case for exercising conceptual discrimination, going beyond linguistic similarity. Sure enough, the exclusionary perspective can be very useful in some contexts, but it can also be linguistically invoked even when it adds little to what is already well understood without reference to relational features. Investigative usefulness is partly a matter of judgement, but it is important that critical scrutiny is exercised in deciding whether to invoke the powerful—sometimes bewitching—rhetoric of social exclusion.

An example may help to illustrate the distinction. Consider the deprivation involved in being hungry or starving. It is easy enough to use the language of exclusion to say that involuntary starvation (as opposed to fasting) "can be seen as being excluded from access to food." Such a sentence makes good sense, but it does not, in itself, add anything much to what we already knew, to wit, the involuntarily hungry do not get enough food to eat. Since the real merit in using the language of exclusion is to draw attention to the relational features in a deprivation, it is crucial to ask whether a relational deprivation has been responsible for a particular case of starvation or hunger.

There are, of course, relational features that may be central to a case of hunger. First, since food is often used—especially in many traditional societies—as a means of social intercourse (celebrations, mournings, or even standard communications may depend on food being served to guests), a family may suffer from food shortage precisely because of the constitutively relational role of exchange of food. Second, even in having enough food for consumption within the family, causal influences may relate to relational features in a significant way. For example, when some groups are made to go hungry when other groups command most of the food (through bureaucratic arrangements or through superior market power), then there is a sense in which the idea of exclusion can be seen to be relevant even in examining a deprivation that is not constitutively of the relational kind. Such "food battles" can be an important element in the causation of hunger when supply is inflexible, and cases of this kind have received attention in the context of studies of famines and undernourishment.

With relational deprivations that are not constitutively significant, it is necessary to see whether any process that can be helpfully called "exclusion" is playing a significant part in causally generating other deprivations that may be ultimately important. This leads to a typology of causation that can be sensibly and fruitfully used to supplement the analysis of traditionally recognised deprivations.

For example, hunger and starvation relate to entitlement failure that can result from a variety of causes. To consider a few alternative cases, take the following:

(1) hunger caused by a crop failure that makes a peasant family lose its traditional food supply;

(2) hunger resulting from unemployment through the loss of purchasing power;

(3) hunger induced by a fall in real wages as a result of relative price changes, resulting from asymmetric increase in the economic power of, and increased food demand from, other groups; and

(4) hunger precipitated by the removal of food subsidies to a particular group on which that group may standardly rely.

While each of these developments can be described in the language of exclusion, to wit, respectively: (1) being excluded from enjoying a normal crop, (2) being excluded from employment, (3) exclusion from the food market because of low purchasing power, (4) exclusion from food subsidy arrangements, they involve quite different causal patterns, some of which are more fruitfully described in the language of exclusion than others.

For example, the removal of food subsidies to an excluded group involves an active form of exclusion that is central to the development in question. On the other side, the failure of a crop from which a peasant family suffers is not easily seen as an exclusion—or even as a relational failure—in a significant way (no matter what liberty our language may give us to dress up any failure as an "exclusion").

Hunger resulting from unemployment raises a more difficult issue. In some contexts a person's inability to get a job may be helpfully analysed in terms of exclusion, for example when the available employment tends to be reserved for—or allocated to—people of particular types, leaving out others. This can be important in understanding, say, high levels of unemployment of minority groups, or women, in societies which reserve the jobs—or at least the better jobs—to majority groups or to men. But, in general, the *causation* of unemployment need not be seen to be resulting invariably—or even typically—from any exclusionary process. Whether hunger resulting from unemployment can be helpfully analysed in terms of instrumentally important social exclusion would, thus, depend on the exact nature of the causal processes involved.

The inability of a person to buy enough food because of a fall in his or her real wages again requires more causal probing to see whether the idea of exclusion will be usefully employed or not in that particular context. What made the real wages fall? Since such declines in real wages have often been causally connected even with famines, causal analysis here can be particularly important. To cite a particular example, the decline in the real wages of rural labourers that played a crucial part in the genesis of the Bengal famine of 1943 was closely connected with the asymmetric nature of the war-expenditure-based boom in the economy of Bengal— a boom that boosted the incomes of many urban dwellers but excluded the rural labourers. The analysis of entitlement failure of rural labourers can be fitted into a reasoning in which the idea of exclusion can be given a useful part. And the same applies, to an even greater extent, to the entitlement failure of fishermen and river-based transport workers, since they suffered not only from being left out of the war boom, but also from the British Raj's decision to sink the normally-used boats in the area, which it feared would be soon overrun by the invading Japanese army. This did not do much to hinder the already overstretched Japanese army, but it surely did actively exclude many fishermen and boat operators from carrying out their normal business.

The real relevance of an exclusionary perspective is, thus, conditional on the nature of the process that leads to deprivation—in this case, to a sharp fall in the purchasing power of the affected population. This kind of discrimination is important to undertake in order to separate out (1) the conceptual contribution that the idea of social exclusion can make and the constructive role it can play, and (2) the use of social exclusion merely as language and rhetoric. Both can be effective, but conceptual creativity must not be confused with just linguistic extension.

Constitutive and Instrumental Importance of Social Relations

In this section and in the next one, I investigate two particular *distinctions* within the general category of social exclusion. The distinction between the two ways in which social exclusion can lead to capability deprivation is worth clarifying more precisely and also worth investigating further.

Being excluded can sometimes be in itself a deprivation and this can be of intrinsic importance on its own. For example, not being able to relate to others and to take part in the life of the community can directly impoverish a person's life. It is a loss on its own, in addition to whatever further deprivation it may indirectly generate. This is a case of *constitutive relevance* of social exclusion.

In contrast, there are relational deprivations that are not in themselves terrible, but which can lead to very bad results. For example, not using the credit market need not be seen by all to be intrinsically distasteful. Some do, of course, enjoy borrowing or lending, while others do not feel this to be a matter of inherent importance one way or the other, while still others are happy enough to follow Polonius's advice: "Neither a borrower, nor a lender be." But, not to have access to the credit market can, through causal linkages, lead to *other* deprivations, such as income poverty, or the inability to take up interesting opportunities that might have been both fulfilling and enriching but which may require an initial investment and use of credit. Causally significant exclusions of this kind can have great *instrumental importance:* they may not be impoverishing in themselves, but they can lead to impoverishment of human life through their causal consequences, such as the denial of social and economic opportunities that would be helpful for the persons involved.

Landlessness is similarly an instrumental deprivation. A family without land in a peasant society may be deeply handicapped. Of course, given the age-old value system in peasant societies, landlessness can also have constitutive importance in a world that values a family's special relation with its land: to be without land may seem like being without a limb of one's own. But, whether or not a family attaches direct value to its relation with its "own land," landlessness can also help to generate economic and social deprivations. Indeed, the alienation of land has been—appropriately enough—a much-discussed problem in the development literature.

Clearly, particular relational deprivations may, easily enough, have both constitutive and instrumental importance. For example, not to be able to mix with others may directly impoverish a person's life, and also, additionally, reduce economic opportunities that come from social contact. Indeed, quite often different aspects of capability deprivation and social exclusion may go together. However, they can also appear singly, and as and when they are relevant, we have to pay attention to each possibility within the general categories of constitutively important deprivations and instrumentally significant handicaps. When a deprivation does not have constitutively relational importance, it may still be fruitful, in many cases, to use the perspective of social exclusion, on instrumental grounds, to analyse it, *if* the causal process can be better understood through invoking the idea of exclusion. The nature of the causal process is crucial for deciding the relevance of each perspective.

Active and Passive Exclusion

The distinction between constitutive relevance and instrumental importance is only one of the distinctions that can be fruitfully used to understand and analyse the nature and reach of social exclusion. Another potentially useful distinction is that between *active* and *passive* exclusion. When, for example, immigrants or refugees are not given a usable political status, it is an active exclusion, and this applies to many of the deprivations from which minority communities suffer in Europe and Asia and elsewhere. When, however, the deprivation comes about through social processes in which there is no deliberate attempt to exclude, the exclusion can be seen as a passive kind. A good example is provided by poverty and isolation generated by a sluggish economy and a consequent accentuation of poverty. Both active and passive exclusions may be important, but they are not important in the same way.

The distinction can be relevant for causal analysis as well as for policy response. Relational exclusions may, in some cases, be brought about by a deliberate policy to exclude some people from some opportunities. For example, the decision of the United States Congress a couple of years ago to exclude permanent residents who were not US citizens from certain types of federal benefits was clearly an *active* exclusion, since it came about through policies directly aimed at that result.

In contrast, the macroeconomic circumstances that may lead to a significant level of unemployment may not have been devised to bring about that result. Also, when particular groups—such as the young and the less skilled—suffer especially from being left out of the employment process, it is possible that the economic conditions causing that result (and even the economic policies precipitating those conditions) may not have been, in any sense, aimed at excluding these vulnerable groups from employment. The absence of direct aiming does not, of course, absolve the government involved from responsibility, since it has to consider what bad things are happening in the economy and how they can be prevented and not merely the things that are directly "caused" by its own policies. Nevertheless, for causal analysis, it may be important to distinguish between the active fostering of an exclusion—whether done by the government or by any other wilful agent—and a passive development of an exclusion that may result from a set of circumstances without such volitional immediacy.

Sometimes, an active exclusion can bring about other exclusionary consequences that were not part of the plan of exclusion but nevertheless are results of the directly aimed exclusion, even though they may not have been clearly anticipated or not at all foreseen. Let us illustrate this with an example of political exclusion in Europe that has, received less attention than it deserves.

Recently, the targeting of settled immigrant population in Germany and France by right-wing extremists has received much political attention. The question is sometimes raised as to why Britain has, to a great extent, escaped this problem, even though decades ago when the large-scale immigration took place, Britain had strong anti-immigrant sentiments as well. But, in the event, those sentiments seem not to have caused the kind of flourishing of right-wing extremism and severe targeting of immigrants that have occurred in Germany and France.

It is generally argued argue that the explanation lies partly in the political exclusion from voting rights from which most of the settled immigrants in Germany and France suffer. Indeed, in much of Europe, legally settled immigrants do not have the political right to vote because of the difficulties and delays in acquiring citizenship. This keeps them outside the political process in a systematic way—this is clearly an *active exclusion.* In France, the required qualification for acquiring French citizenship is quite exacting. In Germany the situation is worse, in this respect; German citizenship is very difficult to obtain even for the long-run residents from elsewhere. This political exclusion results in disenfranchisement of the immigrants, even long-term settled immigrants, and this in turn makes their social integration that much harder. However, since the first version of this paper was presented in September 1998, the newly elected German government has declared its intention to ease the process of acquiring voting rights by settled immigrants. If the argument presented here is correct, this change, if carried out, will contribute to the integration of the settled immigrant population with the rest of the population of the country and also help to reduce the political targeting of the immigrant population by anti-immigrant activists.

Because of an imperial tradition, taken over by the Commonwealth, the right to vote is determined in the United Kingdom not exclusively by British citizenship, but also by the citizenship of the Commonwealth. Indeed, any citizen of the Commonwealth—any subject of the Queen as the head of the Commonwealth—immediately acquires voting rights in Britain on being accepted for settlement. Since most of the nonwhite immigrants to Britain have come from the Commonwealth countries (such as the West Indies, India, Pakistan, Bangladesh, Nigeria, Ghana, Kenya, and Uganda), they have had the right of political participation in Britain immediately on arrival on a permanent basis. The absence of this political exclusion has the effect of drawing the settled immigrants directly into British politics, where their votes are sought and taken into account.

If right-wing extremists in Germany make strongly anti-immigrant statements, they do not lose the votes of immigrants (who have none), whereas they pick up votes of those who are inclined in the same anti-immigrant direction. In Britain, in contrast, such statements would immediately bring in a backlash from immigrant voters, even when they are not British citizens. This has made the British political parties quite keen on wooing the immigrant vote, and this clearly has served as a brake on the earlier attempts at racist politics in Britain. It is commonly argued that this is certainly among the reasons why Britain has, to a great extent, been able to avoid the persistence of racist extremism that had threatened the country in the early postwar years. The political incentive to seek support from immigrant communities (rather than "targeting" them for attack) has been a factor of some importance both in the political freedom and in the social integration of immigrants in Britain. The exploitation of "the immigrant issue" in French or German politics turns on the asymmetric political power of the anti-immigrants over the settled immigrants.

Even though the political exclusion of immigrants from voting rights was not devised to bring about the kind of social exclusion related to anti-immigrant extremism that one sees in Germany and France, it seems plausible to argue that the active political exclusion has had the effect of helping further social exclusion in those countries. Since the issues of political integration and of voting rights also arise in other parts of the world, including in Asia, this connection between active and passive exclusions may have a much wider relevance than the European nature of this example may initially suggest.

Unemployment and Exclusion

In investigating the reach of the idea of social exclusion, it is useful to examine the specific role of economic events of the kind that may be particularly associated with the development of an excluded population. An especially apt example is the important phenomenon of long-term unemployment. Indeed, in contemporary Europe, the extraordinary prevalence of unemployment and worklessness is perhaps the single most important contributor to the persistence of social exclusion in a large and momentous scale. With double-digit unemployment rates across many countries in Europe (running between 10 and 12 percent of the workforce in France and Germany as well as Italy, and higher in Spain), the basis of self-reliant and self-confident economic existence of a great many Europeans is severely undermined. This is in sharp contrast not only with the contemporary experience of other economically developed countries, including Japan and the United States (with very much lower unemployment), but also with Europe's own achievements of remarkably low unemployment not so long ago (with unemployment rates between 1 and 3 percent).

Oddly enough, the state of affairs with persistently high unemployment seems to have become "acceptable" in Europe— feeble protests are typically combined with remarkable resignation. There is also an insufficient acknowledgement of the torments and disintegrations caused by high levels of unemployment and inadequate assessment of different types of social exclusion that are brought about by the persistence of high levels of unemployment. We have to take fuller note of the many different ways in which the wide prevalence of joblessness blights lives and liberties in Europe.

The point is sometimes made that unemployment is not—"any longer"—really such a social problem in Europe because of a functioning social security system that offers unemployment insurance and income support for all. This argument is deeply defective for several distinct reasons. First, social security and unemployment insurance cost public money, and the fiscal burden involved has many adverse consequences on the operation of the economy. Second, the evil effects of unemployment are not confined only to the lowness of income with which jobless may be associated. To compensate for the lost income (or, more accurately, for a part of the lost income) does not do away with the other losses that also result from the persistence of unemployment. Some of these losses can be more fully understood in the perspective of social exclusion.

Let us list some of the other effects—other than the loss of income associated with unemployment. Some of these effects can be helpfully analysed with the help of the idea of social exclusion.

Loss of Current Output: Unemployment involves wasting of productive power, since a part of the potential national output is not realised because of unemployment. This magnitude can clearly be quite large when unemployment rates are very high.

Skill Loss and Long-run Damages: People not only "learn by doing," they also "unlearn" by "not doing," that is, by being out of work and out of practice. Also, in addition to the depreciation of skill through nonpractice, unemployment may generate loss of cognitive abilities as a result of the unemployed person's loss of confidence and sense of control. In so far as this leads to the emergence of a less skilled group—with merely a memory of good skill—there is a phenomenon here that can lead to a future social exclusion from the job market.

Loss of Freedom and Social Exclusion: Taking a broader view of poverty, the nature of the deprivation of the unemployed includes the loss of freedom as a result of joblessness. A person stuck in a state of unemployment, even when materially supported by social insurance, does not get to exercise much freedom of decision, and attitudinal studies have brought out the extent to which this loss of freedom is seen by many unemployed people as a central deprivation. Unemployment can be a major causal factor predisposing people to social exclusion. The exclusion applies not only to economic opportunities, such as job-related insurance, and to pension and medical entitlements, but also to social activities, such as participation in the life of the community, which may be quite problematic for jobless people.

Psychological Harm and Misery: Unemployment can play havoc with the lives of the jobless, and cause intense suffering and mental agony. Empirical studies of unemployment have brought out how serious this effect can be. Indeed, high unemployment is often associated even with elevated rates of *suicide,* which is an indicator of the perception of unbearability that the victims experience. The effect of *prolonged* joblessness can be especially damaging for the morale.

Youth unemployment can take a particularly high toll, leading to a long-run loss of self-esteem of young workers and would-be workers such as school leavers. There is some considerable evidence that this damaging effect is particularly severe for young women and it has to be examined whether a similar thing would apply to Europe as well. Youth unemployment has become a problem of increasing seriousness in Europe, and the present pattern of European joblessness is quite heavily biased in the direction of the young. The connection with the emergence of a problem of social exclusion is obvious enough.

Ill-health and Mortality: Unemployment can also lead to clinically identifiable illnesses and to higher rates of mortality (not just through more suicide). This can, to some extent, be the result of loss of income and material means, but the connection also works through the dejection and lack of self-respect and motivation generated by persistent unemployment. This is not, in itself, a problem of social exclusion, but of course ill health can make social relations much more problematic. So there is an indirect connection here.

Loss of Human Relations: Unemployment can be very disruptive of social relations and of family life. It may also weaken the general harmony and coherence within the family. To some extent these consequences relate to the decline of self-confidence (in addition to the drop in economic means), but the loss of an organised working life can also generate problems of its own. This is a relational failure and, thus, within the immediate domain of social exclusion.

Motivational Loss and Future Work: The discouragement that is induced by unemployment can lead to a weakening of motivations and can make the long-term unemployed very dejected and passive. There is clearly some psychological potential here for a motivational collapse that can be devastating on its own and also conducive to further social exclusion later on. The "social psychological" effects of unemployment include the breeding of further unemployment in the future. The impact of prolonged unemployment can be severe in weakening the distinction between (i) being "in the labour force but unemployed," and (ii) being "out of the labour force." The empirical relevance of the distinction between these states and possible transitions from the former state to the latter can be important for the future of the economy as well as the predicaments of the particular persons involved.

Gender and Racial Inequality: Unemployment can also be a significant causal influence in heightening ethnic tensions as well as gender divisions. When jobs are scarce, the groups most affected are often the minorities, especially parts of the immigrant communities. This worsens the prospects of easy integration of legal immigrants into the regular life of the mainstream of the society. Furthermore, since immigrants are often seen as people competing for employment or "taking away" jobs from others, unemployment feeds the politics of intolerance and racism. This issue has figured prominently in recent elections in some European countries, and it is obviously connected with a type of social exclusion.

Gender divisions too are hardened by extensive unemployment, particularly because the entry of women into the labour force is often particularly hindered in times of general unemployment. Also, as was mentioned earlier, the discouraging effects of youth unemployment have been found to be particularly serious for young girls, whose re-entry into the labour market, after a bout of unemployment, is more impeded by early experiences of joblessness.

Weakening of Social Values: There is also evidence that large-scale unemployment has a tendency to weaken some social values. People in continued unemployment can develop cynicism about the fairness of social arrangements, and also a perception of dependence on others. These effects are not conducive to responsibility and self-reliance. The observed association of crimes with youth unemployment is, of course, substantially influenced by the material deprivation of the jobless, but a part is played in that connection also by psychological influences, including a sense of exclusion and a feeling of grievance against a world that does not give the jobless an opportunity to earn an honest living. In general, social cohesion faces many difficult problems in a society that is firmly divided between a majority of people with comfortable jobs and a minority—a *large* minority—of unemployed, wretched, and aggrieved human beings. The engendered sense of isolation may be psychological, but the exclusion resulting from it may be no less real for that reason.

Long though this list is, there are other effects that can also be considered (Sen, 1997a). It should, however, be clear from the list of problems identified here that the persistence of unemployment can cause deprivation in many distinct ways, some of which are emphatically relational and can be sensibly investigated as a part of the process of social exclusion associated with unemployment. The relational exclusions associated directly with unemployment can have constitutive importance through the connection of unemployment with social alienation, but they can also have instrumental significance because of the effects that unemployment may cause in leading to deprivations of other kinds.

Persistent unemployment can, indeed, be an important source of deprivation of capability to live satisfactory lives. While we have particularly emphasised the problem of massive unemployment in Europe, similar issues are important in Asia and Africa as well, even though the overwhelming fact of economic poverty—in the form of low incomes— sometimes leads to the neglect of these problems in social and economic analyses. Even though the European literature on social exclusion has been driven by the European context, it has made an important suggestive contribution to the possibility of analysing poverty in other regions with greater interest in constitutive deprivation associated with exclusions of various types. There are reasons to be grateful for this, while not being overwhelmed by these newer concerns in a way that may lead to the neglect of the Afro-Asian focus on more rudimentary and grosser aspects of general poverty.

European Origin, Universal Importance, and Asian Use

The possibility of variations in regional concerns, briefly touched upon in the last section, is an important issue to address in examining the relevance of the new literature on social exclusion—developed particularly in Europe—for use in other parts of the world, including Asia. In its modern form, the notion of "social exclusion" has had a distinctly European—indeed specifically French—origin. This recognition raises two different types of questions. First, is the European origin, with its cultural specificity, a barrier to the use of the concept elsewhere, including in Asia? Second, does the European, and in particular French, origin give it a conceptual lineage that is worth tracing in assessing the richness of the idea? Also, since the literature on social exclusion has been mainly concerned with problems in European countries, it could be asked whether that literature has anything significant to offer to Asia or Africa.

We consider the second question first. While the French origin may be thought to be entirely accidental, it is, in fact, quite useful not to dismiss this fact altogether. France is a country quite unlike any other, and French culture is a very distinctive part of European civilisation, with a very specific history of events and ideas, including the French Enlightenment and the French Revolution which changed the nature of the world in which we live. Is that specific history of ideas and occurrences important in understanding the demands and reach of the notion of "social exclusion"?

There may well be an important connection here. The demands for "liberty, equality, and fraternity" in the French Revolution and in the related developments in the eighteenth century Enlightenment have had profound influence on the intellectual history of the modern world. The implications of these demands have been variously interpreted in the development of the contemporary world, and the interrelation between these ideas has been intensely investigated.

We would like to argue that the concern for *fraternity* leads to the need for avoiding "exclusion" from the community of people, just as the concern for *equality* pushes us in the direction of a commitment to avoid "poverty." Needless to say, the masculine form of the term "fraternity" (particularly reinforced in the US by the oddities of male communal living in some American universities) is not material here, and should in fact be shunned in extending and generalising this concept, indeed the French revolutionaries did not really aim particularly at male exclusivism, despite the masculine form of the language.

Equality is concerned with *comparisons* of different persons' opportunities, and if we focus, in that context, on the deprivation of opportunities, we move in the direction of the idea of poverty, in particular, to poverty as capability deprivation. In a similar way, fraternity is concerned with the *interrelation* between the opportunities enjoyed by different members of the community, and if we focus instead on the absence of such interrelations, we move in the direction of the idea of social exclusion. This way of looking at the different concepts suggests that we should expect that ideas of poverty and social exclusion would be closely linked (just as equality and fraternity are), without being congruent with each other (just as equality and fraternity are not). The relational failure with which social exclusion is concerned can be seen to be a constitutively significant deprivation ("fraternity" has, here, a directly evaluative importance), and it can also lead to other kinds of deprivation (the failure of fraternal symmetry can be, in many cases, a cause of poverty and inequality of other kinds). The uses to which these concepts can be put in the practical literature are not unrelated to these deeper concerns in European—and French—intellectual history.

The richness of these traditions adds to the importance of the approach of social exclusion, but it would be a mistake to take these norms to be specifically European—or exclusively French—in a way that would not relate to human values in other cultures. We live in a world in which many values that received wholesome formulation and eloquent expression in the Enlightenment literature have become part and parcel of contemporary living. It is indeed possible both to acknowledge and celebrate the particular intellectual history involved in the genesis of these ideas in France and elsewhere and also to accept the claim of these values to be of universal importance. Indeed, the intellectual antecedence of many of the ideas that found their decisive expression in the Enlightenment literature can be traced to many different cultures of the world including some from Asia, even though the particular expressions that have proved to be definitive in the contemporary world have come mainly through the Enlightenment tradition of eighteenth century of which Adam Smith and other leaders of the "Scottish Enlightenment," such as David Hume, were a part.

This issue of intellectual history has some bearing also on the second question, to which I now turn, as to whether the idea of social exclusion—European in origin—can be fruitfully used to understand poverty and deprivation elsewhere, in Asia and Africa in particular. The immediate point to note is that the world in which we live is much more unified today, with shared ideas and concerns, and it would be amazing if socially useful notions developed in Europe would fail to be relevant in Asia just because of their European origin.

The major achievement of the European literature on social exclusion has been the enrichment of the analysis of processes that lead to capability deprivation. Arjan de Haan is right to point out that the literature on social deprivation has helped us to understand better the multidimensional nature of deprivation as well as the importance of causal—and often dynamic—connections. If the constitutive role points at the inescapable necessity to see poverty as being multidimensional (some of the dimensions of which are well reflected by the constitutive role of social exclusions, in addition to the multiplicity of consequences in which we may also take a serious interest), the causal perspective also forces our attention on the importance of processes and changes associated with the emergence and development of capability poverty of particular types. Social analysis and understanding are enriched by both types of contributions, and the investigation of poverty is both internally and externally supplemented in a fruitful way by the use of ideas of social exclusion.

To this general intellectual concern, we must add the contingent empirical fact that many actual problems of deprivation are widely shared across the continents. Unemployment ravages lives both in many European countries and in parts of Asia and Africa. Europe has its refugee problems, but Asia has no less, nor Africa. Questions of the status, seclusion, and social empowerment of immigrants form part of a general concern that should interest Asia and Africa as much as Europe.

Indeed, the idea of social exclusion has recently been used to cover a large variety of "exclusions" particularly important in Asia. There is, in fact, a considerable—and fast growing—literature dealing with one or more of these "exclusions" in Asian countries, such as India, Thailand, Malaysia, Vietnam, the Philippines, and others. The focus has been on *processes* through which deprivation occurs—"through which individuals or groups are wholly or partially excluded from full participation in the society in which they live." There have been things to learn from the European literature on social exclusion, and the learning has been impressively fast in Asia as well.

No sense of Asian "specialness" should make us overlook (I say "us"—asserting my own Asian identity) the things that can be learned from analyses and investigations undertaken in other parts of the world. Indeed, social understanding, like other branches of knowledge, inescapably involves give and take, and an exchange of cognizance and wisdom. It can also be readily pointed out that Europe too has much to learn from Asia. For example, the sharing of social facilities of basic education, in which some parts of Asia have a long tradition, can also offer something of great interest to Europe, for example, to learn a little from the human-development basis of economic and social progress of Japan and East Asia. On the other hand, the absence of "social safety nets" when economic growth falters and lives are battered, probably afflicts Asia and Africa more than western Europe because of the protection offered by certain features of the European "welfare state." There are gains to be made from greater integration of social investigations across regional boundaries, and from examining shared as well as disparate problems faced in different regions of the world.

Practical Reason in a Changing World

The literature of social exclusion addresses two central issues, respectively in epistemology and in practical reason. The epistemic question on which it focuses is how to get a better understanding of the diverse phenomena of deprivation and poverty, focusing particularly on relational obstacles. The challenge of practical reason goes beyond that into policy implications of that understanding. The question there takes the form of asking how to improve policy-making, in light of the understanding generated by studies of social exclusion.

Even though I have, in different ways, tried to address both questions, the balance of attention—so far in this paper—has definitely been more in favour of epistemology than practical reason.

This is, appropriate, since the lessons for policy-making have to be, in an important sense, parasitic on the understanding generated by epistemic investigations. However, for a practical and action-oriented organisation like the Asian Development Bank, the ultimate interest in issues like social exclusion cannot fail to be focused particularly on policy issues and on research directed at practical reason. It is necessary, therefore, not only to gather together the lines of policy analyses already discussed in this paper, but also to explore further the policy issues that need attention at this time, especially in the Asian context.

Before we plunge into that exercise, there are two other issues on which I should briefly comment. First, the world in which we live is not a stationary one; it is changing—often quite rapidly. For example, the forces of "globalisation" are bringing new groups of people into economic, social, and cultural contact with each other. Globalisation is both a threat (especially to traditional ways of earning and living) and an enormous opportunity (especially in providing new ways of being prosperous and affluent). The ability of people to use the positive prospects depends on their not being excluded from the effective opportunities that globalisation offers (such as new patterns of exchange, new goods to produce, new skills to develop, new techniques of production to use, and so on). If people are excluded from these opportunities—either because of international restrictions or due to national or local lack of preparedness—then the overall impact of globalisation may be exclusion from older facilities of economic survival without being immediately included in newer ways of earning and living. The context of global change has to be borne very much in mind in looking for policy implications of the understanding generated by the literature on social exclusion.

Second, while exclusion is one route to capability failure and poverty, what may be called "unfavourable inclusion" can also be a considerable danger. Indeed, many problems of deprivation arise from unfavourable terms of inclusion and adverse participation, rather than what can be sensibly seen primarily as a case of exclusion as such. For example, when there are reasons to complain about "exploitative" conditions of employment, or of deeply "unequal" terms of social participation, the immediate focus is not on exclusion at all, but on the unfavourable nature of the inclusions involved. Anita Kelles-Viitanen has drawn attention to this basic issue.

Given the adaptability of the language of exclusion, it is, of course, possible to make the rhetoric of "social exclusion" cover "unfavourable inclusion" as well. Thus, extended, "exclusion" can include "exclusion from equitable inclusion," or even "exclusion from acceptable arrangements of inclusion." The plasticity of the language easily permits this rhetorical extension. However, it is very important not to be mesmerised into trying to place all problems under the broad umbrella of one general description—in this case of "social exclusion." If we were to take that route, we have, at least, to be aware that what we are doing is to recast a traditionally recognised problem in new terminology, rather than offering any new insight. Those who find the use of linguistic plasticity to be very enlightening, we fear deserve that enlightenment.

Since no great conceptual departure is involved in such a reformulation, I need not argue for an immutable "stand" on an issue of this kind. It is, however, very important to distinguish between the nature of a problem where some people are being *kept out* (or at least *left out)* and the characteristics of a different problem where some people are being included—may even be forced to be included—in deeply unfavourable terms. They are not the same problem, even if we put both under the same linguistic format.

More positively, we have reason to take full note *both* of deprivations that arise from unfavourable exclusion and those that originate in unfavourable inclusion. Once social exclusion is seen *within* the broader concept of capability deprivation, there is no difficulty in seeing the diverse origins of the failure to have adequate basic capabilities. The issue, ultimately, is what freedom does a person have—everything considered. It should come as no surprise that a person's deprivation can have diverse origins and may take disparate forms—unfavourable inclusion as well as prohibiting exclusion.

Also, we have to recognise that the nature of the problems may also change over time. A tied labourer in a backward rural economy may suffer particularly from unequal inclusion and the lack of freedom to go elsewhere, but the same person—once liberated from tied servitude— may have to encounter conditions of sweated labour and exploitative working conditions, because of lack of alternative employment opportunities and the general threat of unemployment. Unemployment is a major cause of social exclusion, and may even—as in this case—cause the person to be subjected to unequal inclusion in an exploitative occupation. There is no conceptual difficulty in seeing the diverse sources of the person's predicament: the unfavourable inclusion of tied labour; the penalty of exclusion from favourable wage employment; the consequent inclusion in exploitative work by the sheer necessity of earning a living. The world may be diverse as well as changing, but there is no basic difficulty in keeping track of what is going on and of the diverse influences that may lead to the person's deprivation, of different kinds. This fuller understanding is important. To find exactly one expression "social exclusion" or any other to describe all this—is not.

Policy Option for Removing Social Exclusion

In identifying policy issues—of particular relevance in Asia—related to the general literature on social exclusion, it is important to pay attention to the distinct types of exclusions and the different ways in which they can impoverish human lives in Asia. Proper identification of the researchability and relevance of diverse problems calls for a much more comprehensive and detailed investigation than we are able to provide in this essay, but we shall take the liberty of mentioning some possible hypotheses and some general lines of inquiry that would seem to be worth examining.

In identifying problems for further investigation and possible action, it is particularly important both to take note of the changing nature of Asian economic experience (including the experience of globalisation and the lessons of the Asian financial and economic crisis) and to reflect specifically on the ways in which the perspective of social exclusion can draw attention to problems that may otherwise be neglected in more traditional studies of poverty and deprivation. The context of this investigation and analysis is as important as the general task of making good use of the diverse literature on social exclusion.

It can be argued that there is a basic dichotomy between two different classes of economic experiences in Asia that makes the nature of the problems of social exclusion faced in the different countries also rather diverse. There are, on the one hand, countries that have achieved major transformations of economic affluence, particularly in the form of massive industrialisation and remarkable enhancement of per capita incomes. Japan is, of course, the pre-eminent example of this, with spectacular progress from low income to one of the highest levels of economic opulence in the world, but many other economies in East and Southeast Asia have also managed to industrialise and to raise their levels of per capita income very substantially. On the other hand, other economies, primarily in South and West Asia have achieved less in these respects, even though some have done more than others to go along that route. The classification is not, of course, very neat, and there are cases that are not clearly on one side or the other of the roughly drawn borderline. But, the overall contrast has some epistemic value and actual relevance for policy analysis.

The social exclusion problems faced in many economies in Asia, mainly in South and West Asia are, as a result, somewhat different from those in many of the countries further east. Indeed, I shall argue that the success of the more eastern economies may have been partly due to their ability to avoid, to a great extent, a specific type of social exclusion— particularly from basic education and elementary social opportunities— that plagues the economies of South and West Asia. The economies in East and Southeast Asia do, of course, face social exclusion problems of their own (even the ones with great progress in per capita income do suffer from various specific exclusions), and the Asian financial and economic crisis has brought out vulnerabilities not adequately identified earlier. We must look at problems of different kinds, but there is something of a general divide in terms of the basic sharing of social opportunities, which has helped to fuel the progress of countries to the east and which has not yet been adequately marshalled in South and West Asia.

Indeed, we have tried to argue elsewhere, that there is an identifiable philosophy on which the success of many of the economies of East and Southeast Asia has been based, and we can even try to identify an "eastern strategy" that first evolved in Japan and then has been practised very successfully elsewhere. Japan's breakthrough into the world of industrialisation and economic development which had been often taken, earlier on, to be reserved for the West was so sure-footed and massive that it cannot but be an irresistible source of learning and understanding about the nature of economic development in general.

The "eastern strategy" has found plentiful use in the remarkable growth achievements of East and Southeast Asia over the last few decades. While many commentators—especially in the West—saw nothing more in these successes than a confirmation of their prior belief in the productivity of international trade (as if there was nothing new in all this), a broader analysis shows that the development process in Japan and in East and Southeast Asia had several strikingly new features.

The new features that were crucial included, first of all, an emphasis on basic education as a prime mover of change. Second, it also involved a wide dissemination of basic economic entitlements (through education and training, through land reform, and through availability of credit), which removed (or substantially reduced) social exclusion from the general opportunities of participating in the market economy. Third, the chosen design of development included a deliberate combination of state action and use of the market economy, in a way that the more laissez faire oriented western modelling of economic development did not adequately seize. Indeed, these successes were based on a basic understanding—which was often implicit rather than explicit—that we live in a multi-institutional environment, and that our ability to help ourselves and to help others depends on a variety of freedoms that we respectively may enjoy. The list of relevant freedoms includes social opportunities as well as market arrangements, and the development of individual capabilities as well as enhancement of social facilities. At a very general level, these changes can be seen as radically countering the social exclusion from participatory growth that plagues economic development in most of the world.

We live and operate in a world of many institutions. Our opportunities and prospects depend crucially on what institutions exist, how they function, and how inclusionary they are. Not only do institutions contribute to our freedoms, their roles can be sensibly evaluated in the light of their contributions to our freedoms. Different commentators have chosen to focus specifically on particular institutions such as the market, or the democratic system, or the media, or the public distribution system, but there is an excellent case for viewing them together, for seeing what they can or cannot do, in combination with other institutions. It is in this integrated perspective that the diverse institutions have to be understood and examined, and their respective contributions and inclusionary functions have to be assessed.

The market mechanism does, of course, arouse passion in favour as well as against, but fundamentally it is no more than a basic arrangement through which people can interact with each other, and undertake mutually advantageous activities. Thus, seen, it is very hard to appreciate how any reasonable critic could be against the market mechanism *in general.* The problems that arise spring typically from other sources—not from the existence of markets per se—and include such concerns as systematic exclusion from the use of the processes and fruits of market operations, insufficient assets or inadequate preparedness to make effective use of market transactions, unconstrained concealment of information by business leaders, or unregulated use of commercial or financial activities that allow the powerful to capitalise on their asymmetric advantage. These have to be dealt with not by suppressing the markets, but by allowing them to function better and with greater fairness and inclusiveness. Here the overall achievements of the market are deeply contingent on the creation of social opportunities. And it is precisely in this connection that the "eastern strategy"—beginning with Japan nearly a century ago—can be seen as having achieved quite a breakthrough.

Remarkably rapid successes have been achieved by the market mechanism under those conditions in which the opportunities offered by it have been widely shared, rather being reserved for an exclusive elite. In making this possible, universal arrangements for basic education, widespread provision of elementary medical facilities, and radical land reforms that provide a basic resource (central for agriculture) to the poorer sections of the rural economy can be quite crucial. They call for appropriate public policies (involving schooling, health care, land reform, and so on) that open the doors of economic participation to the broad masses. Even when the need for "economic reform" in favour of allowing more room for markets is paramount, these nonmarket facilities require careful and determined public action.

Consider the experience of Japan. Even in the middle of the nineteenth century, at the time of Meiji restoration, Japan already had a higher level of literacy than Europe, even though Japan had not yet had any industrialisation or modern economic development, which Europe had experienced, by then, for a century. The emphasis on developing productive human capability was intensified in the early period of Japanese development, in the Meiji era. For example, between 1906 and 1911, education consumed as much as 43 percent of the budgets of the towns and villages, for Japan as a whole. Already by 1906, there is evidence—based on army recruitment information—to suggest that there was hardly any potential recruit even from rural Japan who was not literate. In fact, by 1913, though Japan was economically still quite underdeveloped, it had become one of the largest producers of books in the world— publishing many more books than did Britain (then the leading capitalist economy on the globe) and, indeed, more than twice as many as the United States. The priority to shared basic education and human development came very early to Japan, and even though it is massively high today, the important thing to note is that this relative priority goes back more than a century, and has not, comparatively speaking, intensified as Japan has grown richer and much more opulent.

A similar priority can be seen, to varying extents, all over East and Southeast Asia, though often this came rather more hesitantly and slowly. The Republic of Korea, Singapore, Thailand, and Taipei, China, and the former city state of Hong Kong, as well as other economies in the region— most importantly the People's Republic of China—have made excellent use of this general approach.

The so-called "East Asian miracle" was, to a great extent, based on the reach and force of "the eastern strategy" of focusing on shared— non-exclusionary—human development. In contrast, the persistence of illiteracy in many parts of Asia is a matter of great importance in generating social exclusion and economic deprivation that have both constitutive significance and instrumental consequence. The basic capabilities to lead a life with elementary freedom tend to be severely compromised by keeping large sections of the population out of educational opportunities, and in addition, these exclusions also contribute to making the process of economic growth less participatory in some regions (for example, in South and West Asia, compared with East Asia). Other limitations of social opportunities, such as the lack of land reform and unavailability of micro credit, can also have similarly exclusionary effects.

Asian Crisis and Protective Security

In the preceding analysis, the achievements of East and Southeast Asia were highlighted and suggested how the rest of Asia (indeed the rest of the world) can learn a great deal from their successful use of nonexclusionary expansion of human development. However, not everything in the experience of this region has been so positive and successful, and some of the problems have been strongly brought out by the recent Asian financial and economic crisis.

We may usefully begin with the general recognition that the heady days of unmitigated success—with things going up and up and nothing ever falling down—are over. Even though, much of Asia is already well on the way to recovery from the crisis that hit it two years ago, the sense of invulnerability has not survived. There was no basis for assuming such immunity from vulnerability. Crises can—and do—occur even in the most buoyantly growing economies, and there is no real ground for assuming the continuity of unobstructed economic progress that many Asian countries took for granted.

This makes it absolutely obligatory to see *shared security* as a central part of development. Even though development is often judged by long-run trends in growth averages and by the strength of upward tendencies, this "trend-oriented view" misses out something truly central to the process of development, viz. protection against the "down-side" risk at every moment of time. This immediately suggests the need to see inclusion and exclusion in a somewhat different way, in the specific context of down-side risks and the sharing of arrangements for social security when things do go wrong.

It is, indeed, the case that different groups may all happily benefit together when rapid progress is occurring, and in this particular way the interests of the distinct classes and sections of the population may appear to be substantially congruent. But, nevertheless, when a crisis hits, different groups can have very divergent predicaments. United we may be when we go up and up, but divided we fall when we do fall. The unreal belief in the harmony of interests of different classes and groups may be torn rudely asunder when things start unravelling and collapsing.

Consider, for example, the crises in Indonesia, or in Thailand, and earlier on, in the Republic of Korea. It is not silly to ask (given the dominance of trend-oriented reasoning in economic analysis) why it should be so disastrous to have, say, a 5 or 10 percent fall in gross national product in one year when the country in question has been growing at 5 to 10 percent *every year for decades.* At the purely *aggregate* level this is not quintessentially a disastrous situation. However, if that 5 or 10 percent decline is not shared evenly by the population, and if some are excluded altogether from the part of the economy that survives the crisis, then that group may have very little income left (no matter what the overall growth performance might have been in the past).

As a result, the sharing of "protective security" is an important instrumental freedom, and nonexclusionary social arrangements for safety nets cannot but be an integral part of development itself. It is worth noting here that even the highly illuminating literature on "sustainable development" often misses out the fact that what people need for their security is not only the sustainability of *overall* development, but also the need for guaranteed social protection when people's predicaments diverge and some groups are thrown brutally to the wall while other groups experience little adversity.

There is, in fact, an important need to think of equity and economic inequality in quite a different way in the context of security from the way they are standardly treated in the development literature in the context of long-run growth. It is necessary to go well beyond the analysis and rhetoric of "growth with equity", which have been so often invoked in the development literature—not least in explaining the success of the economies in East and Southeast Asia. That large literature is, of course, conceptually rich and practically important, and is particularly suited to analyse the big—but *different*—problem of eliminating endemic poverty.

In contrast, the problem of sudden destitution can have a very different nature, and may involve quite disparate causal processes from persistent deprivation and endemic poverty. For example, the fact that the Republic of Korea has had economic growth with relatively egalitarian income distribution has been extensively—and rightly—recognised. This, however, was no guarantee of equitable influence in a crisis situation. For example, the Republic of Korea did not have, when the crisis hit it, any ongoing system of social safety nets, nor any rapidly responding system of compensatory protection. The emergence of fresh inequality and the destitution of the socially excluded can coexist with a very distinguished past record of "growth with equity." Divergent problems call for different analyses and understanding, and this applies to the disparate problems included in the broad category of social exclusion as well.

Democracy and Political Participation

We have not so far discussed the issue of exclusion from political participation and from democratic rights. How does the issue of democracy relate to the problems of deprivation, security, and crises that I discussed in the last section? Of course, it can be argued that social exclusion from political participation is itself a deprivation, and a denial of basic political freedom and civil rights directly impoverishes our lives. Prime Minister Keizo Obuchi of Japan, in his insightful "Opening Remarks" to an "Intellectual Dialogue on Building Asia's Tomorrow," has eloquently emphasised the need to take a broad view of security:

It is our deepest belief that human beings should be able to lead lives of creativity, without having their survival threatened or their dignity impaired. While the phrase "human security" is a relatively new one, we understand that it is the keyword to comprehensively seizing all of the menaces that threaten the survival, daily life, and dignity of human beings and to strengthening the efforts to confront these threats.

It is not unreasonable for human beings—the social creatures that we are—to value participation in political and social activities without restraint. Also, informed and *unregimented formation* of our values requires openness of communication and arguments, and political freedoms and civil rights can be central to this process. Furthermore, in order to express effectively what we value and to demand that attention be paid to it, we need free speech and democratic choice. Exclusion from the process of governance and political participation is indeed an impoverishment of human lives, no matter what our per capita income may be.

But, going beyond this foundational role of inclusion and participation in political processes, there is also an instrumental role that must be examined in this context. Indeed, there is a foundational connection with the issue of security. This involves the need for political incentives that may operate on governments and on the persons and groups who are in office. The rulers have the incentive to listen to what people want if they have to face their criticism and seek their support in elections. It is, thus, not astonishing at all that no substantial famine has ever occurred in any independent country with a democratic form of government and a relatively free press. When things are routinely good and smooth, the protective role of democracy may not be desperately missed. But, it comes into its own when things get fouled up, for one reason or another. And then the political incentives provided by democratic governance acquire great practical significance.

Many economic technocrats recommend the use of economic incentives (which the market system provides) while ignoring political incentives (which democratic systems could guarantee). However, economic incentives, important as they are, are no substitute for political incentives, and the lacuna of the absence of an adequate system of political incentives cannot be filled by the operation of economic inducement. The recent problems of East and Southeast Asia bring out, among many other things, the penalty of limitations on democratic freedom.

Two distinct issues are particularly important to consider here, viz. "protective security" and "transparency guarantee." Taking the issue of protective security first, once the financial crisis in this region led to a general economic recession, the protective power of democracy—not unlike that which prevents famines in democratic countries—was badly missed in some countries in the region. The newly dispossessed did not have the hearing they needed. The vulnerable in Indonesia or the Republic of Korea may not have taken very great interest in democracy when things went up and up. But, when the unequally shared crisis developed, that lacuna kept their voice muffled and weak. The protective role of shared democratic rights is strongly missed when it is most needed. Not surprisingly, democracy has become a major issue precisely at a time of crisis, when the economically dispossessed felt strongly the need for a political voice. Indeed, the Republic of Korea has already greatly advanced in that direction, and there are changes in Indonesia as well. Inclusive democratic rights are receiving more explicit consideration in public discussions elsewhere in Asia also including in the Philippines and Thailand.

The second connection between the lack of democracy and the nature of the recent financial and economic crisis concerns the issue of transparency. The financial crisis in some of these economies (such as the Republic of Korea or Indonesia) has been closely linked with the lack of transparency in business, in particular the lack of public participation in reviewing financial and business arrangements. The lack of a shared and inclusive democratic forum has been consequential in this failing. The opportunity that would have been provided by democratic processes to challenge the hold of exclusive families or groups could have made a big difference.

Democratic rights and shared opportunities of political participation can, of course, be important in many other contexts as well. For example, in India, Bangladesh, and Pakistan these rights are being more and more invoked in recent agitations involving gender equity and also justice to the lower strata of society. As was discussed earlier, exclusions of different kinds may link with each other, and progress in inclusion in one field may help to advance inclusion in other areas. These connections call for more extensive investigations, but it is important to note that even in the economically successful region of East and Southeast Asia, where scepticism about shared democratic and civil rights had often been aired in the past, there is more and more recognition of the need for political inclusion and participation.

Diversity of Exclusions

Since this study is becoming very large, we must discuss only rather briefly some other issues of social exclusion that we do want to identify. It is particularly important to recognise the diverse ways in which social exclusion can cause deprivation and poverty. Here are some examples.

Inequality and Relational Poverty: The pioneering analysis of Adam Smith on the possibility of absolute capability deprivation resulting from relative poverty applies as much to Asia today as it did to Britain or France in his time. This kind of constitutively relevant deprivation also relates to new styles of consumption that may get established in a poorer country as a result of the influence or imitation of consumption levels in richer countries, as is happening much more widely today than in the relatively insular economies with which Smith was familiar. Taking part in the life of the community may be rendered much more expensive by emulative consumption styles in the poorer countries today.

The relativist perspective is also increased in importance when some people are suddenly impoverished because of the reversal of earlier growth processes, as happened in the financial and economic crisis in East and Southeast Asia. The problem of absolute poverty may become much sharper if inequalities increase along with recession. If we take note of the relational issues involved in the Smithian analysis of poverty, the increase in poverty can take a further—and additional—form, with constitutive importance of the exclusionary process.

Labour Market Exclusions: The rejection of the freedom to participate in the labour market is one of the ways of keeping people in bondage and captivity, and the battle against the "unfreedom" of tied labour is important in many developing countries today for some of the reasons for which the American civil war was momentous. The freedom to enter markets can itself be a significant contribution to development, quite aside from whatever the market mechanism may or may not do to promote economic growth or industrialisation. In fact, the praise of capitalism by Karl Marx (not the most extreme admirer of capitalism in general), and his characterisation (in *The Capital)* of the American civil war as "the one great event of contemporary history," related directly to the importance of the freedom of labour contract as opposed to slavery and other enforced exclusion from the labour market. The freedom to participate in labour markets has a basic role in social living and can have both constitutive relevance and instrumental importance.

Credit Market Exclusions: The far-reaching impact of expanding access to credit on the part of poorer people can also be seen in the light of instrumental investigation of social exclusion.

Gender-related Exclusions and Inequality: The persistence of inequality between women and men is a problem that is sharper in Asia than in any other continent in the world. It applies even to sex-related mortality rates, with Asia providing the bulk of the estimated "missing women" in the world. It has been empirically noted that the neglect of the interest of women relates closely to their being excluded from employment opportunities, basic education, and land ownership. These exclusions are, thus, of great instrumental importance.

In fact, there are also other issues of constitutive as well as instrumental importance, closely related to this question. It has been found in international comparisons and also in interregional comparisons within a large country that women's schooling and women's employment opportunities have profoundly powerful effects in reducing not only gender bias in mortality, but also in curtailing fertility. The analysis of these results and related findings regarding fertility reduction suggests that these influences work by giving greater voice to young women in decisions within the family, since (i) young women suffer most from continuous bearing and rearing of children, and (ii) schooling, independent income, and social status tend to increase the decisional power of young women in the household. Since greater gender equality in family affairs and the reversal of the exclusion of women from these decisions are matters of direct importance (in addition to the contribution that these changes may make in reducing fertility rates), positive note may well be taken of the instrumental role of girls' schooling and women's employment opportunities in generating constitutively important social changes within the family (reversing the unjust exclusion of women in matters that concern them most).

There is, of course, the general problem of neglect of schooling of children in many parts of Asia. But, there is, furthermore, a special problem of the particular neglect of education of girls in many countries. In addition to the presence of this problem as a passive failure, which is widespread in many parts of Asia, there has been the recent addition of the *active exclusion* of girls from schools in the declared public policies in Afghanistan.

Health Care: The exclusion of large sections of the population from public health services provided by the State has been a matter of considerable discussion in recent years, since it is an extensive problem in many Asian countries. To this, some scholars have proposed adding the international exclusion involved in the unavailability of modern health care in the poorer regions, often because of high medicinal cost (for example, for the medical care of AIDS patients).

Food Market and Poverty: A rather different type of case is involved in the fact that in some countries that have no observed shortage of food in the market, there remain very large populations with significant undernourishment. These people are passively excluded from translating their unfulfilled needs into effective demand in the food market because of lack of purchasing power. This predicament is the result of a variety of economic disadvantages, some of which can be more directly linked with the relational perspective of exclusion than others.

The level of child undernourishment is larger in India and South Asia generally, despite the fact that these countries are "self-sufficient" in food and there is no substantial unmet demand in the food market. It is interesting that even though it is sub-Saharan Africa that is seen, correctly, as not being self-sufficient in food, in contrast with the self- reliance of India, the incidence of undernourishment is much greater in India than in sub-Saharan Africa. Indeed, judged in terms of the usual standards of retardation in weight for age, the proportion of undernourished children in Africa is 20 to 40 percent, whereas the proportion of undernourished Indian children is a gigantic 40 to 60 percent. About half of all Indian children are, it appears, chronically undernourished, despite there being no "food shortage," and this is a context in which the instrumental role of being excluded by penury from the food market can be fruitfully invoked to clarify the nature of the food situation in India.

In choosing these examples for illustrative purposes, we have been guided not merely by the seriousness of the deprivations involved, but also by the need to exemplify different types of exclusions, with and without constitutive importance, and with varying instrumental connections and disparate extents of active exclusion involved in the emergence and sustaining of these deprivations.

Conclusion

While the underlying idea behind the concept of social exclusion is not radically new, the growing literature on the subject has helped to enrich causal understanding and empirical analysis of certain aspects of poverty and deprivation. To be excluded from common facilities or benefits that others have can certainly be a significant handicap that impoverishes the lives that individuals can enjoy. No concept of poverty can be satisfactory if it does not take adequate note of the disadvantages that arise from being excluded from shared opportunities enjoyed by others.

In this study, we have tried to examine critically the idea of social exclusion, particularly in the context of deprivation and poverty. How much additional ground it breaks must depend on what our pre-existing concept of poverty was. If (as is the case in many traditional analyses of deprivation and underdevelopment) poverty is seen in terms of income deprivation only, then introducing the notion of social exclusion as a part of poverty would vastly broaden the domain of poverty analysis. However, if poverty is seen as deprivation of basic capabilities, then there is no real expansion of the domain of coverage, but a very important pointer to a useful investigative focus. In this essay, social exclusion has been placed within the broader perspective of poverty as capability deprivation, and this conceptual linkage both provides more theoretical underpinning for the approach of social exclusion and helps us to extend the practical use of the approach.

The nature of poverty analysis can, we have argued, substantially benefit from the insights provided by the perspective of social exclusion. Its forceful pointer to the multidimensionality of deprivation and its focus on relational processes are both quite important. We have to distinguish between substantive contributions of this type, from mere changes of language in which old issues are sometimes terminologically recast in the literature on social exclusion. While rhetoric does have its own significance and power, it is the former—more substantive—contributions on which we have concentrated in the analysis presented here.

The perspective of social exclusion is broad and inclusive, but need not lack coherence or cogency, if used with discrimination and scrutiny. It is, however, necessary to make some crucial distinctions to clarify the varying reach of the analysis of social exclusion. It is important, in particular to distinguish (1) between the *constitutive relevance* and the *instrumental importance* of exclusion (section 5); and (2) between *active* and *passive* exclusions (section 6). The different categories, which we have discussed conceptually as well as empirically, involve rather distinct types of cases, though they can also overlap. Even though *relational* roots of deprivation are present, in different ways, in each case, their disparities are no less important than their similarities.

What is particularly important to study is the linkage between exclusions in different spheres of interindividual and interfamily interactions, involving both overlap and causal linkages. Many illustrations have been given to exemplify the type of social, economic, and political analyses that can be used to apply the "social exclusion perspective" in investigating deprivations of different kinds.

The applications of the approach also prove to be useful in discriminating between disparate economic experiences in different parts of Asia (for example, East and Southeast Asia on the one hand, and South and West Asia on the other). The patterns of exclusion have varied, and there is much to learn from the experiences of different economies within Asia. Also, investigation of the recent Asian financial and economic crisis helps to bring out the role played by social exclusions of specific types that proved to be particularly damaging both in the genesis of the crisis and in the penalties generated by it. There are other distinctions related to economic, social, and political exclusions that have operated in diverse ways in different economies of Asia.

The perspective of social exclusion reinforces—rather than competes with—the understanding of poverty as capability deprivation. We have argued that if the idea is carefully used, there is much to be gained from using the perspective of social exclusion in analysing the deprivation of basic capabilities and in assessing the policy issues that follow from these diagnoses. Even the clearly European origin of the concept does not compromise its usefulness in other parts of the world, including Asia.

Rather than trying to see social exclusion as a brand new concept, which it is not, the basic idea has to be assessed in terms of the particular focus of attention it helps to generate and the contribution it makes to the understanding of relational aspects of deprivation by adopting a somewhat more specialised perspective. Also, the use of the idea of social exclusion as a deprivation need not serve as a barrier to continuing to take interest in other types of deprivation (including those associated with *unfavourable inclusion),* which may be best investigated in more traditional lines of analysis. The embedding of social exclusion in the wider perspective of capability deprivation makes the reach of this broadened analysis particularly effective. The programme is to look for what the social exclusion perspective *adds* to the literature on deprivation, rather than what it subtracts—or demolishes. In fact, it does little of the latter.

Also, the analysis of capability deprivation in general and that of social exclusion in particular have to take adequate note of the fact that the world that is being interpreted and examined in these studies is itself changing—often quite rapidly. The reach and versatility of the respective investigations must depend crucially on taking adequate note of the forces of change—arising from globalisation and other causes—that characterise the contemporary world.

The real issue is not whether the idea of "social exclusion" deserves a celebratory medal as a conceptual advance, but whether people concerned with practical measurement and public policy have reason to pay attention to the issues to which the idea helps to draw attention. The answer, we believe, is in the affirmative, despite the misgivings that the somewhat disorganised and undisciplined literature has often generated.

The misgivings may have their usefulness as cautious reminders of the need for critical scrutiny. But, it is important to recognise and affirm the basic significance of the perspective of social exclusion. Its importance does not lie in its conceptual novelty—indeed, it is best seen within a broadly Aristotelian framework of freedoms and capabilities. But, in that framework and with adequate critical examination, focusing on social exclusion can substantially help in the causal as well as constitutive analyses of poverty and deprivation. The perspective of social exclusion does offer useful insights for diagnostics and policy.

NOTES AND REFERENCES

Adelman, Irma. 1975. Development Economics—A Reassessment of Goals. *American Economic Review,* Papers and Proceedings 65.

—, and Cynthia T. Morris. 1973. *Economic Growth and Social Equity in Developing Countries.* Stanford: Stanford University Press.

Agarwal, Bina. 1994. *A Field of One's Own: Gender and Land Rights in South Asia.* Cambridge: Cambridge University Press.

Alesina, Alberto, and Dani Rodrik. 1994. Distributive Politics and Economic Growth. *Quarterly Journal of Economics* 108.

Anand, Sudhir, and Martin Ravallion. 1993. Human Development in Poor Countries: On the Role of Private Incomes and Public Services. *Journal of Economic Perspectives* 7 (Winter).

Appasamy, Paul, S. Guhan, R. Hema, Manabi Majumdar, and A. Vaidyanathan. 1995. Social Exclusion in Respect of Basic Needs in India. In *Social Exclusion: Rhetoric, Reality, Responses,* edited by Gerry Rodgers, Charles Gore, and Jose Figueiredo. Geneva: International Institute for Labour Studies. Asian Development Bank. 1997. *Emerging Asia: Changes and Challenges.* Manila:

Asian Development Bank. Atinc, Tamar Manuelyan, and Michael Walter. 1998. *East Asia's Social Model after the Crisis.* Washington DC: World Bank.

Bardhan, Kalpana, and Stefan Klasen. 1999. Women in Emerging Asia. *Asian Development Review* (Forthcoming).

Bardhan, Pranab. 1984. *Land, Labour and Rural Poverty.* New York: Columbia University Press.

Basu, Kaushik. 1990. *Agrarian Structure and Economic Under-development.* Chichester: Harwood.

Behrman, Jere R., and Anil B. Deolalikar. 1988. Health and Nutrition. In *Handbook of Development Economics,* edited by Hollis Chenery and T.N. Srinivasan. Amsterdam: North-Holland.

Beneria, O., ed. 1992. *Women and Development: The Sexual Division of Labour in Rural Societies.* New York: Praeger.

Birdsall, Nancy. 1993. Social Development Is Economic Development. Policy Research Working Paper 1123. Washington DC: World Bank.

—, and Richard H. Sabot. 1993a. Virtuous Circles: Human Capital, Growth and Equity in East Asia. Washington DC: World Bank. (Mimeograph)

—, and Richard H. Sabot, eds. 1993b. *Opportunity Forgone: Education, Growth and Inequality in Brazil.* Washington DC: World Bank.

Boserup, Ester. 1970. *Women's Role in Economic Development.* London: Earthscan Publications.

Caldwell, J.C., R.H. Reddy, and P. Caldwell. 1989. *The Causes of Demographic Change.* Madison: University of Wisconsin Press.

Chen, Lincoln. 1998. Globalisation: Health Equity or Social Exclusion? Keynote address at the Conference of the International Health Policy Association, Perugia, Italy, 23 September 1998.

Chichilnisky, Graciala. 1980. Basic Needs and Global Models: Resources, Trade and Distribution. Alternatives 6, da Costa, Alfred Bruto. 997. Social Exclusion and the New Poor: Trends and Policy Initiatives in Western Europe. In Social Exclusion and Anti-Poverty Policy, edited by Charles Gore and Jose B. Figueiredo. Geneva: International Institute of Labour Studies.

Deininger, Klaus, and Lyn Squire. 1996. *New Ways of Looking at Old Issues: Inequality and Growth.* Washington DC: World Bank. (Mimeograph)

Desai, Meghnad. 1995. *Poverty, Famine and Economic Development.* Aldershot: Elgar.

Do Duc Dinh. 1995. *The Social Impact of Economic Reconstruction in Vietnam: A Selected Review.* Discussion Paper 81. Geneva: International Institute of Labour Studies.

Dowler, Elizabeth. 1998. Food Poverty and Food Policy. In *Poverty and Social Exclusion in North and South*, edited by Arjan de Haan and Simon Maxwell. IDS Bulletin 29 (1). (January).

Doyal, L. and I. Gough. 1991. *A Theory of Human Need.* New York: Guilford Press.

Drèze, Jean, and Amartya Sen. 1989. *Hunger and Public Action.* Oxford: Clarendon Press.

—, and Amartya Sen, eds. 1990. *The Political Economy of Hunger.* Oxford: Clarendon Press.

—, and Amartya Sen. 1995. *India: Economic Development and Social Opportunity.* Delhi: Oxford University Press.

Earls, Felton, and Maya Carlson. 1993. *Towards Sustainable Development for American Families.* Daedalus 122.

—, and Maya Carlson. 1994. Promoting Human Capability as an Alternative to Early Crime Prevention. Boston: Harvard School of Public Health and Harvard Medical School.

Evans, Martin. 1998. Behind the Rhetoric: The Institutional Basis of Social Exclusion and Poverty. In Poverty and Social Exclusion in North and South, edited by Arjan de Haan and Simon Maxwell. *IDS Bulletin* 29 (1). (January). Figueiredo, J.B., and Arjan de Haan, eds. 1998. Social Exclusion: An ILO Perspective. Geneva: International Labour Organisation.

Fishlow, Albert, C. Gwin, S. Haggard, D. Rodrik, and S. Wade. 1994. *Miracle or Design? Lessons from the East Asian Experience.* Washington DC: Overseas Development Council.

Foucauld, J.-B. de. 1992. Exclusion, inegalites et justice sociale. Esprit 182 (June). Gluck, Carol. 1985. *Japan's Modern Myths: Ideology in the Late Meiji Period.* Princeton: Princeton University Press.

Goldsmith, A., J.R. Veum, and W. Darity, Jr. 1996. *The Psychological Impact of Unemployment and Joblessness.* Journal of Socio-Economics 25.

Gore, Charles. 1995a. (with J.B. Figueiredo and G. Rodgers). Introduction: Markets, Citizenship and Social Exclusion. In Social Exclusion: Rhetoric, Reality, Responses, edited by Gerry Rodgers, Charles Gore, and Jose Figueiredo. Geneva: International Institute for Labour Studies.

—. 1995b. Social Excluson and Social Change: Insights in the African Literature. In Social Exclusion: Rhetoric, Reality, Responses, edited by Gerry Rodgers, Charles Gore, and Jose Figueiredo. Geneva: International Institute for Labour Studies.

—, and Jose B. Figueiredo, eds. 1997. Social Exclusion and Anti-Poverty Policy. Geneva: International Institute of Labour Studies.

Griffin, Keith, and Aziz Khan, eds. 1977. *Poverty and Landlessness in Rural Asia.* Geneva: International Labour Organisation.

—, and J. Knight, eds. 1990. *Human Development and the International Development Strategies for the 1990s.* London: Macmillan.

de Haan, Arjan. 1997. Poverty and Social Exclusion: A Comparison of Debates on Deprivation. Working Paper No. 2, Poverty Research Unit at Sussex. Brighton: University of Sussex.

—, and Simon Maxwell, eds. 1998a. Poverty and Social Exclusion in North and South. *IDS Bulletin* 29 (1). (January).

—, and Simon Maxwell, 1998b. Editorial: *Poverty and Social Exclusion in North and South.* In de Haan and Maxwell (1998a).

—, and Pulin Nayak. 1995. Social Exclusion and South Asia. Discussion Paper 77. Geneva: International Institute of Labour Studies.

Hirschman, Albert. 1958. *The Strategy of Economic Development.* New Haven, CA: Yale University Press.

—. 1970. *Exit, Voice and Loyalty: Responses to Declines in Firms, Organisations and States*. Cambridge: Cambridge University Press.

—. 1981. *Essays in Trespassing*. Cambridge: Cambridge University Press.

Ishi, Hiromitsu. 1995. *Trends in the Allocation of Public Expenditure in Light of Human Resource Development* — Overview in Japan. Manila: Asian Development Bank. (Mimeograph)

Jalal, K.F. 1998. Opening and Welcoming Remarks. *Asian Development Bank Seminar on Inclusion or Exclusion: Social Development Challenges for Asia and Europe,* Geneva, 27 April.

Jarvis, Sarah, and Stephen P. Jenkins. 1998. *Low Income Dynamics in 1990s Britain.* In Poverty and Social Exclusion in North and South, edited by Arjan de Haan and Simon Maxwell. IDS Bulletin 29 (1). (January).

Kelles-Viitanen, Anita. 1998. *Discussant's Commentary. Asian Development Bank Seminar on Inclusion or Exclusion: Social Development Challenges for Asia and Europe*, Geneva, 27 April.

Lenoir, René. 1974/1989. *Les Exclus: Un Francais sur Dix. Paris*: Editions du Seuil.

Maurer, Jean-Luc. 1998. *Tentative Brainstorming for an Advancement of the Debate. Asian Development Bank Seminar on Inclusion or Exclusion:* Social Development Challenges for Asia and Europe, Geneva, 27 April.

Maxwell, Simon. 1998. *Comparisons, Convergence and Connections: Development Studies in North and South. In Poverty and Social Exclusion in North and South, edited by Arjan de Haan and Simon Maxwell.* IDS Bulletin 29 (1). (January).

Obuchi, Keizo. 1999. *Opening Remarks. In The Asian Crisis and Human Security.* Tokyo: Japan Center for International Exchange.

Ogata, Sadako. 1998. *Statement. Asian Development Bank Seminar on Inclusion or Exclusion: Social Development Challenges for Asia and Europe,* Geneva, 27 April.

Patterns and Processes of Social Exclusion in Thailand. *In Social Exclusion: Rhetoric, Reality, Responses, edited by Gerry Rodgers, Charles Gore, and Jose Figueiredo. Geneva: International Institute for Labour Studies.*

Rodgers, Gerry. 1995a. *What is Special about a Social Exclusion Approach. In Social Exclusion: Rhetoric, Reality, Responses, edited by Gerry Rodgers, Charles Gore, and Jose Figueiredo.* Geneva: International Institute for Labour Studies.

Schokkaert, E., and L. Van Ootegem. 1990. *Sen's Concept of the Living Standard Applied to the Belgian Unemployed. Recherches Economques de Louvain* 56.

Sen, Amartya. 1980. *Equality of What? In Tanner Lectures on Human Values, vol. I, edited by S. McMurrin. Cambridge:* Cambridge University Press, and Salt Lake City: University of Utah Press.

Tinker, Irene, ed. 1990. *Persistent Deprivations.* New York: Oxford University Press.

Wolfe, Marshall. 1994. *Some Paradoxes of Social Exclusion. Discussion Paper 63.* Geneva: International Institute of Labour Studies.

You, Jong-il. 1998. *Income Distribution and Growth in East Asia. Journal of Development Studies* 34.

Yunus, Mohammad. 1998. *Statement. Asian Development Bank Seminar on Inclusion or Exclusion: Social Development Challenges for Asia and Europe*, Geneva, 27 April.

World Bank. 1993. *The East Asian Miracle. Oxford:* Oxford University Press.

2

THEORIES OF SOCIAL CHANGE

Over a century ago, Nietzsche berated the modern scientist's narrow "factualism" and "renunciation of all interpretation," and a few decades later Weber declared the age of the generalist to be over. Extreme specialisation, self-enclosed disciplinary jargons, and narrowly focused technical work have since transformed these prescient visions into observable realities. Responding to the dominant forms of a theoretical, empirical work and a historical "general theory" in post-World War II American social thought, C. Wright Mills asked: "Where is the intelligentsia that is carrying on the big discourse of the Western world and whose work as intellectuals is influential among parties and publics and relevant to the great decisions of our time?" In his view, professional social science was guilty of "pretentious triviality" and incapable of grasping the growing threats to freedom and reason. Around the same time, Raymond Aron argued that classical social theorists shared "a certain solidarity" deriving from their "global historical interpretations of the modern age": a broad vision which has been regrettably lost.

From this perspective, classical social theory provided comprehensive analyses of the core features, central processes, and imminent threats and possibilities of modernity and in this study we argue that such broad and wide-ranging discourse is still useful and needed today. As a matter of fact classical social theory is primarily a theory of modernity and that the classical tradition of modern social theory raised fundamental questions concerning the nature, structure, and historical trajectories of modern societies. By putting modern societies in broad historical perspective, by emphasising the linkages between their differentiated social institutions, and by expressing the potentialities for normatively guided social change, classical theorists such as Marx, Durkheim, Weber, and Dewey developed a discourse that facilitated comprehension and discussion of, and posed responses to, the rise of modernity and its problematic social conditions.

In recent years, however, there have been a series of attacks on the allegedly foundationalist, essentialist, reductionist, totalising, and positivist features of classical social theory; these critiques have challenged contemporary theorists to probe their metatheoretical assumptions and to articulate and defend the project of social theory against often strong and compelling criticisms by postmodernists, poststructuralists, post-Marxists, feminists, historical sociologists, and others who have called attention to overgeneralised and hyper-rational features of modern philosophy and classical social theory. But, comprehensive theories of big historical trends and structures are too often rejected in toto on the grounds that they liquidate the local and particular and have affinity for totalitarian social movements and political regimes that do the same. Indeed, these critics themselves frequently rely on undertheorised global notions about the complex and fragmentary nature of new transnational structures and the dynamics of the so-called "late modernity," "postmodernity," or the end of history.

In particular, postmodernist and poststructuralist critics have implicitly, and sometimes explicitly, attacked the metatheoretical foundations of classical theory, scuttling its presuppositions concerning representation, the coherence of the social, and the subject. As part of their broadside against the totalising features of Enlightenment rationalism, Jean Baudrillard, Jean-Francois Lyotard, Jacques Derrida, and others deny social theory's capacity to articulate modernity's complex contours and to contribute to progressive social change. Postmodernists contend that critical perspectives on contemporary society require the demolition of the grand narratives and totalising theories of the modern tradition.

In this study, we shall argue that the postmodern critique of modern social theory is excessive and throws out the valuable aspects of classical theories, along with their problematical features. We claim that the substantive analyses of postmodern theory culminate in a one-sided emphasis on cultural and social fragmentation that ignores societal interdependencies and that devalues social solidarities. Against postmodern theory, we argue that while positivist and hyperrationalist elements abound in classical theory, contrary themes suggest much more modest assumptions and metatheoretical positions that anticipated the postmodern critique.

Moreover, classical theorists conceptualised the interdependent and integrative features of modernity, as well as the forms of disintegration and fragmentation, providing illuminating and broad perspectives on contemporary social formations. Thus, although postmodernists point correctly to dogmatic features of classical social theory that should be abandoned, their caricature of the tradition and call for a radical break with all modern social theory ignores the extent to which classical theories continue to provide resources for the projects of social theory and social reconstruction. Our argument is that the critical aspects of classical social theory must be reappropriated to provide adequate theoretical perspectives on contemporary society and constructive responses to the postmodern critique.

POSTMODERN CRITIQUE OF CLASSICAL SOCIAL THEORY

Postmodernists attack classical social theorists' claims about mapping the social totality, detecting social conditions that guarantee "historical progress," and facilitating progressive social change. Since many postmodern critics are former Marxists who now reject radical politics, socialism, and even welfare state reformism, they advance especially scathing criticism of Marxism's claims concerning history and universal emancipation.

The postmodern critique holds that virtually all modern social theory springs from Enlightenment faith in science and reason and leads to "grand narratives" that legitimate political repression and cultural homogenisation. Postmodernists argue that the totalising features of social theory have affinity for centralised systems of power and social planning that liquidate particularity and block the creative forces of language and desire.

Rejecting classical social theory's meta-assumptions about representation, social coherence, and the subject, postmodernists argue that radical cultural criticism must depart from new bases outside the Enlightenment tradition. Postmodern theorists adopt the poststructuralist strategy of severing the connection between signs and their referents, abandoning modern theory's efforts to represent the "real." For example, Derrida views language as a form of "free play," independent of a "transcendental signified," and rejects claims about the capacity of language to objectively represent extralinguistic realities.

And an extreme postmodernist like Baudrillard evaporates "reality" into a contingent play of simulacra. While modern epistemology focuses on the correspondence of representations to external objects, Baudrillard argues that signs and images have recently replaced "the real." Speaking explicitly of a new postmodern age, Baudrillard states: "We are in a logic of simulation which has nothing to do with a logic of facts and an order of reasons". In his view, the proliferation of contradictory images and messages "implodes" the boundaries between signs and referents, as well as between reality and fiction, dissolving truth and meaning.

Postmodernists also emphasise pervasive cultural fragmentation and social distintegration, rejecting social theory's metatheoretical assumptions concerning the coherence of society and, in extreme cases, the very concept of the social. They conceive of postmodernity as an exceedingly complex matrix of discontinuous processes involving ubiquitous, instantaneous, and disjunctive changes; dispersed and overwhelming space; multiple spectacles and discordant voices; contradictory images and messages; and an overall schizophrenic fragmentation of experience. The extreme cultural incoherence of postmodernity supposedly renders obsolete modern theory's discourses about obdurate social structures (e.g., class hierarchy, gender structure, complex organisation) and patterned social processes (e.g., integration, domination, exploitation).

In addition, postmodernists contend that the philosophic subject which undergirded the conceptions of representation and social coherence in modern philosophy and social theory is in eclipse. In the Cartesian tradition of modern epistemology, Enlightenment thinkers implied that people were capable of being rational subjects who, after grasping the "foundations" of knowledge, could achieve a relatively unambiguous understanding of the external world and could use this to transform the social conditions of their existence. Postmodern theorists, in contrast, present the subject as a fictive construct, arguing that the myth of subjectivity serves a control function that represses human spontaneity and difference. In this regard, Foucault interprets the subject as a construct of power and discipline and Baudrillard has declared that in the postmodern era the "drama of the subject at odds with his objects and with his image" is over.

Postmodern theory, thus, rejects the basic meta-assumptions of modern social theory, putting its entire project into question. While taking this postmodern challenge seriously, we argue that classical social theorists anticipated some of the recent attacks on modern theoretical practices without renouncing altogether the vocation of depicting social reality and serving as an instrument of social change. In the following discussion, we argue that the tradition of modern social theory contained "dogmatic" as well as "critical" features, and that there are thus themes in classical theory which provide both critical perspectives on Enlightenment rationalism and positivistic scientism, as well as resources to help develop a critical theory of the present age. Consequently, since nearly all classical theories contained both dogmatic and critical features (both originating in the Enlightenment heritage), any effort to reappropriate this tradition must itself be critical and reconstructive and not celebatory.

CRITICAL VERSUS DOGMATIC THEMES IN CLASSICAL THEORY

Classical theorists initiated the tradition of modern social theory by attempting to grasp the long-term movement from traditional society to modernity. They usually created polar ideal types (e.g., gemeinschaft/gesellschaft, mechanical/organic solidarity, feudalism/capitalism, agricultural/commercial society, military/industrial society) to describe the dominant social structures of the old and new societies and to specify the primary developmental processes that were transforming social life from the local to the international level. Classical theory was centrally concerned with developing broad and comprehensive perspectives on modernity, focusing on the nascent forms of economy, polity, society, and culture. The new social order was shaped by social differentiation, rationalisation, individuation, class structuration, democratic state formation, urbanisation, and industrial revolution. Classical social theory attempted to theorise the trajectories of change, producing the new institutions, practices, ideas, and everyday life, that together constitute modernity.

Classical theorists presumed that they could represent macroscopic social realities, portray coherently the linkages between new forms of social organisation, interdependence, and fragmentation. They also believed that their approaches would guide the efforts of historical subjects to actively regulate or to transform their social worlds. These meta-assumptions were sometimes employed narrowly and dogmatically and, at other times, reflexively and self-critically. In effect, classical social theorists reproduced the contradictory ethos of the Enlightenment, sometimes mechanistically reproducing its excessive faith in science and reason and, at others, employing its critical rationality and self-reflexivity to their own theories and to the social world.

Dogmatic positivistic themes treated science as if, it were a new religion with the power to conjure up a magnificent order behind the chaos and to provide guaranteed solutions to the new social disjunctions. Theorists like Comte and Spencer combined this excessive faith in science with a belief that reason could precisely represent the broadest features and trends of social development. They implied that social theory could unproblematically grasp reality, provide an exact system of knowledge, and serve as an instrument of enlightenment and social change. All the gaps in knowledge about the social world were, in their view, merely a product of the level of the newness of their science and would be mechanically overcome by further technical development. The dogmatic arguments of these theorists grossly exaggerated theory's powers of representation, overstated the integration of society, and attributed too much rationality to the subject. In addition, they often spoke deterministically about homogeneous paths of development, ignoring regional and national differences. Their implicit idea of modernity was too general, lacking sufficient sensitivity to particularity and differences within national and regional cultures.

Although, their approaches were not wholly free of these problematic features, some classical theorists acknowledged the limits of representation, while expressing a dialectical vision of society as an unstable unity of integrating and fragmenting conditions. Critical moments within classical theory articulated a socially differentiated subject whose limited rationality and partial integration depends on its always problematic adjustments to changing historical conditions, and whose thought and action is mediated by material/organisational resources, power, and communication. Yet, contrary to the postmodernists, classical theorists believed that their approaches could be rationally justified and critically compared on empirical-historical grounds. Moreover, they concurred that systematic conceptualisation based on careful empirical inquiry would represent with reasonable accuracy the salient attributes of extralinguistic as well as linguistic social realities. Especially in regard to macroscopic issues concerning large institutions or entire societies, many classical theorists understood that their theories could never capture social reality in all its richness, particularity, and complexity. In their critical moments, classical theorists understood that their approaches were tentative arguments subject to revision or disconfirmation. Despite his positivistic proclivities, even Durkheim contended that "collective representations" have a "relative independence" from their "substructures".

Yet, classical social theorists seldom addressed the limits of representation and the inherent uncertainties that characterise all judgments about the relationship of theory to social reality. Their tendency to see social science as a perfectable and cumulative enterprise understated the complexity, emergent features, and historicity of social phenomena. While defending the validity of their substantive positions, they often spoke too boldly about the powers of their new science, perpetuating the uncritical Enlightenment faith in science and reason.

Classical theory's dogmatic currents often implied an absolute divide between subject and object, treating "facts" as if they were unaffected by interpretation. The Cartesian emphasis on the capacities and clarity of the impartial scientific observer resulted in an uncritical one-sidedness being granted an objectivity and universality that shielded them from genuine empirical inquiry, discussion, and criticism. Marx's critique of Hegel's theory of the state and of the German "ideologists" raised this issue early in the classical tradition. But, Marx himself made essentialist errors (e.g., his belief in historical materialism's capacity to represent unerringly the class interests of the proletariat and the direction of history) that derived partly from his overweening confidence in the representational powers of historical materialism). Moreover, other thinkers, such as Max Weber and John Dewey, were more sensitive to the inherently perspectival, interpretive, and uncertain nature of all theoretical practices.

Most classical theorists emphasised some sensitivity to the limits of knowledge, emphasising that all representations of society are imperfect and ought to be subject to continual inquiries that could lead to their disconformation. Indeed, Marx's repeated emphasis on the "historical" nature of social phenomena referred primarily to the need for continuing empirical investigations and not to Hegelian stages of history. This empirical translation of Cartesian doubt contributed to the overthrow of the fixed ideals of foundationalism, substituting an open-ended discourse that viewed social theories as incomplete and necessarily changing expressions of social conditions.

Although, Hegelian and Spencerian teleology had a great impact on late 19th and early 20th century social theory, a countervailing Darwinian emphasis on the specific, particular, and nonlinear nature of history and social development broke radically with the idea of progress. When they operated within this lens, social theorists' claims about complicated social phenomena (e.g., classes, status orders, complex organisations, social movements, and long-term social change) as inherently complicated and uncertain. Moreover, some theorists also recognised that their practices were mediated by linguistic frameworks and were inextricably entwined with social interests and ideological presuppositions. This critical side of the classical theory approach contradicted positivist themes about "exact" and "objective" representation of an unproblematic social world. However, none of these theorists rejected representation entirely; they understood that if portrayals of social reality were treated merely as narratives, the nonarbitrary, intersubjective bases for discussing, evaluating, comparing, and disconfirming social theories would be eliminated.

Classical theorists viewed society as a differentiated structural whole. Countering the unmediated idea of social totality as an organic whole, as well as the utilitarian individualism of the market, was the Darwinian idea of individuals and subgroups being linked by determinate relations and specific historical conditions to interdependent material and social contexts. Despite strong disagreement about the level of interdependence and types of connectedness, many classical theorists still attempted to address the complex interrelations between individuals and their multileveled and diverse social and environmental contexts, as well as between major institutions and macro developmental processes that linked smaller groupings into networks of regional, societal, and even trans-societal interdependence.

In contrast to postmodernists, classical theorists believed that the social world has a coherence that could be expressed theoretically. But, they sometimes spoke as if the individual and subgroup were completely absorbed in the totality, and then were not always mindful of the problematic boundaries and unevenly differentiated features of large social structure. For example, the organic metaphor, employed by many theorists, reified "society" and social "development" or evolution and underplayed their discontinuities and reliance on coercion and domination. From the start, many theorists framed their arguments too broadly without historical specificity; nearly all classical theorists spoke about traditional societies in too homogeneous a fashion and about the rise of modernity as if it spread (with some lag) uniformly throughout Europe and North America.

This tendency was especially manifested in the many different theories of social evolution that treated modern societies as if they had identical developmental patterns and institutions. But, some classical theorists, such as Weber, anticipated the postmodern analysis of fragmentation and destruction of meaning. Broad societal or trans-societal theorising cannot avoid a precarious balancing of the general and the specific. Nor can it ever solve completely the problems of understating particularity and overstating coherence. To seek perfection in this regard would mean being silent about collective life. Instead, modern social theorists attempted to recognise these limits and inherent difficulties, and thus condition their claims accordingly.

The classical theorists' assumptions about representation and coherence go hand in hand with their implicit view of individuals, or "subjects," as being capable of instrumentally and normatively comprehending, representing, and transforming their worlds. But, classical theorists often privileged the homogenising features of socialisation, equating social consciousness with the passive reception of social norms and values. Conformist ideas of socialisation exaggerated societal integration and consensus, while understating the particularity and differences of individuals and subgroups—themes that remain central to much contemporary social theory.

Debates over the subject as well as the individual-society relationship have been a particularly controversial issue among neo-Marxists, post-structuralists, and feminists because of the assumption in Marxism and other theories of social change that "emancipation" requires rational human agency. Orthodox Marxists spoke confidently about overcoming "false consciousness" and about the fragmented working class inevitably awakening as a unified revolutionary proletariat. Class fragmentation and political, ethnic, religious, and gender segmentation were at first dismissed as epiphenomena that merely postponed the revolutionary proletariat's unification and triumph. But, when it became obvious that capital's homogenising power was not sufficient to eradicate these obdurate social distinctions and modes of association and identification, some Western Marxists searched for a substitute emancipatory subject, or a plurality of subjects, and, more recently, debated whether the conception ought to be dispensed with entirely.

Other modern social theorists had already developed a more critical conception of the social self contradicting conformist and homogeneous portrayals of the subject. For example, Simmel and Mead held that socialisation is an individuating as well as a homogenising force. In their view, modernity's highly differentiated social structure produces a highly articulated individuality capable of increasingly self-conscious self-assertion and voluntaristic patterns of association. Mead's view of the subject stands out from the sometimes simplistic, hyperrationalist, and conformist version implied by many other classical theorists. Here the postmodernist criticism points to serious deficiencies.

However, they go too far in rejecting the individual's capacity for autonomy and rational action, substituting schizophrenically fragmented or robotised experience and behaviour. Postmodernists seem to be amnesiac about the Counter-Enlightenment reactionaries who used the alleged irrationality of the subject to justify the need for authoritarian moralism and social control. Despite its shortcomings, some current of classical theory suggested a more balanced view of the self, abandoning the imperious vision of rationality and maintaining a conditioned idea of autonomy. Approaches that speak of the disappearence of, or radical fragmentation of, the subject cannot account for uncoerced collective action. Such extreme views are not only empirically misguided, but can easily be turned around to support the types of repression that postmodernists themselves oppose.

Classical theorists saw the new types of mass social organisation and consequent interdependences to be dialectically related with opposing forces producing social and cultural fragmentation. They produced standpoints for criticising society and suggesting social changes from the interplay of these integrating and fragmenting conditions. In particular, the "immanent" criticism of social theorists emphasised the contradictions between emergent democratic ideals and possibilities of modernity and the new types of oppression, inequality, and polarisation. As with their central metatheoretical assumptions, this historical method of social criticism sometimes resulted in dogmatic pseudosociological pronouncements (e.g. about the "inevitable" direction of history), and, at others, expressed critical sensitivity pointing to concrete resources and possibilities at the heart of nascent social struggles, as well as growing aspirations for a freer and more pacified social life.

In essence, classical social theorists provided languages for discussing societal development, the primary social structures and institutions of modern society, and the most significant possibilities for progressive social change. Such theories provided a basis for cognitively mapping the social order which helps individuals situate themselves meaningfully in their emergent social order. They also encouraged an attitude that society can be understood and transformed through collective action and planning.

Classical social theorists such as Marx, Durkheim, and Dewey exhibited a balanced concern for interdependence and fragmentation and argued that modern social arrangements contain their own historical bases for social criticism. It is true that these theorists sometimes spoke dogmatically about the path of societal development and its significance for realising freedom and justice. Although, they claimed to abandon philosophical "grounds," classical theorists often treated the "progressive" features of modernity too optimistically, transforming them into transcendent warranties about a more democratic future.

But, postmodernists, overreacting to this tendency of classical theory, speak of overwhelming social and cultural fragmentation destroying the historical bases of immanent critique and the possibility of progressive social transformation. By dismissing the metatheoretical underpinnings and historical social criticism of modern social theory, postmodernists rule out the strong sociology needed to support their own extremely sweeping claims about a postmodern era, and the exhaustion of theory, collective action, and radical social transformation. They, thus, give up the analytic means for clarifying and elaborating the historical bases of their normative criticisms of modernity. In the end, postmodernists' totalising claims continue in the tracks of classical social theory, but without the conceptual tools and analytical methods to provide a satisfactory account of the alleged postmodern condition.

CONCLUSION

We, thus, conclude that the postmodern critique of contemporary critical social theory undertheorises the current historical conjuncture, overstates its discontinuities with the recent past, and foregoes responsibility for explaining why their views ought to be privileged or even entertained as serious cultural criticism. Still, these approaches do raise important critical questions about the classical tradition and about its complicity in cultural domination. But, their claims that the creative and emancipatory potentials of modernity have already been exhausted and that an entirely new epoch has dawned are highly questionable speculations lacking systematic empirical and theoretical argumentation.

Even if an epochal transformation has not yet occurred, the multiplication of heterodox approaches proclaiming the need for radically new theories, new normative languages, and new politics themselves suggest the possibility of important cultural crises and major social changes. But, theories of broad scope are needed for discussing and assessing recent claims by postmodernists and others about totalising social and cultural change. Thus, the type of social mapping characteristic of classical social theory is necessary again today. Increasingly large publics across the earth sense that a fundamental restructuring of the world order may already be under way. For example, accelerated internationalisation of the economy and the pressing threat of world environmental despoliation highlight increased global interdependence and the need for planning while the political restructuring of Eastern Europe, the tensions in the Arab world manifested in the 1990 Iraqi invasion of Kuwait, and the "postmodern" cultural fragmentation in the West suggest trends toward decentralisation and disintegration. Classical social theory was constructed precisely for making sense out of this type of dialectic of societal integration and fragmentation, and theories of similar scope are needed to do the same for the current macroscopic dynamics.

Furthermore, it is believed that the modern emphasis on theorising society as a whole and of defining its most pressing crises and problems is desperately needed in an era dominated by specialised, disciplinary "middle range" theories and even narrower forms of specialised research. It is widely held that the orientation of competing theories of society in the classical style could contribute significantly to producing discourse over comprehensive social structure and challenging social problems. But, we are not recommending that social theory of the classical type serve as a substitute for specialised social analysis, criticism, and research. Rather, we would hope that specialised sciences be informed by comprehensive and critical theoretical perspectives, and that critical social theory, in turn, be informed by empirical research and results in the special sciences, as well as the experiences of new social movements.

Thus, we believe that contemporary social developments require broad new social theories to help chart out the contours and trajectories of societies at the present moment, much as classical theory provided conceptual delineations of the developmental tendencies and structures of modern societies. Both the capitalist and communist systems are currently undergoing restructuring, relations between the two Cold War enemies have dramatically improved, and new complexities are emerging due to dramatic changes in Europe and turmoil in the Middle East. In such a votile and complex historical conjuncture, comprehensive social theories with a historical vision are needed to make sense of the changes taking place in the contemporary era. Such critical theories of society would incorporate the findings of specialised science into broader perspectives and, at the same time, encourage both social theory and science to engage in increased ethical responsibility and critical awareness of the direction and relevance of its specialised practices.

Such critical theories of society would, therefore, incorporate systematic understanding of national and global social structures and processes and would utilise the technical resources of specialised science to help in this task. It would also attempt to repoliticise critical theory and to orient its theory toward political practice aimed at confronting and dealing with the problems of the present age (economic chaos in the financial and banking system, homeless and growing poverty in an era of intensifying class division, health epidemics in a conjuncture of deteriorating public helath, and so on). We believe that our dangerous historical conjuncture requires a more affirmative (yet still critical) attitude toward science and planning than is suggested by strands of either Frankfurt school critical theory (especially the "dialectic of Enlightenment" tendency) and postmodern theory and that critical social theories of the future should be more open to science and concrete proposals for the restructuring of society than has been the case in the past decades.

Postmodern theory, in contrast, exhibits an exhaustion of theoretical resources and political hope that cavalierly throws away the best of modern theory, especially Marxist and neo-Marxist theories. Reproducing the theoretical despair of Adorno and Horkheimer in Dialectic of Enlightenment in the face of the triumph of fascism, postmodern theory replicates left melancholy after the defeats of the movements of the 1960s and the triumph of conservativism in the 1980s. We believe, however, that the rapidly accelerating crises arising from the breakdown of the postwar structure of accumulation and of the threat of deep recession, environmental destruction, and war demand a reengagement of classical theory and particularly the critical tradition that affirm efforts to rationally grasp large structures and problems and to seek modes of collective resistance, cooperation, and social transformation.

NOTES AND REFERENCES

Anand, Sudhir, and Amartya Sen. 2000. "Human Development and Economic Sustainability." *World Development* 28: 2029-2049.

Banfield, Edward. 1958. *The Moral Basis of Backwardness.* New York: Free Press.

Barnes, Samuel H., Max Kaase, *et al.* 1979. *Political Action.* Beverly Hills: Sage.

Barro, Robert J. 1997. *Determinants of Economic Growth.* Cambridge: MIT Press.

Cummins, Robert A. 1995. "On the Trail of the Gold Standard for Subjective Well-Being." *Social Indicators Research* 35: 179-200.

Cutright, Phillips. 1963. "National Political Development." *American Sociological Review* 28: 253-264.

Dahl, Robert A. 1973. *Polyarchy.* New Haven: Yale University Press.

Dahl, Robert A. 1997. "Development and Democratic Culture." In *Consolidating the Third Wave Democracies*, eds. Larry Diamond, Marc F. Plattner, Yun-han Chu, and Hung-Mao Tien. Johns Hopkins Press, pp. 14-33.

Ersson, Svante, and Jan-Erik Lane. 1996. "Democracy and Development." In *Democracy and Development*, ed. Adrian Leftwich. Cambridge: Polity Press, pp. 45-73.

Estes, Richard J. 1998. "Trends in World Social Development." *Journal of Developing Societies* 14: 11-39.

Foweraker, Joe, and Todd Landman. 1997. *Citizenship Rights and Social Movements*. Oxford: Oxford University Press.

Freedom House. Ed. *Freedom in the World.* Lanham: University Press of America.

Goldstein, Harvey, et al. 1998: A User's Guide to Mlwin. Multilevel Models Project, University of London.

Gurr, Ted R., Keith Jaggers, and Will H. Moore. 1990. "The Transformation of the Western State." *Studies in Comparative International Development* 25: 73-108.

Helliwell, John F. 1993. "Empirical Linkages Between Democracy and Economic Growth." *British Journal of Political Science* 24: 225-248.

Hughes, Barry B. 1999. *International Futures*. Boulder: Westview Press (3rd edition).

Inkeles, Alex, and David H. Smith. 1974. *Becoming Modern.* Cambridge: Harvard University Press.

Inkeles, Alex. 1983. *Exploring Individual Modernity.* New York: Columbia University Press.

Jackman, Robert W., and Ross A. Miller. 1998. "Social Capital and Politics." *Annual Review of Political Science* 1: 47-73.

Kopstein, Jeffrey S., and David A. Reilly. 2000. "Geographic Diffusion and the Transformation of the Postcommunist World." *World Politics* 53: 1-37.

Kurzman, Charles. 1998. "Waves of Democratisation." *Studies in Comparative International Development* 33: 42-64.

Landes, David S. 1998. *The Wealth and Poverty of Nations.* New York: W.W. Norton.

Lasswell, Harold D. 1958. "Democratic Character." In *The Political Writings*, ed. Harold D. Lasswell. Glencoe: Free Press, pp. 465-525.

Muller, Edward N., and Mitchell A. Seligson. 1994. "Civic Culture and Democracy." *American Political Science Review* 88: 635-52.

Nagle, John D., and Alison Mahr. 1999. *Democracy and Democratisation.* London: Sage.

Nevitte, Neil. 1996. *The Decline of Deference.* Ontario: Broadview Press.

Olson, Mancur J., Naveen Sarna, and Anand W. Swamy. 2000. "Governance and Growth." *Public Choice* 102: 341-364.

Page, Benjamin, and Robert Y. Shapiro. 1993. "The Rational Public and Democracy." In *Reconsidering the Democratic Public*, eds. George E. Marcus and Russell L. Hanson. Pennsylvania: Pennsylvania State University Press, pp. 35-64.

Rowen, Henry S. 1996. "World Wealth Expanding." In *The Mosaic of Economic Growth*, eds. Ralph Landau, Timothy Taylor, and Gavin Wright. Stanford: Stanford University Press, pp. 92-125.

Rustow, Dankwart A. 1970. "Transitions to Democracy." *Comparative Politics* 2: 337-363.

Scarbrough, Elinor. 1995. "Materialist-Postmaterialist Value Orientations." In *The Impact of Values*, eds. Elinor Scarbrough and Jan van Deth. Oxford: Oxford University Press, pp. 123-159.

Weber, Max. 1958 [1905]. *The Protestant Ethic and the Spirit of Capitalism*. Boston: Allen and Unwin.

Welzel, Christian, and Ronald Inglehart. 2001. Human Development and the "Explosion" of Democracy. Discussion Paper FS III 01-202. Wissenschaftszentrum Berlin für Sozialforschung (WZB) (forthcoming).

Yi, Feng. 1997. "Democracy, Political Stability and Economic Growth." *British Journal of Political Science* 27: 391-418.

Yule, George U., and Maurice G. Kendall. 1950. *An Introduction to the Theory of Statistics.* London: Griffin.

Zeller, Richard, and Edward G. Carmines. 1980. *Measurement in the Social Sciences.* Cambridge: Cambridge University Press.

3

MOVEMENTS FOR SOCIAL CHANGE

Social movements are large-scale informal groupings of individuals or organisations, which are connected through their shared interests to focus on specific political or social issues, in order to carry out a social change. Multiple alliances may work separately for common causes and still be considered a social movement.

A social movement is a combination of shared ideas and activities that are concerned with changing the patterns of social life (Sinclair). The shared activities or collective action may be defined as "any goal-directed activity jointly pursued by two or more individuals". It should be observed that only a fraction of all collective action involves social movements.

It may also be defined as collectivity acting with some degree of organisation and continuity outside of institutional channels for the purpose of promoting or resisting change in the group, society, or world order of which it is a part..

Qualifications

Some scholars believe that groups sharing the same ideas for change are not social movements—unless they are involved in collective action. These ideas are only pre-conditions. Trends and mass migrations are not social movements. These are uncoordinated activities of individuals. Something with social consequences is not necessarily a social movement. Seeing social movements as mainly outside the established political institutions, they do not accept that interest groups are social movements.

The movements for social change can be forward or backward looking. Social movements develop because there is a perceived gap between the current ethics and aspirations of people and the present reality. There are various levels of social change: individual, organisational and institutional.

Because social movements are the consequences of new elements of civil society, which are not incorporated into the social order, they are always unconventional. Civil society is normally in a state of change, but social structures tend towards stability. That is why social movements almost always exist. If the discrepancy between civil society and social order is large, then social movements are strong and numerous. If the discrepancy is small, then social movements are weak and more conventional.

This 'disenfranchisement' leads to mobilisation—first organisational, where resources are harnessed in support of the cause. Resources include: people, time, skills/expertise and funds. Then mass mobilisation, where society is recruited behind the cause.

There is inevitable resistance to social change. Many do not want their vested interests or status quo threatened. There is also simple inertia.

Tactics of Change: non-violence includes negotiation, direct action, events/media stunts, demonstrations, propaganda, strikes, boycotts, non-co-operation, civil disobedience, parallel structures. Violent breakaways undercut the movement's legitimacy.

Actions undertaken by civil society to effect change are generally informed by strategic thought. In thinking strategically, social change activists try to identify the nature and causes of social problems and then choose specific targets that are deemed the most likely people or organisations to resolve those problems. One of the keys to a successful strategic approach is in maintaining effective communication with, and among, members of the public. It is readily acknowledged by leading social theorists that just and effective democracies require a strong and functional public sphere. The public sphere operates best where citizens, as individuals or in groups, are informed about the social, political and corporate affairs that affect their interests, and enter into public discussion about the plans, policies and activities of those in power whose decisions affect the public interest. This on-going discussion provides the feedback and direction needed for healthy governance.

History of the Social Movement

Political movements that evolved in late 18th century, like those connected to the French Revolution and Polish Constitution of May 3rd 1791 are among the first documented social movements. The labour movement and socialist movement of the late 19th century are seen as the prototypical social movements, leading to the formation of communist and social democratic parties and organisations.

From 1815, Britain after victory in the Napoleonic Wars entered a period of social upheaval and change, caused by returning soldiers and unemployment. This resulted in class struggle in the Peterloo Massacre, the Reform Act of 1832, disputes over the Corn Laws. Other European countries, such as France, began to see the emergence of political and social movements in the 19th Century. These social movements set the background to which Karl Marx attempted to analyse social theory more generally. 1861 saw the beginning of the reform movements in Russia, as the feudal system was abolished. Unions, or Soviets were formed from 1905 as pressure for reform continued, resulting in the collapse of the Russian State at the end of the First World War.

In 1945, Britain after victory in the Second World War entered a period of radical reform and change, as a workers rights social movement dominated politics until the election of Margaret Thatcher in 1979. In the 1970s, women's rights, peace, civil rights, and environmental movements emerged, often dubbed *New Social Movements.* They lead inter alia to the formation of green parties. Some find in the end of the 1990s the emergence of a new global social movement, the anti-globalisation movement.

Factors Contributing to Social Movements

Several key processes lie behind the history of the social movements. The process of urbanisation, which created large cities, facilitated social interaction between scores of people. It was in cities, where people of similar goals could find each other, gather and organise, that those early social movements first appeared.

Similarly, the process of industrialisation, which gathered large masses of workers in the same region, was responsible for the fact that many of those early social movements addressed matters important to that social class. Many other social movements were created at universities, where the process of mass education brought many people together.

With the development of communication technologies, creation and activities of social movements became easier—from printed pamphlets circulating in the 18th century coffeehouses to newspapers and Internet, all those tools became important factors in the growth of the social movements.

Finally, the spread of democracy and political rights like the freedom of speech made the creation and functioning of social movements much easier.

Social Movement Organisations

Organising New Social Change Activities: The surplus energy accumulated by the society and given expression through the initiative of pioneers and their followers does not gain momentum until it becomes accepted and organised by society. The process of organisation may take many different forms. It may occur by the enactment of new laws or regulations that support the activity or it may be in the form of a new system or accepted set of practices. Each development advance of the society leads to the emergence of a host of new organisations designed to support it and puts pressure on existing organisations to elevate their functioning to meet the higher demands of the new phase.

***Integrating the Organisation with Society*:** The organisation is the mechanism by which the surplus energy in society is harnessed, mobilised, directed and channelled to produce greater results. The organisation derives energy from being integrated with the society in which it functions. The energy of society comes from its needs and aspirations. This energy pervades the social organisation established to meet these needs. The more finely the organisation is attuned to fulfil underlying social aspirations, the greater *the energy flowing through it.*

The will of society changes over time as old attitudes and goals are replaced with new ones. Organisations that adapt to these changes continue to thrive. Those that remain fixed in the past decline, become ineffective, and are eventually discarded or fade away.

Interest Groups and Organisation

It should be observed that it is difficult to distinguish between a social movement and an interest group if we insist that social movements must operate outside political institutions. (Interest groups normally operate inside existing structures.) This is especially true for movements that focus on partial change—the vast majority. *E.g,* the environmental movement & Sierra Club, Greenpeace or the World Wildlife Fund.

Note that many social movements are associated with one or more formal organisations (SMOs).

Relevant Actors

The types of individuals or activists in the social movements can be classified as followings:

Protagonists: all who support the movement or whom it claims to represent.

Adherents: activists and less involved constituency members.

Constituency: those whom movement claims to represent, usually beneficiaries. The beneficiary may be the whole public rather than a particular segment.

Conscience adherents: those who support a movement but are not beneficiaries if it is successful.

Antagonists: those who oppose the movement—targets and counter-movements.

Bystanders: those with no obvious stake or immediate interest.

Types of Social Movements

David Aberle (1966) described four types of social movement including: alterative, redemptive, reformative, and revolutionary social movements, based upon two characteristics: (1) who is the movement attempting to change and (2) how much change is being advocated.

Alternative Social Movements are looking at a selective part of the population, and the amount of change is limited due to this. Planned Parenthood is an example of this, because it is directed toward people of childbearing age to teach about the consequences of sex.

Redemptive Social Movements also look at a selective part of the population, but they seek a radical change. Some religious sects fit here, especially the ones that recruit members to be 'reborn'.

Reformative Social Movements are looking at everyone, but they seek a limited change. The environmental movement fits here, because they try to address everyone to help the environment in their lives.

Revolutionary Social Movements want to change all of society. The Communist party is an example of wanting to radically change social institutions.

Social movements can also advocate minor changes (e.g., tougher restrictions on drunk driving).

Reform Movements—movements dedicated to changing some norms, usually legal ones. Examples of such a movement would include a trade union with a goal of increasing workers rights, a green movement advocating a set of ecological laws, or a movement supporting the introduction of capital punishment or right to abortion. Some reform movements may advocate a change in custom and moral norms, for example, condemnation of pornography or proliferation of some religion. The Polish *Solidarnoœœ* movement of 1980s was an important factor in the fall of the Soviet Union

Radical Movements—movements dedicated to changing some value systems. It directs to the creation of new social order and the destruction of existing social order. Those are usually much larger in scope then the reform movements, Examples would include the American Civil Rights Movement which demanded full civil rights and equality under the law to all Americans, regardless of race, or the Polish Solidarity movement which demanded the transformation of communist political and economy system into democracy and capitalism.

Target Audience—Social movements can be aimed at change on an individual level or change on a broader, group or even societal level.

Group-focussed Movements—focused on affecting groups or society in general, for example, advocating the change of the political system. Most of such groups eventually transform into or join a political party.

Individual-focussed Movements—focused on affecting individuals. Most religious movements would fall under this category. Those movements rarely transform into political parties.

Methods of Work

Peaceful Movements—opposed to using violent means. The American Civil Rights movement, Polish Solidarity movement, or Mahatma Gandhi civil disobedience movements would fall into this category

Violent Movements—various armed resistance movements up to and including terrorist organisations. Examples would include the Palestinian Hezbollah, Basque Euskadi Ta Askatasuna *(ETA)* or Ireland's Provisional Irish Republican Army *(IRA)* movements.

Old and New

Old Movements—most of the 19th century movements that recruited their followers from a specific social class (only workers, only peasants, only whites, only Aristocrats, only protestants, etc.). They were usually centered on some materialistic goals like improving the living standard of the given social class.

New Movements—movements which became dominant from the second half of the 20th century—like the civil rights movement, environmental movement, gay rights movement, peace movement, anti-nuclear movement, anti-globalisation movement, etc. Sometimes they are known as postmodernism movements. They are usually centered on a non-materialistic goal.

Dynamics of Social Movements

Social movements are more likely to evolve in the time and place which is friendly to the social movements: hence their evident symbiosis with the 19th century proliferation of ideas like individual rights, freedom of speech and civil disobedience. They are more likely to form in the societies and cultures allowing expression of ideas by individuals -like most of the Western culture, which explains why most of social movements exist in the United States and Europe, and fewer in more autocratic places like Russia or China. Such friendly context and environment is only a background facilitating the creation of the social movement. There must also be polarising differences between groups of people: in case of 'old movements', they were the poverty and wealth gaps. In case of the 'new movements', they are more likely to be the differences in customs, ethics, and values.

Finally, the birth of a social movement needs what sociologist Neil Smelser calls an *initiating event:* a particular, individual event that will begin a chain reaction of events in the given society leading to the creation of a social movement. For example, American Civil Rights movement grew on the reaction to black women, Rosa Parks, riding in the whites-only section of the bus. The Incident of Rosa Parks who was arrested for refusing to give up her seat to make room for white people sparked the American Civil Rights Movement. The Polish Solidarity movement, which eventually toppled the communist regimes of the Eastern Europe, developed after trade union activist Anna Walentynowicz was fired from work. Such an event is also described as a *volcanic model*—a social movement is often created after a large number of people realise that there are others sharing the same value and desire for a particular social change.

Thus, one of the main difficulties facing the emerging social movement is spreading the very knowledge that it exists. Second, is overcoming the free rider problem—convincing people to join it, instead of following the mentality 'why should I trouble myself when other's can do it and I can just reap benefits after their hard work'.

Modern social movements became possible through education (the wider dissemination of literature), and increased mobility of labour due to the industrialisation and urbanisation of 19th century societies. The freedom of expression, education, and relative economic independence are required for organised social structures like political societies and popular movements.

Other Contributing Factors: Power and Authority

Power Means: "being influential, having control, being effective. Sociologists usually define **power** as the ability to impose one's will on others, even if those others resist in some way. More generally, one could define 'power' as the potential to bring about significant change, usually in people's lives, through the actions of oneself or of others.

Such influence, control effectiveness involves the consideration of authority which is an accepted source of expert information, a conclusive statement or decision that may be taken as a guide or precedent, power to influence or precedent resulting from knowledge or experience.

Authority can take three forms:

(1) Regulatory, based on one's formal position and status in relation to others (employer-employees, teacher-student, police officer-citizen);

(2) Expert knowledge, where the expert may possess the power to define ordinary people or to withhold knowledge from those whose well being is affected by it. Vast bodies of technical regulations exist whose application becomes the responsibility of the political technician; and

(3) Relationship ability or interpersonal skills, where power comes from interpersonal influence based on abilities to work with people. Obviously one may have one kind of power and authority and not others or may have all three in various degrees.

Government exercises authority over its citizens through laws, administration, and enforcement. Society exercises a far more persuasive authority over its members through its ideas, attitudes, customs, and values. Different societies may develop at very different rates and in different directions under very similar forms of government, due to differences in social and cultural authority.

Modern societies are far more free and tolerant than those of previous centuries, yet they continue to exert a very powerful force on their members—but the character of that force has changed. From being predominantly negative in the form of prohibitions and strictures, now the force of social authority acts far more as a spur to initiative, than a bar. The pressure felt by middle and working class families to conform to social norms has become pervasive throughout the world.

The spread of education tends to enhance this tendency. Apart from the practical knowledge and skills it imparts, modern education also instills a greater sense of individual self-respect and social rights that impels the individual to seek and maintain status in society.

There are many theories and discourses focusing on the subject of 'power' and 'authority'. However, it is vital to recognise these two concepts and its interrelation with the social movements.

Organising vs. Mobilising mobilising refers to the process by which inspirational leaders or other persuaders can get large numbers of people to join a movement or engage in a particular movement action, while organising refers to a more sustained process whereby people come to deeply understand a movement's goals and empower themselves to continued action on behalf of those goals.

Stages of Social Movements

After the social movement is created, there are two likely phases of recruiting. The first phase will gather the people deeply interested in the primary goal and ideal of the movement. The second phase, which will usually come after the given movement had some successes and its fame increased, will gather people whose primary interest lie in joining the movement for 'being in it'—because it's trendy, it would look good on a resume. People who joined in this second phase will likely be the first to leave when the movement suffers any setbacks and failures.

Eventually, the social movement will move towards a crisis. If it has achieved its intended goal, then it's called a *victory crisis,* as most members leave the movement assuming there is no longer any need for its continued existence. This will likely be opposed by a minority of members, for whom the existence of the very movement have become the primary goal itself, and likely the source of their income. Few social movements have survived a *victory crisis,* often merging with other similar movement or transforming into a tiny, caricature form of their early selves. Other type of crisis is *a failure crisis,* which can be seen in increasing demoralisation and disenchantment of members, when they loose faith in the possibility that the primary goal of the movement can be ever achieved. *Failure crisis* can be encouraged by outside elements, like opposition from government or other movements. However, many movements had survived a failure crisis, being revived by some hardcore activists even after several decades.

Blumer, Mauss and Tilly have described different stages social movements often pass through. Movements emerge for a variety of reasons, coalesce, and generally bureaucratise. At that point, they can take a number of paths, including: finding some form of movement success, failure, co-optation of leaders, repression by larger groups, or even the establishment of the movement within the mainstream.

Theories of Social Movement

A variety of theories have attempted to explain how social movements develop. The many approaches to the explanation of the phenomenon of social movements suggest that no one of them is able to explain everything. All the approaches may be correct in their local sphere, but they either stress attention to specific types of social movements and consider them as universal or put all the attention on a single aspect of the phenomenon of social movements and ignore others. Different accents give diverse outcomes. Some of the better-known approaches are outlined below.

Collective Behaviour (Old Social Movement Theory)

'Collective behaviour' theory is still recognised as a dominant theory in studies of social movements. The supporters of this approach consider social movements as semi-rational responses to abnormal conditions of structural strain between the major societal institutions; that strain causes malfunctioning of the whole social system. In general, according to the collective behaviour approach, social movements are the symptom and manifestation of a sick society. A healthy society does not have social movements; it has a conditional form of political and social participation.

Resource Mobilisation Theory (RMT)

This school of social movement analysis, developed from the 1960s onward, has been and remains the dominant approach among sociologists, though it has increasingly been challenged in recent years.

'Resource mobilisation' theorists point out that social movements are rational and novel responses to new situations and new opportunities in society. Movements are seen as innovative forms of political participation, which create and tap new political resources available in modern democratic societies. They are treated as emerging pressure groups or as embryonic parties. Social movements are no longer seen as symptomatic of social malfunction or pathology. They appear as a part of the political process.

RM theory stresses the ways in which movements are shaped by and work within limits set by the resources available to the group and the organisational skills of movement leaders in utilising those resources. Resources are understood here to include: knowledge, money, media, labour, solidarity, legitimacy, and intern and external support from power elite. The emphasis on resources offers an explanation why some discontented/deprived individuals are able to organise while other are not.

Political Process Theory

Political process theory in some way is similar to resource mobilisation, but tends to emphasis different components of social structure that is important for social movement development: political opportunities. Political process theory argues that there are three vital components for movement formation: insurgent consciousness, organisational strength, and political opportunities.

Organisational strength falls inline with resource-mobilisation theory, arguing that in order for a social movement to organise it must have strong leadership and sufficient resources.

Insurgent consciousness refers back to the ideas of deprivation and grievances. The idea is that certain members of society feel like they are being mistreated or that somehow the system is unjust. The insurgent consciousness is the collective sense of injustice that movement members or potential movement members feel and serves as the motivation for movement organisation.

Political opportunity refers to the receptivity or vulnerability of the existing political system to challenge. This vulnerability can be the result of any of the following or a combination thereof.

One of the advantages of the political process theory is that it addresses the issue of timing or emergence of social movements. Some groups may have the insurgent consciousness and resources to mobilise, but because political opportunities are closed, they will not have any success. The theory, then, argues that all three of these components are important.

Critics of the political process theory and resource-mobilisation theory point out that neither theory discusses movement culture to any great degree. This has presented culture theorists an opportunity to expound on the importance of culture.

An additional strength of this model is that it can look at the outcomes of social movements not only in terms of success or failure but also in terms of consequences (whether intentional or unintentional, positive or negative) and in terms of collective benefits.

New Social Movement

New social movement theory developed initially in Europe to help explain a host of new movements that emerged in the 1960s and 1970s that did not seem to fit a model of Marxian class conflict that had been the predominant model in much European social movement theory.

The newness of the putatively new social movements is said to consist of such things as a greater emphasis on group or collective identity, values and lifestyles rather than or in addition to developed ideologies, and a tendency to emerge more from middle than working class constituencies. The Green Party in Germany with its emphasis on environmental and peace issues, feminism, and alternative non-consumerist lifestyles is often portrayed as the umbrella group representing a synthesis of new social movements aimed at a broad, general social liberation.

Some new social movement theorists emphasise a change in the economic structure of the First World from an industrial, heavy manufacturing based 'Fordist' (after Henry Ford's assembly line) to a 'post-industrial,' 'postmodern' or 'post-Fordist' economy centered more around the service sector (i.e. fast food restaurants) and computer-based information industries as a structural force shaping the new movements. New social movements, in contrast to old social movements, are produced by new contradictions of society, contradictions between individual and state. 'New values' theorists also stress that the condition of economic prosperity and political stability allow them to de-emphasise material values and lead them to embrace post-materialist values, reflecting 'higher' aesthetic, self-realisation, and creative needs. These approaches change class interests or transform them into non-class but 'universal human' interests.

There first three approaches have been particularly influential in the USA, the fourth has been mainly associated with European scholars. In some extends it can be seen as an 'American' and a 'European' approach to the study of social movements.

Examples of Social Movements: Gandhi and Non-Violence

Gandhi's greatest achievement was to develop the philosophy of non-violent action, and spread this concept throughout the world. Born on October 2, 1869, Mohandas Karamchand Gandhi struggled to find freedom for his Indian countrymen and to spread his belief in non-violent resistance.

Part of the inspiration Gandhi's policy of non-violence came from the Russian writer Leo Tolstoy, whose influence on Gandhi was profound. Gandhi also acknowledged his debt to the Bhagavad Gita, the teachings of Christ and to the 19th-century American writer Henry David Thoreau, especially to Thoreau's famous essay 'Civil Disobedience'.

Gandhi considered the terms passive resistance and civil disobedience inadequate for his purposes, however, and coined another term, Satyagraha (Sanskrit, "truth and firmness").

It was in South Africa that Gandhi first experienced racial discrimination. There he began his fight to end prejudice and achieve equality for people of all races. Using marches, letters, articles, community meetings and boycotts, he protested. These protests often led to his arrest.

After 21 years in South Africa, Gandhi returned to India to fight for Indian independence from Great Britain. In addition to the methods he used in South Africa, Gandhi would add fasting, prayer, and to his system of non-violence.

The six strategic steps on non-violent action were:

Investigate

Get the facts. The complexity of society today requires patient investigation to accurately determine responsibility for a particular injustice.

Negotiate

Meet with opponents and put the case to them. A solution may be worked out. If no solution is possible, let your opponents know that you intend to stand firm to establish justice, but that you are always ready to negotiate further.

Educate

Keep campaign participants and supporters well informed about the issues, and spread the word to the public.

Demonstrate

Picketing, vigiling, mass rallies, and leafleting are the next steps.

Resist

Non-violent resistance is the final step, to be added to the first four as a last resort. This may mean a boycott, a fast, a strike, tax resistance, a non-violent blockade or other forms of civil disobedience. Planning must be carefully done, and non-violence training is essential. When properly carried out, actions of resistance build a position of moral clarity, which will strengthen your own courage and create widespread respect for your campaign.

Be patient

Meaningful change cannot be accomplished overnight. To deepen ones analysis of injustice and oppression means to become aware of how deeply entrenched are the structures, which produce them. These structures can be eliminated, but this requires a long-term commitment and strategy.

Gandhian principles played a part in inspiring similar movements throughout the world, removing dictators over the last 15 years in countries as far apart as the Philippines and Poland, while providing the inspiration for the American civil rights leader, Martin Luther King. In 1959, Dr. and Mrs. King spend a month in India studying Gandhi's techniques of non-violence as guests of Prime Minister Jawaharal Nehru.

The American Civil Rights Movement

The civil rights movement in the United States was a struggle by black Americans to gain full citizenship rights and achieve racial equality. Individuals and organisations challenged discrimination with a variety of activities, including protest marches, boycotts, and refusal to abide by segregation laws. Many believe that the movement began with the bus boycott in Montgomery, Alabama, in 1955 and ended with the Voting Rights Act of 1965, though some argue that it has not ended yet.

The movement had two clear strands:

- *Reform:* The Southern Christian Leadership Council. Luther King's non-violent approach.
- *Revolutionary*: The Black Panthers, Malcolm X.

Malcolm X rejected non-violence as a principle, but he sought co-operation with Martin Luther King and other civil rights activists who favoured aggressive non-violent protests. To thousands of black people around the world, he personified revolution. He was able to appeal to ordinary people and to articulate the anger and frustration they felt. Above all, he symbolised unyielding defiance and resistance in the face of prejudice, discrimination, and repression.

Martin Luther King, and his policy of non-violent protest, was the dominant force in the civil rights movement during its decade of greatest achievement, from 1957 to 1968. His lectures and remarks stirred the concern and sparked the conscience of a generation. The movements and marches he led brought significant changes in American life.

King summoned together a number of black leaders in 1957 and laid the groundwork for the organisation now known as the Southern Christian Leadership Conference (SCLC). King was elected its president, and he soon began helping other communities organise their own protests against discrimination.

Dr. King's concept of '*somebodiness*' gave black and poor people a new sense of worth and dignity. His philosophy of non-violent direct action, and his strategies for rational and non-destructive social change, electrified the conscience of this nation and re-ordered its priorities. The Voting Rights Act of 1965, for example, went to Congress as a result of the Selma to Montgomery march. His wisdom, his words, his actions, his commitment, and his dreams for a new cast of life fired the movement. His 1963 T Have a Dream' speech dealing with peace and racial equality is one of the most powerful speeches in American history.

The major principles of King's non-violence movement were:

- Non-violence is a way of life for courageous people.
- Non-violence seeks to win friendship and understanding
- Non-violence seeks to defeat injustices, not people.
- Non-violence holds that suffering for a cause can educate and transform.
- Non-violence chooses love instead of hate.
- Non-violence holds that the universe is on the side of justice and that right will prevail.

The tactics employed included:

In 1960, four black students asked to be served at Woolworth's lunch counter in Greensboro, reserved for white customers only. When refused they staged a sit-in protest. By 1961, 70,000 had taken part in similar sit-ins. These protests gained publicity for the plight of blacks in the South.

Freedom Riders

These were groups of black and white protesters who rode segregated buses across the Southern States. Sometimes, they were ambushed and attacked by white youths. When they reached their destination—usually a heavily segregated town, they would organise sit-ins. Freedom riders got great publicity for the civil rights cause.

Demonstrations and Marches

Peaceful demonstrations and marches were very powerful civil rights tactics. When demonstrators were attacked by white police forces e.g. Birmingham, Alabama, April 1963, (dogs, fire hoses and cattle prods used) public opinion came down on the civil rights protestors, rather than bigoted police chiefs.

King was recipient of the 1964 Nobel Peace Prize, which increased his credibility enormously. After 1965 the focus of the civil rights movement began to change. Martin Luther King, Jr., focused on poverty and racial inequality in the North. Younger activists criticised his interracial strategy and appeals to moral idealism. In 1968, King was assassinated by a gunman in Memphis, Tennessee.

For many, the civil rights movement ended with the death of Martin Luther King, Jr. Some argue that the movement is not yet over because the goal of full equality has not been achieved. Racial problems still existed after 1968, and urban poverty among blacks represented a worsening problem.

King's legacy has lived on. In 1969, his widow, Coretta Scott King, organised the Martin Luther King Jr. Center for Non-Violent Social Change. Today it stands next to the Ebenezer Baptist Church in Atlanta. His birthday, Jan. 15, is a national holiday, celebrated each year with educational programs, artistic displays, and concerts throughout the United States. The Lorraine Hotel where he was shot is now the National Civil Rights Museum. More importantly, he has inspired future social change fighters and citizens.

Extension of civil rights—owning credit card, equal rights, equal pay, education, reproductive and health rights. Women in politics.

Suffragettes

In the UK, the National Union for Women's Suffrage was formed in 1987 by Millicent Fawcett. Their primary aim was to obtain the vote for women, Ms Fawcett believed in peaceful protest.

Progress was slow, and in 1903 the Women's Social and Political Union was founded by Emmeline Pankhurst and her daughters Christabel and Sylvia. They wanted women to have the right to vote and they were not prepared to wait. The Union became better known as the Suffragettes. Members of the Suffragettes were prepared to use violence to get what they wanted.

In fact, the Suffragettes started off relatively peacefully. It was only in 1905 that the organisation created a stir when Christabel Pankhurst and Annie Kenney interrupted a political meeting in Manchester to ask two Liberal politicians if they believed women should have the right to vote. Neither man replied. As a result, the two women got out a banner that had on it 'Votes for Women' and shouted at the two politicians to answer their questions. Such actions were all but unheard of then when public speakers were usually heard in silence and listened to courteously even if you did not agree with them. Pankhurst and Kenney were thrown out of the meeting and arrested for causing an obstruction and a technical assault on a police officer. Both women refused to pay a fine preferring to go to prison to highlight the injustice of the system as it was then.

The Suffragettes burned down churches as the Church of England was against what they wanted; they vandalised Oxford Street, apparently breaking all the windows in this famous street; they chained themselves to Buckingham Palace as the Royal Family were seen to be against women having the right to vote; they hired out boats, sailed up the Thames and shouted abuse through loud hailers at Parliament as it sat; others refused to pay their tax. Politicians were attacked as they went to work. Their homes were fire bombed. Golf courses were vandalised.

Suffragettes were quite happy to go to prison. Here they refused to eat and went on a hunger strike. The government was very concerned that they might die in prison thus giving the movement martyrs. Prison governors were ordered to force feed Suffragettes but this caused a public outcry as forced feeding was traditionally used to feed lunatics as opposed to what were mostly educated women.

The government of Asquith responded with the Cat and Mouse Act. The Cat and Mouse Act allowed the Suffragettes to go on a hunger strike and let them get weaker and weaker. Force-feeding was not used. When the Suffragettes were very weak... they were released from prison. If they died out of prison, this was of no embarrassment to the government. However, they did not die but those who were released were so weak that they could take no part in violent Suffragette struggles. When those arrested had regained their strength, they were re-arrested for the most trivial of reason and the whole process started again. This, from the government's point of view, was a very simple but effective weapon against the Suffragettes.

As a result, the Suffragettes became more extreme. The most famous act associated with the Suffragettes was at the June 1913 Derby when Emily Wilding Davison threw herself under the King's horse. She was killed and the Suffragettes had their first martyr. However, her actions probably did more harm than good to the cause, as she was a highly educated women. Many men asked the simple question—if this is what an educated woman does, what might a lesser-educated woman do? How can they possibly be given the right to vote?

It is possible that the Suffragettes would have become more violent. They had, after all, in February 1913 blown up part of David Lloyd George's house—he was probably Britain's most famous politician at this time and he was thought to be a supporter of the right for women to have the vote!

However, Britain and Europe was plunged into World War One in August 1914. In a display of patriotism, Emmeline Pankhurst instructed the Suffragettes to stop their campaign of violence and support in every way the government and its war effort. The work done by women in the First World War was to be vital for Britain's war effort. In 1918, the Representation of the People Act was passed by Parliament.

Environmental Movement

From the late nineteenth century until the nineteen sixties, 'environmentalism' was generally understood to refer to a set of movements made up overwhelmingly of people from the better off sectors of society, who were concerned about issues of preservation or management of the wilderness, and whose critique of society did not generally go beyond these concerns.

Although, it had its roots dating back into the 1890s, the modern environmental movement did not develop until the 1960s—which was an era of real social change (free speech, civil rights, women's rights, anti-war etc.).

Rachel Carson's book 'Silent Spring' in 1963 was a real 'wake-up' call. Its exposure of the effects of DDT (a 'pest' pray that killed insects, entered the food chain and caused cancer and genetic damage) led to it being banned from the market. The crises that triggered change were the toxic smogs, starting with the 1948 Pennsylvania smog followed by others in New York and London in the 1950s and 60s.

In the sixties and seventies a radical environmental movement began to emerge made up of groups concerned with the degradation of the environment not as a wilderness issue, but as a part of daily life. Recycling was promoted, and wider issues such as the dangers of chemicals in the food chain, polluted air and water etc. were promoted to persuade people that protection of the environment was an important issue. Most of the people involved in these groups were young people, influenced by the antiwar movement and by the counterculture.

Around the same time, some progressive labour activists were beginning to raise issues having to do with occupational safety and health, with the presence of toxic chemicals and other environmental hazards in the workplace. Both labour environmentalism and radical environmentalism (or ecology, as it was usually called) were concerned not only with protecting the wilderness, but also with the impact of environmental degradation on people's daily lives.

In the seventies, both radical and mainstream environmentalism grew, but both sectors of environmentalism remained overwhelmingly white and, except for efforts by labour activists around occupational safety and health, overwhelmingly composed of middle and upper-middle class people, especially students and professionals.

It was in the late seventies and early eighties that a new grassroots environmental movement began to emerge involving constituencies previously distant from environmentalism: lower middle class and working class whites, coloured people and rural communities.

Growth of environmental organisation membership increased enormously from the early 60s to the present day. The number of environmental organisations also grew rapidly. These groups cover a number of types of approaches, for example:

- Mainstream/conservative ecology: The Sierra Club
- Populist ecology: Earth Day
- Radical ecology: Greenpeace, GAIA (eco-feminists)

The range of environmental issues that organisations campaign about is vast (covering issues such as water, air, forests, wetlands, animals and habitats, anti-war and anti-nuclear, and wastes).

Environmentalism, unlike most social change movements, has the benefit of extremely concrete benchmarks, things like tons of CO2 emissions prevented; acres of rainforest and coral reef preserved; species saved from extinction etc. However, in terms of the ultimate conservation objective of building a civilisation that can thrive on this planet without destroying it, then the movement is failing. Analyses indicate the need to tap more into other higher need—and individually more urgent concerns—such as prosperity, security, health, fashion/luxury, success/progress etc. in order for the movement to continue to thrive.

NOTES AND REFERENCES

Alston, P. 1988. 'Making Space for New Human Rights: The Case of the Right to Development', *Harvard Human Rights Yearbook*, 1: 3–40.

Ama Ankumah, E. 1992. 'Universality of Human Rights and the African Charter on Human and Peoples' Rights', in *Universaliteit en Mensenrechten. Fundamenteel en Controversieel*, pp. 23–38. Leiden: NJCM.

Barbero, J.M. 1993. *Communication, Culture and Hegemony. From the Media to Mediations*. London: Sage Publications.

Barker, C. 2000. *Cultural Studies. Theory and Practice*. London: Sage Publications.

Baxi, U. 2002. *The Future of Human Rights*. New Delhi: Oxford University Press.

Bell, D.A. 1996. 'The East Asian Challenge to Human Rights: Reflections on an East West Dialogue', *Human Rights Quarterly*, 18(3): 641–667.

Benhabib, S. 1995. 'Cultural Complexity, Moral Interdependence, and the Global Dialogical Community', in M. Nussbaum and J. Glover (eds). *Women, Culture and Development. A Study of Human Capabilities*, pp. 235–255. Oxford: Clarendon Press.

Carrier, J.G. 1995. *Occidentalism. Images of the West*. Oxford: Clarendon Press.

Donders, Y. 1999. Human Rights, Culture and Development. Report of the conference organised by Women for Women's

Human Rights and Novib, Istanbul, 25–27 November 1998. The Hague: Novib.

Donnelly, J. 1989. *Universal Human Rights in Theory and Practice*. Ithaca: Cornell University Press.

—. 1993. *International Human Rights*. Boulder: Westview Press.

Foucault, M. 1980. *Power/Knowledge: Selected Interviews and Other Writings 1972–1977*, in C. Gordon (ed.). Translated by

Galtung, J. 1994. *Human Rights in Another Key*. Cambridge: Polity Press.

Geertz, C. 1973. *The Interpretation of Cultures*. London: Fontana Press.

Gupta, A. and J. Ferguson. 1997. 'Beyond "Culture": Space, Identity, and the Politics of Difference', in A. Gupta and

Hamelink, C.J. 2004. *Human Rights for Communicators*. Cresskill: Hampton Press.

Hannerz, U. 1996. *Transnational Connections*. London: Routledge.

Harindranath, R. 2006. *Perspectives on Global Cultures*. Berkshire: Open University Press.

Howard, M. 1993. *Contemporary Cultural Anthropology*. New York: Harper Collins.

Igantieff, M. 1998. 'Out of Danger. Human Rights at 50: Overview', *Index on Censorship*, 27(3):21–29.

Jones, P. 1999. 'Human Rights, Group Rights, and Peoples' Rights', *Human Rights Quarterly*, 21(1):80–107.

Kagitçibasi, C. 1997. 'Individualism and Collectivism', in J.W. Berry, M.H. Segall and C. Kagitçibasi (eds). *Handbook of Cross-Cultural Psychology, 3, Social Behaviour and Applications*, pp. 1–49. Boston: Allyn & Bacon.

Koh, T. 1999. 'Differences in Asian and European Values', *Asian Mass Communication Bulletin*, 29(5):10–11.

Komin, S. 1988. 'Thai Value System and Its Implications for Development in Thailand', in D. Sinha, D. and H. Kao (eds). *Social Values and Development. Asian Perspectives*. New Delhi: Sage Publications.

—. 1991. *Psychology of the Thai People. Values and Behavioural Patterns*. Bangkok: National Institute of Development Administration.

Linden, A. 1997. 'Communication and Human Rights in Developing Countries', *Culturelink*, August, 22:149–166.

Lukes, S. 1993. 'Five Fables about Human Rights', in. S. Shute and S. Hurley (eds). *On Human Rights: Oxford Amnesty Lectures*, pp. 19–40. New York: Basic Books.

Mani, L. 1987. 'Contentious Traditions: The Debate on Sati in Colonial India', *Cultural Critique*, 7:119–157.

Miller, D. (ed.). 1995. *Worlds Apart. Modernity through the Prism of the Local.* London: Routledge.

Mutua, M. 2002. *Human Rights. A Political and Cultural Critique.* Philadelphia: University of Philadelphia Press.

Narasimhan, S. 2002. *Sati. Widow Burning in India.* New York: Doubleday.

Narayan, U. 1997. *Dislocating Cultures. Identities, Traditions and Third World Feminism.* New York: Routledge.

Perez De Cuéllar, J. (ed.). 1995. *Our Creative Diversity. Report of the World Commission on Culture and Development.* Paris: UNESCO.

Postel-Coster, E. 1994. 'Women and Culture: An Ambivalent Relationship', *Culture Plus,* 14:7–10.

Preis S., A.B. 1996. 'Human Rights as Cultural Practice: An Anthropological Critique', *Human Rights Quarterly*, 18(2): 286–315.

Ravindran, D.J. 1998. *Human Rights Praxis: A Resource Book for Study, Action and Reflection.* Bangkok: The Asian Forum for Human Rights and Development.

Said, E. 1995. *Orientalism.* Harmondsworth: Penguin Books.

Samuels, H. 1999. 'Hong Kong on Women, Asian values and the Law', *Human Rights Quarterly*, 21(3):707–734.

Servaes, J. 1989. 'Cultural Identity and Modes of Communication' in J. Anderson (ed.). *Communication Yearbook*, 12, pp. 383–416. Beverly Hills: Sage Publications.

—. 1999. *Communication for Development. One World, Multiple Cultures.* Creskill: Hampton Press.

Servaes, J. and R. Lie (eds) 1997. *Media and Politics in Transition. Cultural Identity in the Age of Globalisation.* Leuven: Acco.

Suu Kyi, A.S. 1995. *Freedom from Fear* (Revised Edition). London: Penguin Books.

Symonides, J. 2000. 'Towards a Human Rights Agenda for the 21st Century', in J. Servaes (ed.). *Walking on the Other Side of the Information Highway. Communication, Culture and Development in the 21st Century*, pp. 74–85. Penang: Southbound.

Tomasevski, K. 1993. *Development Aid and Human Rights Revisited.* London: Pinter.

Tomlinson, J. 1997. *Internationalisation, Globalisation and Cultural Imperialism.* London: Pinter.

Werbner, P. and T. Modood (eds). 1997. *Debating Cultural Hybridity. Multi-cultural Identities and the Politics of Anti-racism.* London: Zed Books.

4

EVOLUTION OF SOCIALISM

Social Conditions for Human Evolution

Before proceeding now to the further consideration of the laws which underlie the complex social phenomena that present themselves in the civilisation around us, it will be well to look for a moment backwards, so as to impress on the mind the more characteristic features of the ground over which we have travelled. We have seen that progress from the beginning of life has been the result of the most strenuous and imperative conditions of rivalry and selection, certain fundamental physiological laws rendering it impossible, in any other circumstances, for life to continue along the upward path which it has taken. Man being subject like other forms of life to the physiological laws in question, his progress also was possible only under the conditions which had prevailed from the beginning. The same process, accordingly, takes its course throughout human history; but it does so accompanied by phenomena quite special and peculiar.

The human intellect has been, and must necessarily continue to be, an important factor in the evolution which is proceeding. Yet, the resulting self-assertiveness of the individual must be absolutely subordinated to the maintenance of a process in which the individual himself has not the slightest interest, but to the furtherance of which his personal welfare must be often sacrificed. Hence the central feature of human history, namely the dominance of that progressively developing class of phenomena included under the head of religions whereby this subordination has been effected. Hence, also, the success of those forms which have contributed to the fullest working out of that cosmic process which is proceeding throughout human existence, just as it has been proceeding from the beginning of life.

What we have, therefore, specially to note before advancing further is that it is this cosmic process which is everywhere triumphant in human history. There has been no suspension of it. There has been no tendency towards suspension. On the contrary, throughout the period during which the race has existed, the peoples amongst whom the process has operated under most favourable conditions have always been the most successful. And the significance of that last and greatest phase of social development which has taken place in our Western civilisation, in which all the people are being slowly brought into the rivalry of life, consists simply in the fact that this process tends to reach therein the fullest and completest expression it has ever attained.

Emergence of Socialist Movement in Europe and America

Keeping these facts in mind, let us now proceed to consider the significance of that great social movement which is beginning to exert a gradually deepening influence on the political life of our period. The uprising known throughout Europe, and in America, as the socialist movement is the most characteristic product of our time. Nothing is, however, more remarkable than the uncertainty, hesitation, and even bewilderment with which it is regarded, not only by those whose business lies with the practical politics of the current day, but by some of those who, from the larger outlook of social and historical science, might be expected to have formed some conception of its nature, its proportions, and its meaning.

Local Environment and its Impact on Solid Movement

In attempting to examine this movement, it is a matter of no small importance to carefully consider the environment in which it is to be studied; for a very brief reflection makes it clear that many of the phenomena associated with it in various parts of our civilisation are due to local causes that have no essential connection with the movement in general Thus, if France is chosen as the locality in which to study the movement, it sooner or later becomes clear that that country, despite its early and trenchant experiments in democratic government, is not by any means a favourable one in which to observe the progress of modern socialism. The process of social development therein, although rapid, has been too irregular, and its people have too completely broken with the past to allow for an exact comparison of the relationship to each other of the developmental forces at present at work. In the recent history of the country, the old spirit and the new have tended to confront each other in extremes; and we must remember that, despite the genuine triumph which democracy obtained in the period of the Revolution, it is in France that we have witnessed within the nine-teenth century attempts to revive, on a most ambitious scale, that ancient spirit of military Cæsarism which is altogether foreign to our civilisation.

In Germany, again, we have a country which in many respects must be considered the true home at the present day of social democracy. Yet, it may be noted that even there the causes which have contributed most effectively to swell the proportions of the existing movement are largely local and peculiar. Placed, as the German people are, between a neighbour like France on the one side, and a country like Russia in a far earlier stage of social evolution on the other, they have developed, through force of circumstances, an extensive militaryism which, while essentially defensive and therefore characteristically different from the older type, tends, nevertheless, to retard the process of social expansion which is in progress, and to develop features which are incompatible with the spirit underlying this expansion.

In many of its social features, Germany is still backward, although it is difficult to believe, as M. Leroy-Beaulieu asserts, that it remains, despite the rapid advance made by socialism therein, the one country in Europe, excluding Russia, which is most under the sway of old influences. Social development in Germany is, in fact, proceeding unevenly. It is advanced as regards ideas, but in arrear as regards practice; and such a situation does not offer the most favourable conditions for estimating the character and the destiny of the movement with which the extreme party in that country is identified.

Again, in the United States of America, where we have the most typical democracy our civilisation has produced, we are also under some disadvantage in the study of the forces that lie behind modern socialism. The social question in America is, in all essential respects, the same question as in any other part of our Western civilisation. It is probable too that nowhere else will the spirit which is behind socialism measure itself with greater freedom from disturbing influences against certain opposing forces which are the peculiar product of our modern free communities, than in that country. Yet, the special conditions of "newness" which are present largely interfere to prevent the essential character of the social question as a phase of an orderly development which has been long in progress, from being so clearly distinguished in the United States, and, therefore, from being so profitably studied there as elsewhere. Taking all these considerations into account we shall probably not be able to do better than to follow the lead of Marx in choosing England as the best country in which to study the developments of the modern spirit. We may do so, not only for the reason which influenced Marx, namely, that it is the land in which modern capitalism and industrialism obtained their earliest and fullest expression; but also because, in this country, the process of social development has been less obscured by local causes and less interrupted by disturbing events. It has, on the whole, proceeded by regular, orderly, and successful stages in the past, and it shows no signs of weakening or cessation in the present. For these reasons it would appear that the relationship of the present to the past and the future may be more profitably studied in England that anywhere else in our Western civilisation.

Now, there is an aspect of the British political life at the end of the nineteenth century which will, not improbably, at a later period, absorb the attention of the historian. This is the remarkable change that at the present time is slowly and silently taking place within that great political party which has led the van of progress during the past one hundred and fifty years, and which, during the lifetime of the last few generations, has added to the statute-book a list of progressive measures that, taken all together, constitutes in effect one of the greatest revolutions through which any country has passed in so brief a period. At first sight, the change in progress has all the appearance of being a process of disintegration, and one of its results for the time being must undoubtedly be to strengthen, in some measure, the opposing ranks. It is not that the party of progress has been rent with feuds, or that its strength has been undermined by malign influences.

On the contrary, not only has it fought a good fight, but it has kept the faith. It is rather that events appear to have outgrown the faith; and slowly and almost imperceptibly the depressing and dispiriting feeling has spread throughout the ranks that the old watchwords are losing their meaning, and that the party is at length confronted with problems which the well-tried formulæ of the past have no power to solve. The unusual and exceptional nature of the crisis through which political life in England is passing at the present time, is only brought into greater prominence on a closer view. It may be observed that the development which the Liberal Party has been working out in the British public life throughout the nineteenth century has been but the latest phase of that great social movement, the progress of which we traced in the last chapter throughout the history of our Western civilisation; and in this stage it has at length almost accomplished the emancipation of the individual and the establishment of political equality throughout the entire social organisation. Since the early part of the century, we have had, for instance, in England a series of measures following each other at short intervals extending the political franchise until it now nearly includes the adult male population. Side by side with these we have had a number of measures emancipating trade and commerce from the control of the privileged classes, who, under the cover of protective laws, made largely in their own interests, were enabled to tax the community for their benefit.

Similarly, during the century, a long list of measures has aimed at the curtailment and abolition of class privileges. Local popularly-elected bodies of all kinds have been everywhere created, the tendency of which has been to greatly restrict, and even to extinguish, the undue local influence previously exercised by wealth. The voting power of the property-owning classes has been gradually curtailed until it has been reduced almost to the level of the humblest class of citizens. The state services have been thrown open, instead of being practically reserved for the friends of the privileged classes; all comers have been placed on a footing of equality, and unexampled purity of administration has been secured throughout the public services.

There has been also a great number of measures which have aimed at rendering this state of political equality, not only theoretical, but real and effective. The extension of the franchise has been accompanied by measures like the Ballot Act and the Bribery Acts, intended to protect the weakest and poorest class of the people from being interfered with in the exercise of their political rights; and, lastly, we have had a succession of Education Acts which have aimed at qualifying every citizen to understand and value for himself his rights and position as a member of a free community. It has to be specially noted now that the political doctrine which lay behind all this extensive list of reforms has had certain clearly defined limitations. The acknowledged aim of the political party, under whose influence or direction most of these measures were carried, has always been kept clearly in the foreground. It hag been to secure *equal political rights* for all. The first article of faith behind this programme was that, this end being secured, the highest good of the community was then to be secured by allowing the individuals to work out their own social salvation amid the free and unrestricted play of natural forces within the community, hampered by the least possible interference from government. It has been held in England by the Progressive Party, as a fundamental principle, that "a people among whom there is no habit of spontancous action for a collective interest—who look habitually to their government to command or prompt them in all matters of joint-concern, who expect to have everything done for them in all matters of joint-concern, who expect to have everything done for them except what can be made an affair of mere habit and routine—have their faculties only half developed; their education is defective in one of its most important branches."[1] The end consistently aimed at was, therefore, the "restricting to the narrowest compass the intervention of a public authority in the business of the community."[2] Mill urged with emphasis that the *onus* of making out of a strong case in respect of this intervention, should further be placed, not on those who resisted it, but on those who recommended it, and he insisted without compromise that letting alone should be the general practice," and that every departure from it, unless required by some great good, is a certain evil."[3]

Such has been the great British political doctrine of Laissez-faire. To the development, expansion, and application thereof, one of the most distinguished group of political leaders and social, political, and philosophical writers that any country has ever produced, has for a long period contributed. Under it the unexampled English expansion of the nineteenth century has taken place, and it has undoubtedly been an important factor in producing that expansion. Taken with all its faults and limitations, it has been one of the most characteristic products of the political genius of the Englishspeaking peoples. Its spirit still pervades the entire political life of all the lands into which these peoples have carried their institutions. In what respect, therefore, have we outgrown it? What is the import in relation thereto of that socialistic movement which is now so deèply affecting the minds of certain sections of the population amongst the Western peoples? Whither beyond it is that evolution which we have traced throughout the history of these peoples now carrying us?

In order to answer these questions, it is necessary to examine the forces at work in British political life at the present time. We have already found that the real impelling force which lies behind the political advance that we, in common with most European peoples, have been making in recent times, has its seat in the development the altruistic feelings have attained amongst us, and in the deepening and softening of character which has accompanied the change. It is these feelings that have found a vehicle for expression in that body of public opinion which, moving slowly in the past but more quickly in our own time, has brought about the gradual political emancipation of the individual from the rule of the privileged classes. What we have, however, now to particularly note, is that the movement which has carried us so far shows no signs of staying or abating; the same feelings continue to supply an impelling force that threatens to drive us, and that actually is driving us, onwards far beyond the limits which the political doctrines of the recent past prescribed.

Political Emancipation of the Masses in Britain

It may be noticed in England that the political emancipation of the masses, the last stage of which in this country has occupied almost an entire century, is now well-nigh accomplished. The shreds of political measures necessary to complete it—which are all that those who adhere to the progressive faith of the past have to offer—form so slender a programme as scarcely to excite any real enthusiasm amongst the followers of those leaders whose mental horizon is still bounded by the old ideals of the political enfranchisement of the people. On the other hand, an immense number of larger and greatly more important questions have arisen which press for attention. In the unparalleled expansion which has taken place, new and vast problems that the old leaders did not foresee have been born, and it may be noticed that the free and unrestricted play of forces within the community is producing results against which the public conscience, still moved by the altruistic feelings, has been slowly but surely rising in revolt.

In England, within the last decade, descriptions of how the poor live in our great cities, and the revelations made through inquiries like that conducted by the Sweating Commission, or more recently through that instituted on so extensive a scale by Mr. Charles Booth into the condition of the London poor, have deeply stirred the public mind. It is being gradually realised that there are great masses of the people who, amid the unrestricted operation of social and economic forces, and under a regime of political liberty, have never had any fair opportunity in life at all, and who have been from the beginning inevitably condemned to the conditions of a degraded existence. It seems to be already generally felt that something more than mere political liberty is demanded here.

Again, trade and commerce have been to a large extent freed from the control of the privileged classes of the past; but, in the unrestricted expansion which has followed, the capitalist classes appear to have inherited a very large share of the rights and powers of their predecessors. They have even become possessed of others in addition, while the personal sense of relationship which introduced a modifying sense of duty in the past, tends to become more and more attenuated. Political liberty has not enabled the poorer classes to make headway against the enormous influence which these classes wield, to the extent to which many of the older reformers expected. By the combination of the capitalist classes into rings, trusts, syndicates, and like associations for the universal control of production and the artificial keeping up of prices, the community finds the general welfare threatened by a complication which the reformers of the past can scarcely be said to have counted upon. We have also great organisations and combinations of labour against these capitalist classes, whereby the life of the community is disturbed and disorganised to a serious extent, and to which it seems to be increasingly difficult to apply the old doctrine of the restricted nature of the duty of the state. It is evident, moreover, that in these recurring struggles the combatants, if left to themselves, are often unequally matched; for the weapon on one side is merely the power to reduce profits, while on the other it is the right to impose actual want and hunger on large numbers of our fellow-creatures. We have, therefore, public opinion tending more and more to side with the inherently weaker cause, and, under the stimulus of the altruistic feelings, coming to propose measures that leave the *laissez-faire* doctrine of the past far behind.

It may be observed, that the public opinion, which earlier in the century regarded with suspicion (as tending to the infringement of the prevailing theories as to the restricted nature of the duty of the state) even the attempt to regulate the hours of women and children in factories and mines, has already come to view as within the realm of reasonable discussion proposals to strengthen the position of the working classes by enforcing a legal eight hours day and even a minimum wage in certain occupations. The public conscience, which is moving fast in these matters, has all the appearance of being destined to move far. We are not without growing evidence that our education laws will not stop with providing the bare rudiments of education for the people, nor with providing them on the grounds mentioned by Mill:—that others are liable to suffer seriously from the consequences of ignorance and want of education in their fellow-citizens.[4] Nor would indications seem to show that we have reached finality in our poor laws in simply guaranteeing the bare necessities of existence.

We have evidence everywhere along the line, not only of a movement towards the general abandonment of the doctrine of the non-interference of the state in social matters, but of a more significant tendency that seems to be associated with it—*a tendency to strengthen*and equip at the general expense the lower and weaker against the higher and wealthier classes of the com*munity*. We have, it is evident, already progressed a considerable distance beyond the doctrine, that the end of endeavour is to secure political equality for all. Yet, whither are we travelling?

Another feature of the times which we may notice is that under the outward appearance of action, the great political party which has carried progress so far in England stands in reality doubting and confused in mind. It moves, it is true, but rather because it is thrust forward; the enthusiasm, the robust faith, the clearly defined conviction that marked its advance through the early and middle decades of the nineteenth century seem to be wanting. The ranks move, but irresolutely. They still appear to wait for the vibrant call of a leader upon whom a larger faith has descended. While the party of progress in England advances, thus, falteringly, and with eyes cast backwards rather than forwards, the most remarkable political phenomenon of the time is rising into prominence in another quarter.

The socialist movement which has languished through various phases, and fitfully occupied attention in various parts of Europe since the beginning of the century, has entered on a new stage, and has taken the field with a definite political programme. The leaders of the movement, no longer ignoring politics and political methods, now appear to have set before themselves the task of reforming the state through the state. The Utopian projects which distinguished the writings of its earlier advocates have disappeared, and even the essential ideals of the movement tend to be kept in the background, to be discussed amongst the faithful as the ultimate goal rather than with the adversary as the immediate end of endeavour. We have not to deal with mere abstract and transcendental theories, but with a clearly-defined movement in practical politics appealing to some of the deepest instincts of a large proportion of the voting population, and professing to provide a programme likely in the future to stand more and more on its own merits in opposition to all other programmes whatever.

Yet, more remarkable still, one of the signs of the times in England is the attitude of the advanced wing of the great progressive party of the past to this new movement. It appears to be slowly wheeling its forces into line with those of this socialist party. To the bewilderment of many of the old leaders, that party whose central article of political faith in the past, namely, the untrammelled freedom of the individual, has given a distinctive colouring to the political life of the whole English-speaking world, is now asked apparently to turn its face in a direction opposite to that in which it has been previously set, and contrary to that in which the evolution of our civilisation has, so far, progressed. The advance in the new direction, it appears to those who still hold to the old faith, must inevitably involve the weakening, if not the ultimate abandonment, of the principles for which the party has fought so long and so sturdily in the past. The individualism which they held so highly, and which has been so markedly associated with the stress and energy of life amongst the advanced peoples, must apparently, if the new views are to prevail, be given up. The play of the competitive forces which has so largely contributed to the extraordinary expansion of the past, must be, it appears to them, not only restricted, but perhaps ultimately suspended in an era of soul-deadening and energy-restricting socialism on the one side, and general confusion and political insolvency on the other.

The question which now presents itself is: What is the significance of this situation, and of that remarkable period of transition through which political life in England, as in most countries where our civilisation has reached an advanced stage, is passing? Let us proceed, as a means of throwing light on the subject, to examine the leading features of the most prevalent and influential form of socialism at the present day, namely, the "scientific socialism" of the German school more particularly associated with the names of two of its exponents, Marx and Engels. One of the first things to be noticed by any one who undertakes an examination of the socialistic phenomena of our time, is the remarkable number of schemes, projects, and measures, loosely described as socialist or socialistic, that have nothing whatever of an essentially socialist character about them. Without going so far as to accept Proudhon's definition of socialism as all aspiration towards the improvement of society, a large number of persons appear to make only a slight reservation, and regard it as all aspiration towards the improvement of society by society.

True socialism has, however, one invariable characteristic by which it may be always recognised, whether it take the form advocated by the more prevalent German school, or by that anarchist section represented by Proudhon and Bakunin, whose ideal, despite their title and methods, is really a morally perfect state in which government, law, and police would be unnecessary. True socialism has always one definite object in view, up to which all its proposals directly or indirectly lead. This is the final suspension of that personal struggle for existence which has been waged, not only from the beginning of society, but, in one form or another, from the beginning of life.[5]

Although, Marx prudently abstained from putting forward any detailed scheme of the social order which he held was to supersede the present capitalist and competitive era, he, as we shall presently see, deliberately leads us up to this culmination. The attainment of the same object is clearly put forward by Engels as the avowed end of endeavour. As a later example we have the same idea in Mr. Bellamy's artistic model of a socialist community in working order,—a community in which children are to become entitled to an equal share of the national wealth in virtue of being born, in which the prices of staples are to grow less year by year, in which there is to be no state legislature and no legislation, in which there are to be no police and no criminal classes, but in which it can be said at last that "society rests on its base, and is in as little need of support as the everlasting hills."[6] Now, directly we come to examine these schemes, a somewhat startling admission has to be made, an admission, however, for which those who have followed the argument developed through the preceding chapters will be prepared. It is that the arguments by which their advocates lead up to them are unanswered, and even unanswerable from the point of view from which the greater number of their critics have assailed them. This admission may appear the more remarkable, when it has to be asserted in the same breath that it is probably true that in all the literature which socialism has produced, no serious attempt has been made, and that probably no serious attempt can be made, to deal with even the initial difficulties in the way of the continued success of a society organised on a socialist basis. At the outset, underneath all socialist ideals, there yawns the problem of population. Progress so far in life has always been, necessarily associated with the inexorable natural law over which man has no control, and over which he can never hope to have any control, which renders selection necessary; and which, therefore, keeps up the stress of life by compelling every type, as the first condition of progress, to continually press upon and tend to outrun the conditions of existence for the time being. One of the fundamental problems which has, therefore, confronted every form of civilisation that has arisen, and which must confront every form that will ever exist, is that arising from the tendency of human reason to come into conflict with nature over this requirement.

Under the Utopias of socialism, one of two things must happen: either this increase must be restricted or not. If it be not restricted, and selection is allowed to continue, then the whole foundations of such a fabric as Mr. Bellamy has constructed are bodily removed. Even if we imagine the competitive forces suspended for a time between the members of the community, the society as a whole must, sooner or later, come into active competition with other ocieties, and so begin once more one of the phases through which human society has already passed.

But, if, on the other hand, the increase of population is to be restricted, a difficulty no less important presents itself. A considerable number of persons have contemplated the action of a new restrictive influence (although it operated widely in the ancient civilisations) in public opinion and the conditions of life under the new order, anticipating, with a lady writer who has given attention to the subject in England, the growth of a feeling of intellectual superiority to "this absurd sacrifice to their children, of generation after generation of grown people."[7] But, in whatever way restriction which would limit the population to the actual conditions of life might be effected, it is not necessary, after what has been said in previous chapters as to the physiological conditions of the process which has been working itself out throughout life—and nowhere more effectively and thoroughly than in human history—to deal at length with the fate of any people amongst whom the restriction was practised. The conditions of selection being suspended, such a people could not in any case avoid progressive degeneration even if we could imagine them escaping more direct consequences.

In ordinary circumstances they would indubitably receive short shrift when confronted with the vigorous and aggressive life of societies where, other things being equal, selection and the stress and rivalry of existence were still continued. Again, a class of objections, now being temperately discussed in England and Germany, according to which a state organised on a socialist basis would find more immediate difficulties, hindrances, and drawbacks, which would place it at a manifest disadvantage with other communities, have never been seriously dealt with by socialist writers. The enormous pressure, capable of being exercised by the competitive system at its best, operating continually to ensure the most economic and efficient system of production; the accompanying tendency of the best men to find the places for which they are best fitted; the tendency towards the free utilisation of the powers of such men to the fullest degree in the direction of invention, discovery, and improvement, coupled with the difficulty of finding any thoroughly efficient stimulus for the whole of the population to exert itself to the highest degree when the main wants of life were secure, these are all considerations which would, in an earlier stage, tell enormously against a socialist community when matched in the general competition of life against other communities where the stress of life was greater.

It will not help us even if there are to be no competing societies, and if, in the contemplated era of socialism, the whole human family without distinction of race or colour is to be included in a federation within which the competitive forces are to be suspended. We may draw such a draft on our imagination, but our common-sense, which has to deal with materials as they exist, refuses to honour it. We are concerned, not with an imaginary being, but with man as he exists, a creature standing with countless æons of this competition behind him; every quality of his mind and body (even including, it must always be remembered, that very habit of generous thought for others which gives heart to the modern socialistic movement) the product of this rivalry, with its meaning and allotted place therein, and capable of finding its fullest and fittest employment only in its natural conditions.

But, these are the mere commonplaces which only bring us to the crux of the subject. Impressive as such considerations may be to those who have caught the import of the evolutionary science of the time, no greater mistake can be made than to think that they form any practical answer to the arguments of those who would lead us on to socialism. Why? For the simple reason that, as we have throughout insisted, men are not now, and never have been, in the least concerned with, or influenced by, the estimates which scientists or any other class of persons may form of the probable effects of their present conduct on unborn generations. The motives which inspire their present acts are of quite a different kind. But, it is these motives which are shaping the course of events, and it is consequently with these, and these only, that we have to deal if we would gauge the character and dimensions of the modern socialist movement. Let us see, therefore, in what way the conception, of what is called scientific socialism—of modern society developing towards socialism as the result of forces now actually at work amongst us—is justified or the contrary.

According to Marx, the dominant factor in the evolution through which we are passing is the economic one. The era in which we are living began in the mediæval period with the rise of capitalism. To understand what capitalism is—and few writers have grasped more thoroughly than Marx some of the ultimate facts which underlie the institution in the form in which he attacked it—we have to get behind the superficial phrases, and some of the errors of the political economists of the old school. When we reach the heart of the matter we find it to be, according to Marx, a system by which the capitalist is enabled to appropriate the *surplus value* of the work of the labourers, these being able to retain as wages only what represents the average subsistence necessary for themselves and their children in keeping up this supply of labour. There is, thus, an inherent antagonism between the two classes.

As the conflict takes shape, it begins to develop remarkable features. At the one pole, we have the continued appropriation and accumulation of surplus value, with the ever-increasing wealth and power of those in whose hands it is concentrated. At the other end, we have the progressive enslavement and degradation of the exploited classes. As the development continues, the workers, on the one hand, gradually come to recognise their position as a class and become possessed of a sense of their common interests. On the other hand, the competition amongst the capitalist class is great and continually growing; the larger capitalists gradually extinguish the smaller ones, and wealth becomes accumulated in fewer and fewer hands. To quote Marx's words: "Along with the constantly diminishing number of the magnates of capital, who usurp and monopolise all advantages of this process of transformation, grow the mass of misery, oppression, slavery, degradation, exploitation; but with this, too, grows the revolt of the working class, a class always increasing in numbers and disciplined, united, organised by the very mechanism of the process of capitalist production itself."

The monopoly of capital becomes a fetter upon the mode of production, which has sprung up and flourished along with and under it. Centralisation of the means of production and socialisation of labour, at last, reach a point when they become incompatible with their capitalist integument. This integument is burst asunder. The knell of capitalist private property sounds."[8] That is to say, the state of things becomes at length intolerable; there is anarchy in production, accompanied by constantly-recurring commercial crises; and the incapacity of the capitalist classes to manage the productive forces being manifest, public opinion at last comes to a head. The organised workers seize possession of the means of production, transforming them into public property, and socialistic production becomes henceforward possible.

The transformation supposed to be effected in the latter stage of the movement is thus described by Frederick Engels: "With the seizing of the means of production by society, production of commodities is done away with, and, simultaneously, the mastery of the product over the producer. Anarchy in social production is replaced by systematic, definite organisation. The struggle for individual existence disappears. Then, for the first time, man, in a certain sense, is finally marked off from the rest of the animal kingdom, and emerges from mere animal conditions of existence into really human ones. The whole sphere of the conditions which environ man, and which have hitherto ruled man, now comes under the dominion and control of man, who now, for the first time, becomes the real conscious lord of Nature, because he has now become master of his own social organisation.... It is the ascent of man from the kingdom of necessity to the kingdom of freedom."[9]

This is the Marx-Engels theory of our modern civilisation, and of the denouement to which it is hastening, so far as justice can be clone to it in so brief a summary. It is a conception, whatever its shortcomings, of power and originality—displaying, despite its errors, a deep knowledge of social forces and a masterful grasp of some of the first principles underlying our complex modern life. Now, the first fact which it is necessary to keep clearly before the mind in dealing with this theory of society is, that this relationship of capital to labour which Marx has described, is nothing more than the presentday expression of a social relationship which has existed throughout the greater part of human history.

There is nothing new or special about the fact which underlies the theory of surplus value; nor is it peculiar to the capitalist era any more than to any other era. We had what corresponds to the appropriation of the surplus value of the work of the lower masses of the people by the ruling classes in all the early military societies, in the Greek States, and under the Roman Republic and Empire. We had it in a marked form under the institution of slavery, and it continued under the feudal system which preceded the rise of modern capitalism. With the discoveries of science, and their application to the wants of life, we have it only under another phase in the resulting era of expansion and capitalism in which we are now living.[10]

But, while this fact must never be lost sight of, it must, at the same time, be noticed that there is a development taking place in this relationship of labour to capital, a development of the most significant kind which is likely, as time goes on, to control and dominate the entire political outlook. Although, Marx, has been quite mistaken as to the nature of the development which is taking place in our civilisation, and as to the direction in which it is carrying us; it will, nevertheless, in all probability be recognised in the future that he has been much nearer the truth in regarding, as he did, the prevailing relationship of the workers to the capitalist classes, than the hitherto dominant school of political economists have been in regarding it as the natural and normal condition of the two parties, any disturbance of which must involve the dislocation of the entire social machinery of the modern world. Not the least important part of the work which Marx has already accomplished (for to the influence of the socialist party the change is undoubtedly due) is the tendency already visible amongst the younger and rising school of political economists, particularly in England, to question whether this relationship is natural and normal, and whether the extraordinary powers and privileges which capital has inherited from a past order of society—powers begetting, to use words of Professor Marshall, "the cruelty and waste of irresponsible competition and the licentious use ofwealth,"[11]—constitute any necessary feature of the institution of private capital in enabling it to discharge the beneficial function it is held to be capable of performing for society.

Now, the development which Marx contemplated is, it may be observed, thoroughly materialistic; it takes no account of those prime evolutionary forces which lie behind the whole process of our social development. The phenomenon which underlies what has been called the exploitation of labour is, as we have seen, in no way new or special to our time. What then is the special factor in modern life which has enabled Marx to anticipate the growing power of the workers, and as a result to picture with some degree of verisimilitude a stage at which it will become irresistible, and at which they will proceed to seize and socialise the means of production? His followers may reply that it is the inherent tendency of the process of economic evolution actually in progress. Yet, it is nothing of the kind. If any of Marx's followers really hold this view, they are deceiving themselves. The economic problem per se has no inherent tendency whatever which it did not possess under any other phase of society, and from the beginning. The new factor in the problem is one altogether outside of and independent of the economic situation.

If we look round at the position of the workers at the present day, and note their relations to the state and to the capitalist class, it will be seen that the one absolutely new and special feature which distinguishes these relationships now, as compared with all past periods, is, that the exploited classes, as the result of an evolution long in progress, and still continuing with unabated pace, have been admitted to the exercise of political power on a footing which tends more and more to be one of actual equality with those who have hitherto held them in subjection. This evolution has its causes exclusively in that ethical development, the course of which has been traced in the previous chapter. It is the cardinal and essential feature of the situation dominating the entire outlook, but entirely independent of the economic question.

It will help materially towards the clearer understanding of the position, if this feature of the situation is kept well in view. We may perceive the importance of the factor at once if it is taken away. The materialistic evolution of Marx is left without its motive power. For, if we are to have only the frank selfishness of the exploiting classes on the one side, and the equally materialistic selfishness of the exploited classes on the other, the inherent tendency of modern society" disappears. There would remain nothing whatever in the present constitution of society, economic or otherwise, which would lead us to expect any progress towards the culmination which Marx describes, but everything which would lead us to anticipate the repetition of a well-worn tale of history. If we are to have nothing but materialistic selfishness on the one side leagued against equally materialistic selfishness on the other, then the power-holding classes, being still immeasurably the stronger, would be quite capable of taking care of themselves, and would indeed be very foolish if they did not do so. Instead of enfranchising, educating, and raising the lower masses of the people (as they are now doing as the result of a development which Marx has not taken into account), they would know perfectly well, as they have always done in the past, how "to keep the people in their places," i.e. in ignorance and political disability, all the modern tendency of capital towards competition and concentration notwithstanding.

But, it will be answered, the feature of our times, which there is no gainsaying, is the humanitarian tendency in the contrary direction.

The situation with which we have to deal is one in which this materialistic selfishness does not exist. Never in human history have the minds of men been moved with nobler or more generous ideas towards each other; and the whole tendency of our civilisation has been, and continues to be, to develop this disposition. Quite so. This is, indeed, the reason why we are only likely to misinterpret, as Marx has undoubtedly done, the nature and tendency of the economic development we are undergoing, by regarding it apart in itself as the key to the whole situation, instead of as only a subordinate phase of an immensely wider evolutionary process. From the larger outlook the view is immeasurably widened. The development that will fill the history of the twentieth century, will certainly be the change in the relations of capital, labour, and the state; but once we have grasped the fundamental laws behind that development as a whole, it becomes clear that the change, vast and significant as it undoubtedly promises to be, will, nevertheless, be one essentially and profoundly different both in character and results from that which Marx anticipated. To understand the nature of this change, it is desirable now to call to mind once more the leading features of that remarkable process of social development which has been in progress throughout the history of our civilisation. We found this process to consist essentially in the slow disintegration of that military type of society which reached its highest development in the Roman Empire.

The change has been gradually accomplished against the prolonged resistance encountered under innumerable forms of those privileged classes which obtained, under this constitution of society, the influence they have in considerable measure, although to a gradually diminishing extent, continued to enjoy down into the time in which we are living. Let us see then, in the first place, what have been the tendencies of this process so far, for this must evidently be a most important consideration in endeavouring to form an estimate of the direction in which it is carrying us.

If we look at this process as a whole, it will be seen that, so far as it has proceeded, it presents two easily recognised features. There have been two distinct tendencies displayed therein, each constant, growing, unmistakable. In the first place there can be no doubt that, allowing for all disappointments and drawbacks, the social progress, moral and material, which the masses of the people have made since the process commenced has been great, and has been, although interrupted at times, practically continuous. It must be remembered that, at the period at which we take up the process, the lower masses of the people amongst the present European nations possessed scarcely any social or political rights. Great numbers of them lived continually on the brink of starvation; military force was almost the only law society recognised; and slavery, which had hitherto been an almost universal human institution, had behind it not only all the authority of force, but the unquestioned sanction of the highest civilisation which man had so far reached.

The instincts which led men to prey on each other were scarcely more restrained than amongst the lower animals, and it must not be assumed that this was the result of the disorganised state of society; for, following the example of the ancient empires, all associations of men with any definite pretensions to a national existence aspired as a legitimate object to prey on other peoples. The feudal lords, in like manner, preyed on their neighbours whenever their resources and following gave them hope of success, so that scarcely any district was long free from the horrors and outrage of war in one shape or another.

No glamour can hide the wretchedness of the masses of the people throughout the early stages of the history of the present European peoples. Their position was, at best, but one of slavery slightly modified. The worse than animal conditions to which they were subject, the unwholesome food on which they fared, and the state of general destitution in which they lived, must, in all probability, be held to be associated with the general prevalence in Europe late into the Middle Ages of widely prevalent diseases that have since becomeextinct. Theterrible "plague" epidemics periodically devastated Europe on a scale and to an extent which the modern world has no experience of, and which we can only very imperfectly realise. After the break-up of military feudalism the condition of things was little better. The people were crushed under the weight of rents, services, taxations, and exactions of all kinds. Trade, commerce, industry, and agriculture were harassed, restricted, and impoverished by the multitude of burthens imposed on them—burthens which only during the last hundred years have been eased or removed in most Western countries.[12]

Though the improvement in material conditions has been slow, it has been, nevertheless, unmistakable as the people have gradually acquired a larger and larger share of political power; but it has, naturally, been greatest as we approach our own times. No careful student of history can ignore the significance of the improvement in the position of the masses of the people which has taken place in England and France during the nineteenth century; nor of the position the working classes have already come to occupy in the United States and some of the British colonies. In England, the progress, as we approach our own day, has been enormous. At the bottom of the scale we find, as Mr. Giffen showed a few years ago,[13] an almost continuous decrease in the proportion of paupers since 1855. The wages of almost all classes have greatly risen, and their purchasing power is greater. The savings bank deposits and depositors show a progressive increase which is most striking. The houses in which the masses of the people live are better, and continually increase in value; the conditions of life are more healthy and refined, and continually tend towards improvement. The hours of labour are much less, and tend towards further reduction; the conditions of work have been greatly improved; and education, amusement, and recreation are provided for the people on a greatly extended scale. Nay, at last, we have the rising school of orthodox political economists in England already beginning to question whether poverty itself may not be abolished, and whether it is necessarily any more a permanent human institution than was slavery.

It has been the same in France. It must be remembered that we have to compare the present condition of the mass of the population, not with their state under some ideal organisation of society, but with their actual condition in the past. In a very striking comparison of the present and the past in France by Alfred Neymarck, which appeared in the *Journal de la Société de Statistique de Paris* for March 1889, some interesting facts are recorded. "During the last centuries," says the author, "famine, which we now only know by name, and of which we have had no practical experience, was, in some sort, a permanent institution on the fertile soil of France. In the twelfth century it made its appearance over fifty times. Under Louis XIV. in 1663 and 1690, and in 1790, whole populations were absolutely dying of hunger."[14]

A century ago, the peasant in France suffered continual privation; such a condition had become chronic. "White bread was a thing unknown; once or twice a year, at Easter or at other high festivals, a piece of bacon was regarded as a luxury. Oil of rape-seed and beech-oil were used to render the most common vegetables palatable. The ordinary beverage was water; beer was dear, cider not less so, and wine was a luxury exceedingly rare." As against this, the author contrasts the present condition of the lower classes. "One has only to glance at the labouring man when engaged at his work, to see that the quality of his clothing has improved, and that the shoe has replaced the sabot. Instead of the tattered garments, veritable rags in fact, formerly worn by women, has succeeded printed calicoes, wool, and cloth; and in the poorest houses it is a common thing to find linen, clean and white, put away for use on Sundays and *fête* days, and it is by no means unusual to find in a large number of cottages both books and flowers. Wages have increased three, four, five, and even tenfold in certain industries. Formerly a workman barely gained, and that with the hardest labour, from one to two francs a day; he now receives from five, six, eight, and sometimes ten francs." The average duration of life has, the author says, increased; the rate of mortality is lower; the quality of food has improved; house accommodation is better; clothing more healthy; and temperance more extensively practised.

In whatever direction we look, we find evidence of this same tendency. Foreign economic writers are already beginning to remark that one of the most striking of recent economic phenomena in England is the check which appears to have been given to the growth of large fortunes, and the wider and more even distribution of wealth which is taking place. The same tendency is visible in France; M. Claudio Jannet has recently stated that there are not now in France more than 700 to 800 persons with £10,000 a year, and not more than 18,000 to 20,000 with £2000 and upwards. He shows also that whereas the national debt in that country has doubled from

1869 to 1881, the holders have quadrupled. The number of small holders of bonds tends to greatly increase, and he mentions that one-half of the bonds of the city of Paris are owned by holders of a single bond. Other figures quoted are also striking. Out of 8,302,272 inhabited houses in France, he states that 5,460,355, or more than 65 per cent, are occupied by their owners.[15] Some years ago Mr. Goschen furnished as with an equally interesting set of facts exhibiting the tendency to the increase of moderate incomes in England.[16]

The conditions of life of the masses of the people show everywhere a progressive improvement—the improvement, so far, following the development by which the people have attained to a larger and larger share of political power. This feature is sometimes dwelt upon by those who wish to draw conclusions therefrom favourable to the continuance of the existing order of things. But, we must not on that account ignore the facts altogether, as is sometimes done by writers of extreme views on the other side. In estimating the situation, our first duty clearly is to take all its features fairly into account; and when this is done it must be frankly admitted that there is no justification whatever for either thinking or speaking of the past century as a period of progressive degeneration for the working classes.

All the facts point unmistakably the other way. If we look now in another quarter, the second tendency of the developmental tendency which has been, so far, in progress, is even more clearly discernible. The movement which is thus slowly raising the condition of the masses, and bringing about more equal conditions of life amongst the people, has not hitherto operated to suspend the rivalry and competition of life. On the contrary, the more carefully we consider the whole process, the more clearly does it appear that its tendency has been in the opposite direction. It is in countries like England and the United States, where the process has advanced furthest, that the rivalry and competition have such well marked features. The conditions have tended to become freer, fairer, more humanised. But, so also have the stress and energy of life, developed thereby, tended to reach a point distinctly higher than ever before attained in human existence.

The tendency amongst all the advanced peoples appears to be unmistakable. It is everywhere to allow the fullest possible scope for the development of the personality of the individual, and the widest possible range of opportunity to follow wherever his powers or abilities lead him. We have, dwelt upon the extent to which this tendency is displayed in almost every department of life amongst the leading Western peoples, and how unmistakably it constitutes the characteristic feature of the life of those sections of the race which are obtaining the greatest ascendency in the world.

Looking back over the process of evolution, which has been unfolding in our civilisation, there can be no mistaking its nature. The slow break-up of the military type of society out of which it arose; the abolition of slavery; the steady restriction of the power retained over the people by those privileged classes who obtained their rights and influence under an earlier form of society; the disintegration of military feudalism; the slow and painfully-achieved steps in the emancipation (still incomplete) of agriculture, trade, and commerce, from the rights which modified feudalism continued to retain over them; the hard-won stages in the political emancipation of the masses (now approaching completion amongst the Western peoples), accompanied by a gradual improvement in the conditions of life amongst the lower classes—these have all been the well-marked stages in a single developmental process still pursuing its onward course amongst us. The inherent tendency of the process from the beginning has been to ultimately bring all the excluded people into the rivalry of life. But, its significance has consisted in its tendency to raise this rivalry to the highest level of efficiency it has ever reached. It would seem that there can be little doubt as to the nature and the tendency of the development so far. What then, it may be asked, is it destined to accomplish in the future?

The answer must apparently be, that it must complete the process of evolution in progress, by eventually bringing all the people into the rivalry of life, not only on a footing of political equality, *but on conditions of equal social opportunities*. This is the end which the developmental forces at work in our civilisation are apparently destined to achieve in the social life of those people amongst whom it is allowed to follow its natural and normal course uninterrupted by disturbing causes,—an end, when its relationships are perceived, as moving to the imagination, as vast and transforming in character, as that which Marx anticipated. But, it is an end essentially and profoundly different in character. Marx contemplated our Western civilisation culminating in a condition of society which it was difficult, if not impossible, for any one who had realised the essential unity and continuity under all outward forms of the developmental forces at work in human society, to imagine; a state in which the laws that had operated continuously from the beginning of life were to be suddenly interrupted and finally suspended. But, the state towards which we are travelling is apparently not one in which these laws will be suspended; it will be only the highest phase reached in human society of the same cosmic process which has been in operation from the beginning. Great and transforming as the coming changes will in all probability be, no *bouleversement* of society is to be expected. We are moving, and shall merely continue to move, by orderly stages to the goal towards which the face of society has in reality been set from the beginning of our civilisation.

If we endeavour to present clearly to our minds the nature of this process as a whole, we shall find that we are now in a position to understand the meaning of that social development towards which our times are ripening, and with which the history of the twentieth century will undoubtedly be filled. Nay, more, we are enabled to distinguish, with some degree of clearness, the stages through which it must carry us in the immediate future. The period through which we are passing is perceived to be one of transition. A definite, longdrawn-out, and altogether remarkable era in the history of our civilisation is coming to a close amongst the more advanced peoples. We are entering on a new era. The *political* enfranchisement of the masses is well-nigh accomplished; the process which will occupy the next period will be that of their social enfranchisement.

Movement Towards Social Equality

The people have been, at last, admitted to equal political rights; in the next stage they must apparently be admitted to equal social opportunities. When the nature of the transition is perceived, it becomes clear also that the questions around which the conflict of *social* forces must centre in the immediate future are just those questions the socialist movement has brought into such prominence, namely, those affecting the existing rights of capital and the present distribution of wealth.

In one of those frequent flashes wherewith Marx, for a moment, lights up the foundations of present-day society, he asserts that "the economic structure of present capitalist society has grown out of the economic structure of feudal society."[17] This is a fact which has not yet been fully realised by those progressive parties amongst us, who, having for the most part accepted the ideas of the older school of economists as to the relationships of labour, capital, and the state, have obtained therefrom a false sense of the continued normalcy and rigidity of these relationships. We have, however, only to watch closely the wave of change which is passing over economic science in England to learn in what a large measure the truth underlying Marx's statement is already being perceived and applied by the younger and rising school of economists.

There is a growing and highly significant tendency amongst this school to question whether the present "cruelty and waste of irresponsible competition, and the licentious use of wealth," do really form any essential feature of the institution of private capital, or any necessary accompaniment of "the services which competition renders to society, by tending to put the ablest men into the most important posts, the next ablest into the next most important, and so on, and by giving to those in each grade freedom for the full exercise of their faculties."[18] It is being questioned with growing confidence by this school whether, allowing "that industrial progress depends on our getting the right men into the right places and giving them a free hand and sufficient incitement to exert themselves to the utmost," it also follows "that nothing less than the enormous fortunes which successful men now make and retain would suffice for that purpose."

Professor Marshall goes so far as to hold that this last position is untenable, and that "the present extreme inequalities of wealth tend in many ways to prevent human faculties from being turned to their best account." And he continues: "All history shows that a man will exert himself nearly as much to secure a small rise in income as a large one, provided he knows beforehand what he stands to gain, and is in no fear of having the expected fruits of his exertions taken away from him by arbitrary spoliation. If there were any fear of that he would not do his best, but if the conditions of the country were such that a moderate income gave as good a social position as a large one does now; if to have earned a moderate income were a strong presumptive proof that a man had surpassed able rivals in the attempt to do a difficult thing well, then the hope of earning such an income would offer to all but the most sordid natures inducements almost as strong as they are now, when there is an equal hope of earning a large one."[19]

These are all indications of the direction in which we are travelling—and indications of the utmost significance at the present time as coming from the younger orthodox school of economists in England. The position occupied by this party is already clearly defined. "They are most anxious to preserve the freedom of the individual to try new paths on his own responsibility. They regard this as the vital service which free competition renders to progress; and desire, on scientific grounds, to disentangle the case for it, from the case for such institutions as tend to maintain extreme inequalities of wealth; to which some of them are strongly opposed."

The nature of the position which has been reached amongst the advanced sections of the Western peoples thus emerges more clearly into view. Occupied as these peoples have been for a prolonged period in winning and consolidating their political freedom, they as a consequence have tended—no less in the United States than in Germany, France, and England—to magnify as the final end the occupation of a merely preliminary position. We have come to believe that the feudal system is defunct. But, the real fact, as Marx realised more clearly than the older economists, is, that the dead hand of feudalism still presses with crushing weight upon the people through almost all the forms and institutions of present day society. A large part of the existing unregulated and uncontrolled rights of wealth and capital are in reality merely the surviving rights of feudalism adapted to new conditions. Education must in time bring us to see that their continued existence is incompatible with the attainment of the ideal which society will have set more and more clearly before it in the stage of development upon which we are entering.

How far we are at present from the realisation of this ideal of equality of opportunity, we shall probably perceive more clearly as the development continues. Future generations may regard with some degree of surprise, and may even smile at our conceptions of present-day society as a condition in which we secure the full benefits of free competition; in which we get the right men into the right places and give them sufficient inducements to exert themselves; and in which we have obtained for all members of the community the necessary opportunity for the full exercise of their faculties. It requires but little reflection to see how wide of the mark such a conception really is.

A large proportion of the population in the prevailing state of society take part in the rivalry of life only under conditions which absolutely preclude them, whatever their natural merit or ability, from any real chance therein. They come into the world to find the best positions not only already filled but practically occupied in perpetuity. For, under the great body of rights which wealth has inherited from feudalism, we to all intents and purposes allow the wealthy classes to retain the control of these positions for generation after generation, to the permanent exclusion of the rest of the people. Even from that large and growing class of positions for which high acquirements or superior education is the only qualification, and of which we, consequently (with strange inaccuracy), speak as if they were open to all comers, it may be perceived that the larger proportion of the people are excluded—almost as rigorously and as absolutely as in any past condition of society—by the simple fact that the ability to acquire such education or qualification is at present the exclusive privilege of wealth.

Before the rivalry of life can be raised to that state of efficiency as an instrument of progress towards which it appears to be the inherent tendency of our civilisation to continue to carry it, society will still have to undergo a transformation almost as marked as any through which it has passed in previous stages. We have evidence of the beginning of this transformation in that trend of present-day legislation which appears so puzzling to many of the old progressive school, who have not realised the nature of the process of development in progress. It may be noticed that the characteristic feature of this legislation is the increasing tendency to raise the position of the lower classes *at the expense of the wealthier classes.* All future progressive legislation must apparently have this tendency.

It is almost a *conditio sine quâ non* of any measure that carries us a step forward in our social develop. ment. This is the real meaning of a large class of proposed measures, amongst others that which aims at securing an eight hours day for adult labour enforced by law—measures, in the present transition period, loosely but inaccurately described as socialist, and still looked at askance by that radical party in England who have not yet clearly perceived that the principles of their faith carry them any further than the mere political enfranchisement of the people.

To shorten the hours of labour in such a manner is, at the present time, primarily and above everything else to raise the conditions of life of the workers at the expense of wealth; and, consequently, ultimately to place the workers more on a footing of equality in the rivalry of life with those above them. It is this principle also that is behind various recent measures in England—limited in character but tending to gradually and greatly extend in scope—which aim at bettering at the public expense the condition of the lives of the lower classes of workers. It underlies the demand for graduated taxation, which may be expected to increase in strength and importunity; and demands which may be expected to take practical shape in the near future, for the revision of the hereditary rights of wealth and the conditions under which great fortunes are transmitted from generation to generation. The same principle will apparently underlie our education legislation in future. We must expect to have to meet, before long, demands for a very considerable extension of the education provided by the state and for state control in the interests of the people of higher as well as of elementary education. It may be remarked that over no other question is the struggle between the old spirit and the new likely to be more severe and prolonged than over this question of education. It is in reality one of the last principal strongholds of the retreating party. It is not yet clearly perceived by the people that there is not any more natural and lasting distinction between the *educated* and the *uneducated* classes of which we hear so much nowadays, than there has been between the other classes in the past. Citizen and slave, patrician and plebeian, feudal lord and serf, privileged classes and common people, leisured classes and working masses, have been steps in a process of development. In the "educated classes" and the "uneducated classes" we have only the same distinction under a subtler and even less defensible form; for the right to education in its highest forms now remains largely independent of any other qualification than the possession of mere riches to secure it; it constitutes, in fact, one of the most exclusive, and at the same time one of the most influential, of the privileges of wealth.

There is also another aspect of the subject which we must be prepared to find coming into increasing prominence. It is a fact, the full significance of which has not yet been perceived by the masses, that the condition of society which renders the right of entry to the institutions for higher education the almost exclusive privilege of wealth, tends, from the close connection of these institutions with the intellectual life of society, to render them (however much they may, and do, from the highest motives endeavour to resist such tendency) influences retarding to a considerable degree the progress of the development which society is undergoing. We have, consequently, at the present day, in most of our advanced societies the remarkable phenomenon of the intellectual and educated classes, at first almost invariably condemning and resisting the successive steps in our social development, uttering the most gloomy warnings and forebodings as these steps have been taken—and then tardily justifying them when they have become matters of history; that is to say, when approval or disapproval has long ceased to be of practical importance.

It has to be confessed that in England during the nineteenth century, the educated classes, in almost all the great political changes that have been effected, have taken the side of the party afterwards admitted to have been in the wrong —they have almost invariably opposed at the time the measures they have subsequently come to defend and justify. This is to be noticed alike of measures which have extended education, which have emancipated trade, which have extended the franchise. The educated classes have even, it must be confessed, opposed measures which have tended to secure religious freedom and to abolish slavery. The motive force behind the long list of progressive measures carried during this period has in scarcely any appreciable measure come from the educated classes; it has come almost exclusively from the middle and lower classes, who have in turn acted, not under the stimulus of intellectual motives, but under the influence of their altruistic feelings. We have evidence of the same development towards securing equality of opportunity in that tendency towards the extension of the interference of the state, which appears so revolutionary to politicians of the old *laissez-faire* school.

The progressive interference of the state (mostly in the interests of the weaker classes, and at the expense of wealth and privilege) in departments now looked upon as quite outside the sphere of such action, is apparently inevitable. We do not yet fully realise that with the completion of the political enfranchisement of the people, the state itself will have undergone a profound transformation. Its new relationship to the people must be quite different from any that has ever before prevailed in history. The spirit which produced the old *laissez-faire* doctrine has, in all probability, still a great part to play in our social development; but the doctrine itself is, in reality, what the party previously identified with it in England has for some time instinctively recognised it to be—the doctrine of a period beyond which we have progressed. It has served its end in the stage of evolution through which we have passed; for the doctrine of the non-interference of the state was the natural political creed of a people who had won their political freedom through a process of slow, orderly, and hard-fought development, and to whom the state throughout this period represented the powerholding classes whose interests were not coincident with those of the masses of the people.

But, the doctrine has no such part to play in the future. In the era upon which we are entering, the long uphill effort to secure equality of opportunity, as well as equality of political rights, will ot necessity involve, not the restriction of the interference of the state, but the progressive extension of its sphere of action to almost every department of our social life. The movement in the direction of the regulation, control, and restriction of the rights of wealth and capital must be expected to continue, even to the extent of the state itself assuming these rights in cases where it is clearly proved that their retention in private hands must unduly interfere with the rights and opportunities of the body of the people. But, the continuity of principle may be expected to remain evident under the new appearances. Even in such cases the state will, in reality, assume such functions in order to preserve or secure free competition rather *than to suspend it*. Hence, the general tendency must be expected to be towards state interference and state control on a greatly extended scale rather than towards state management.

It may, perhaps, be inferred from this that the development of society in the direction indicated will be itself a movement towards socialism. This is not so. The gulf between the state of society towards which it is the tendency of the process of evolution now in progress to carry us, and socialism, is wide and deep. The avowed aim of socialism is to suspend that personal rivalry and competition of life which not only is now, but has been from the beginning of life, the fundamental impetus behind all progress. The inherent tendency of the process of social development now taking place amongst us is (as it has been from the beginning of our civilisation) to raise this rivalry to the very highest degree of efficiency as a condition of progress, by bringing all the people into it on a footing of equality, and by allowing the freest possible play of forces within the community, and the widest possible opportunities for the development of every individual's faculties and personality. This is the meaning of that evolutional process which has been slowly proceeding through the history of the Western peoples.

But, in any consideration of the future tendency of our social progress, the overshadowing importance of that ethical development which has supplied the motive power behind the procession of events we call progress, must always be kept in mind. In the process of evolution through which we have passed, the main function of that ethical movement on which our civilisation is founded has been in the first place to provide the sanctions necessary to secure the continued subordination of the interests of the self-assertive individual to the larger interests of society. In the second place, it has been to generate that great fund of altruistic feeling which, gradually saturating our entire sociallife, has slowly undermined the position of the powerholding classes, and so rendered possible the movement which is tending to ultimately bring all the people into the rivalry of life on conditions of equality. The future progress of our social development continues to be indissolubly bound up with this movement. When the fundamental conditions of the problem which underlies human evolution are once clearly understood, it must be perceived that it is in the nature of things impossible for rationalism by itself to provide such sanctions or to generate, or even to keep up, this fund of altruistic feeling.

The process which is proceeding in human society is always progressively developing two inherently antagonistic tendencies; namely, the tendency requiring the increasing subordination of the individual to society, and the rationalistic tendency leading the individual at the same time to question, with increasing insistence, the authority of the claims requiring him to submit to a process of social order in which he has absolutely no interest, and which is operating largely in the interests of unborn generations. In a healthy and progressive society, the fundamental principle of its existence is, that the second tendency must be continually subordinated to the first. But, as has been throughout insisted, the intellect has no power to effect this subordination. With the decay of the ethical influences in question, we may imagine the cynical indifference, nay, the cultivated intellectual pride, with which a vigorous character would regard its emancipation from what it must, in such circumstances, regard as a mere vulgar thraldom. If our conscious relationship to the universe is measured by the brief span of individual existence, then the intellect can know of only one duty in the individual, namely, his duty to himself to make the most of the few precious years of consciousness he can ever know. Every other consideration must appear dwarfed and ridiculous in comparison.

Every pain avoided, every pleasure gained in these few years, is a consideration, beside which the intellect must count any aspiration to further a process of cosmic evolution in which the individual has no interest as mere dust in the balance. We must expect wealth and power, in such circumstances, to be grasped at with a fierce earnestness, not for what are called sordid motives, but for intellectual motives over and above all others; that is to say, for the command of the pleasures and gratifications which they alone can secure. And it must be remembered that the universal experience of mankind has been, and is still, that wealth and power divorced from the control of ethical influences of the kind in question have not sought to find satisfaction in what are called the higher altruistic pleasures, but that they have rather, as evolutionary science would have taught us, sought the satisfaction of those instincts which have their roots deepest in our natures. Voluptuousness and epicureanism in all their most refined forms have everywhere been, and everywhere continue to be, the accompaniments of irresponsible wealth and power, the corresponding mental habit being one of cultured contempt for the excluded and envious masses. Nor, as already pointed out, must any weight be attached to the argument that would ask us to take note of the many exceptions to such a tendency to be found in present society, in individuals of the highest motives and purest lives, who are not in any way under the influence of the religious movement upon which our civilisation is founded.

Once we have grasped the conception of our civilisation as a developing organic growth, with a life-history which must be studied as a whole, we perceive how irrational it is to regard any of the units as independent of the influence of a process which has operated upon society for so many centuries. We may also argue that because the fruit survives for a time when removed from the tree, and even mellows and ripens, that it was, therefore, independent of the tree. In this connection it should be remarked that the relationship between true socialism and rationalism, casually noticed by many observers, is not accidental as it is often stated to be. It has its foundation deep seated in the very nature of things. The conflict between the forces shaping the course of the development we are at present undergoing, and the materialistic socialism of Marx, is but the present-day expression of that conflict in which we have seen man engaged against his own reason throughout the whole course of his social development. Socialism in reality aims at exploiting in the interests of the existing generation of individuals that humanitarian movement which is providing a developmental force operating largely in the interests of future generations. It would, in fact, exploit this movement while it cut off the springs of it. Genuine socialism of the German type must be recognised to be ultimately as individualistic and as *anti* social as individualism in its advanced forms. Scientifically, they are both to be considered as the extreme logical expression of rationalistic protest by the individual against the subordination of his interests to the process of progressive development society is undergoing from generation to generation.

But, though we have thus to identify socialism with political materialism, no greater mistake can be made than to suppose that the ultimate triumph of materialism in our Western civilisation would imply the realisation of the ideals of socialism. The state to which we should probably attain long before reaching this stage would be one in which the power-holding classes, recognising the position, would with cynical frankness proceed to utilise the inherent strength of their own position. Instead of slowly yielding their position as they are now doing, under the softening influence upon general character of an ethical movement—which by undermining their faith in their own cause has deprived them of the power of making effective resistance—they might be expected to become once more aggressive in the open profession of class selfishness and contempt for the people.

History presents a melancholy record of the helplessness of the latter when society has reached this stage. The deliberate effectiveness with which the power holding classes in ancient Rome dealt with the rights of the people in such circumstances in the long downward stage under the Empire is instructive, and bears its moral on the surface. In such a state of society, the classes who have obtained wealth and power, and all other classes in turn, instead of acting, as they now do, under the influence of an evolutionary force operating largely in the future interests of society, come to hold it as a duty to themselves to serve their own present interests by such direct means as may be available. In vague popular phraseology, society in this stage is said to be irremediably corrupt: strictly speaking the social organism has exhausted its physiological capital, and has, therefore, entered on the downward stage towards disintegration.

NOTES AND REFERENCES

1. J.S. Mill, *Principles of Political Economy*, Book v. chap. xi.
2. *Ibid.*
3. *Ibid.*
4. Vide *Principles of Political Economy*, Book v. chap. xi.
5. The existence of an inherent principle of antagonism between true socialism and that class of proposals which currently pass under the name of "State Socialism" was uncompromisingly maintained by Herr Leibknecht in his speech at the Social Democratic Congress held at Berlin in November 1892. "Social democracy," said Herr Leibknecht, "has nothing in common with the so-called state socialism, a system of half-measures dictated by fear, and aiming merely at undermining the hold of social democracy over the working classes by petty concessions and palliatives. Such measures social democracy has never disdained to promote and to approve, but it accepts them only as small instalments, which cannot arrest its onward march towards the regeneration of the state and of society on socialistic principles. Social democracy is essentially revolutionary: state socialism is conservative. As such they are irreconcilably opposed."
6. Vide *Looking Backward*, by Edward Bellamy.
7. Mrs. Mona Caird, *Nineteenth Century*, May 1892.
8. *Capital*, by Karl Marx, English translation (Swan Sonnenschein & Co., 1887), vol. ii. pp. 788, 789.
9. *Socialism, Utopian and Scientific*, by Frederick Engels, translated by Edward Aveling, 1892.
10. The younger school of economists in England have not yet quite done justice to Marx's conception of the state of capitalistic society which he describes. It is quite true, as Professor Marshall remarks ("Some Aspects of Competition," *Journal Roy. Stat. Soc.* December 1890), that socialist schemes founded thereon "seem to be vitiated by want of attention to the analysis which the economists of the modern age have made of the functions of the undertaker of business enterprises," and that they "seem to think too much of competition as the exploiting of labour by capital, of the poor by the wealthy,

and too little of it as the constant experiment by the ablest men for their several tasks, each trying to discover a new way in which to attain some important end." But, it must also be kept well in mind—and the rising school of economic science can do nothing but good in keeping the fact always clearly in view—that the rights and privileges of capital and wealth have hitherto been much more than those which necessarily attach to "the function of the undertaker of business enterprises" in order to obtain the highest possible efficiency. Marx went much too far, but the idea underlying his conception of the exploitation of labour in the past is, in the main, sound and scientific.

11. *Journal of the Royal Statistical Society*, December 1890, p. 643. Reprint of Address as President of Economic Section, British Association, Meeting September 1890.

12. In the *Journal de la Société de Statistique de Paris*, March 1889, Alfred Neymarck enumerates some of the burthens imposed on the peasant in France one hundred years ago. "Without taking into account services to be paid for in kind, he was called upon to pay *dîmes, tailles, capitations, vingtièmes*, and *centièmes, corvées, aides, gabella*, etc. If he was (desirous of selling in the markets open to him the produce of his labour, he was forced to pay the dues on *mesurage, piquetage, minage, sterlage, palette, écuellée, pied fourchu, angayage, eprouvage*, and *étalage*; that is to say he was mulcted for each measure of grain sold; for each cow, pig, or sheep; for each load of wheat brought in by strangers; for each basket containing fowls, eggs, butter, and cheese, and for each horse examined and sold" (see translation of paper in *Journal of the Royal Statistical Society*, June 1889). See also Mill *Political Economy*, Book v. chap. xi., for an account of the restrictions and burthens which the state formerly placed upon commerce and manufactures.

13. Vide *Journal of the Royal Statistical Society*, December 1887; Presidential Address, Economic Section, British Association, Meeting 1887.

14. *Vide* Translation, *Journal Royal Statistical Society*, June 1889.

15. See *Le Capital*, p. 30.

16. Vide *Journal of the Royal Statistical Society*, December 1887.

17. *Capital*, vol. ii. chap. xxvi. English translation, Swan Sonnenschein and Co.

18. *Vide* "Some Aspects of Competition," by Professor Alfred Marshall, *Journal of the Royal Statistical Society*, December 1890. Reprint of Address as President of Economic Section, British Association, 1890.

19. *Vide* "Some Aspects of Competition," by Professor Alfred Marshall, *Journal of the Royal Statistical Society*, December 1890. Reprint of Address as President of Economic Section, British Association, 1890.

5

SOCIALISM AND RELIGION

It is sometimes said that socialism is neither religious nor irreligious. This does not or should not mean that socialism fails to come into contact with the views of the world and of life which the current religions provide, or that at a particular stage in its progress it may not take up a position even of active hostility to those religions. What it means is that socialism implies a state of society out and away beyond the barren speculative polemics of the hoar.

The popular "secularism" or "freethought" is simply the obverse side of the popular "dogmatic theology." In this it has the "reason of its being." With theology played out, secularism is also played out. Like the two Kilkenny cats, theology and secularism must, in the long run, mutually devour each other. Socialism is essentially neither religious nor irreligious, inasmuch as it re-affirms the unity of human life, abolishing the dualism which has lain at the foundation of all the great ethical religions. By this dualism, we mean the antithesis of politics and religion, of the profane and the sacred, of matter and spirit, of this world and the "other world," and the various subordinate antagonisms to which these have given rise, or which they implicitly contain. Hitherto, the whole tendency of our society and thought has been to make of aspects of things, distinguishable if you will, but not legitimately separable, separate and more or less opposed principles. We will take only the instance which most concerns the subject-matter of these remarks. Those feelings, aspirations, emotions after the ideal which constitute the "religious sentiment" are very easily *distinguishable* from the impulses of kindliness, friendship, duty, etc., to individuals which ought to animate our daily life. They are distinguishable but not separable. Yet, the current religions erect them into distinct principles, severing the "religions sentiment" from all connections with the world and human society, and transferring it to an imagined supernatural "world," which is nothing but a grotesque travesty of the relations of this world.

It is curious to trace how this came about. In the most ancient civilisations there is no separation between the political or social and the religious, simply because religion was then nothing more than the propitiation of dead ancestors, powers of nature, fetiches or other supposed supernatural agents (whose existence passed unquestioned to the human mind in its then stage) in the interests of the society. These ancestral ghosts, personified powers, or animated fetiches were as often immoral as not; in fact, it would be more correct to say that for them morality and immorality had no existence. The worshipper possibly cared not one jot for them or they for him—his worship was a social duty.

The only way in which they possessed any human interest was as embodying certain powers, which might be noxious or beneficent *to the State*. We have spoken of them as being "propitiated" and "worshipped," but it is doubtful if those terms can be applied with regard to the ancient religious cults more than very partially. The practices they embodied were rather those of compulsory invocation or regulation by means of magical spells and incantations than prayers and "services" such as are understood to-day. The social festivals were as much religious as they were political. Political and religious functions were necessarily united in the same persons since every religious act was political, every political act also religious. The foregoing remarks apply in all essentials to every primitive civilisation, to ancient India, Egypt, China, Syria, Palestine. Even in later classical times, religion was still a social and political matter, a thing of this world only or mainly. The most sacred forms of the Greek and Roman cults were those identified with the preservation of the city, of the tribe, and of the *gens*. Undoubting as was men's belief in the existence of the supernatural, it only interested them in so far as they conceived it to affect the community of which they were a part. The supernatural, too, was as yet imperfectly distinguished from the natural. There was no religion of the supernatural *as such*. But, with the decay of the old civic morality and the absorption of the small free States into centralised monarchies and finally into the Roman Empire, men came to care less and less for the body politic, and fell back more and more upon themselves as individuals.

At first, this individualism took the form of a search among the leisured and educated class for the higher life of wisdom. The Stoic, the Epicurean, and the Cynic had each his special receipt for slipping through life as comfortably as possible. But, this, though satisfactory for a time, palled in the long run. The Roman Empire got ever more corrupt, its corruption ramifying through all its branches; public life became more and more vapid; the old religious, once instinct with meaning, were but empty forms; the newer panaceas of the philosophers failed to afford satisfaction. The utmost they promised was to make the best of the doubtful bargain—life.

But, the sense of individualism was too strong for this merely negative creed. Men sought in vain for an object in life, collective or individual. In this state of mind they are confronted by a new Asiatic sect. They become initiated. At once the scene changes. This life is indeed pronounced hopelessly worthless. There is no citizenship here, no happiness for the individual, not even the apathy of the "wise man." But, as this life crumbles into nothingness, there rises the fair vision of the "city of God," joys beyond imagination, not the "apathy" of "wisdom," but the "peace" of the blest. *Hic Rhodus, hic saltus*! Religion is henceforth separated from life, the religious sphere of *another* world is set over against the irreligious sphere of *this* world. Earth is drained of its ideal to feed Heaven. Society established on this basis involves the antagonisms of "temporal and spiritual" powers, of "world" and Church, of religious and profane, etc.

What is said applies not only to Christianity, but more or less to all the so-called ethical or universal religious, Zoroastrianism, Buddhism, Mahommedanism, etc. They are the expression of the decay of the old life, and hence they one and all centre in the individual and in another world, their concern with this world being purely incidental.

We daily see around us the result of 1,600 years of "other-worldliness" on character and conduct. Men and women upon whom the mere greed for gain palls are driven to the one ideal resource their education has given them or they can comprehend, the hope of a glorified immortality for themselves. Those only who know from bitter experience the smile of honest contempt with which such people greet the idea of the sacrifice of personal or claw privileges, or anything else for a social object, can appreciate the depth to which the canker has eaten into their souls. Yet, it would be unjust to say that these people are bad. They are religious and antisocial, just as there are many others irreligious and antisocial.

In what sense socialism is not religious will be now clear. It utterly despises the "other world" with all its stage properties—that is, the present objects of religion. In what sense it is not irreligious will be also, we think, tolerably clear. It brings back religion from heaven to earth, which, as we have sought to show, was its original sphere. It looks beyond the present moment or the present individual life though not, indeed, to another world, but to another and a higher social life in this world. It is in the hope and the struggle for this higher social life, ever-widening, ever-intensifying, whose ultimate possibilities are beyond the power of language to express or thought to conceive, that the Socialist finds his ideal, his religion. He sees in the reconstruction of society in the interest of all, in the rehabilitation, in a higher form and without its limitations, of the old communal life—the proximate end of all present endeavour. We take up the thread of Aryan tradition, but not where it was dropped. The state or city of the ancient world was one-sided, its freedom was political merely, based on the slavery of the many; that of the future will be democratic and social. It was exclusive, the union within implied disunion without; the life of the future will be international, cosmopolitan, in its scope. Finally the devotion of its members was connected with the existent supernatural belief, and involved a cultus; the devotion of the member of the socialised community, like the devotion of all true socialists to-day, will be based on science and involve no cultus. In this last point the religion of the Socialist differs from that of the Positivist. The positivist seeks to retain the forms after the beliefs of which they are the expression have lost all meaning for him. The socialist whose social creed is his religion requires no travesty of Christian rites to aid him in keeping his ideal before him.

In socialism, the current antagonisms are abolished, the separation between politics and religion has ceased to be, since their object-matter is the same. The highest feelings of devotion to the Ideal are not conceived as different in kind, much lea as concerned with a different sphere, to the commoner human emotions, but merely as diverse aspects of the same fact. The stimulus of personal interest no longer able to poison at its source all beauty, all affection, all heroism, in short, all that is highest in us; the sphere of government merged in that of industrial direction; the limit of the purely industrial itself ever receding as the applied powers of Nature lessen the amount of human drudgery required; Art, and the pursuit of beauty and of truth ever covering the ground left free by the "necessary work of the world"—such is the goal lying immediately before us, such the unity of human interest and of human life which Socialism would evolve out of the clashing antagonisms, the anarchical individualism, religious and irreligious, exhibited in the rotting world of today and what current religion can offer a higher ideal or a nobler incentive than this essentially human one?

NOTES AND REFERENCES

Corijn, M. and E. Klijzing (eds.). 2001. *Transitions to adulthood in Europe. European Studies of Population*, Vol. 10, Kluwer Academic Publishers, Dordrecht.

D'Andrade, R.G. (1984), Cultural meaning systems. In: R.A.Schweder and R.A.Levine (eds.), *Culture theory. Essays on mind, self and emotion.* Cambridge University Press. Cambridge, pp. 88-119.

D'Andrade, R.G (1992), Schemas and motivation. In: R.G. D'Andrade and C. Strauss (eds.), *Human motives and cultural models.* Cambridge University Press, Cambridge, pp. 23-44.

Gauntlett, D. (2002), *Media, Gender and Identity: An Introduction*, Routledge, London and New York.

Gerson, K. (1985), *Hard Choices: How women decide about work, career and motherhood.* University of California.

Kapur, P. (1970), *Marriage and the working women in India.* Vikas Publications, New Delhi.

Morgan, P.S. and R. B. King (2001), Why have children in the 21st century? Biological predisposition, social coercion, rational choice. *European Journal of Population.* 17 (1): pp. 3-20.

Mouzelis, N. (1991), Modernity: a non-European conceptualisation, *British Journal of Sociology*, Routledge, (part of Taylor and Francis Group), 1 March 1999, vol. 50, no. 1, pp. 141-159.

Mydral, A. and V. Klien. (1956), *Women's Two Roles: Home and Work.* London: Routledge and Kegan Paul.

Runyan, W.M. (1984), The life course as a theoretical orientation. In: W.M.Runyan (ed.), *Life histories and psychobiography. Explorations in theory and method.* New York, Oxford University Press.

Ryder, N.B. (1985), The cohort concept in the study of social change, In: W.M.Mason and S.E.Fienberg, (eds.), *Cohort Analysis in Social Research.* Springer Verlag: New York. Reprinted from American Sociological Review, 30 (1965), p. 843-861.

Tandon, R.K. (1998), *Women in Modern India*, Indian Publishers Distributors, Delhi. Thornton, A., W.G.Axinn and J.D. Teachman (1995), The influence of school enrollment and accumulation on cohabitation and marriage in early adulthood, *American Sociological Review.* 60(5): 762-774.

6

ROLE OF NGOS IN SOCIAL CHANGE

Globalisation has shifted the balance of power from public to private interests, including NGOs. However, sustainable development requires a change in power relations that runs much deeper than this: a shift from using power over others to advance our selfish interests, to using power to facilitate the self-development of all. This demands constant attention to personal change, and a series of reversals in attitudes and behaviour. In this study it has been argued that NGOs—as explicitly values-based organisations have a crucial role to play in supporting these changes through their programme activities, constituency-building work, and organisational praxis. The decline of paternalistic foreign aid and the rise of more genuine international co-operation provide an excellent opportunity to advance this agenda. The study provides a detailed rationale for these claims and a set of examples that show how power relations could be transformed by civic-led approaches in economics, politics and the structures of social power.

Changes in the distribution of power and authority are characteristic of the processes we call globalisation (Edwards). The erosion of state sovereignty and the weakening of workers' rights are two obvious examples, but globalising capitalism also re-shapes relations between women and men, adults and children, people of different cultures, and those with varying levels of technological competence. This is not just a "power shift" from public to private interests, as Jessica Mathews has claimed, but a deeper and more complex process in which large numbers of people see their position systematically eroded by economic, social and political forces which work to the benefit of a small proportion of the world's population. Left unchecked, these forces will create an unprecedented degree of inequality and insecurity within and between societies, which will never be sustainable. NGOs who wish to promote "sustainable development" must therefore decide how they are going to address this situation.

At one level, the answers to this question are already apparent: those who are marginalised by global processes must have a "fairer deal" in economics, politics and social policy. However, at another level this is clearly insufficient without much deeper changes which encourage people to conserve scarce resources, share their wealth and opportunities, protect each-others' rights, and co-operate to advance the "common good"—the long term health and welfare of the planet and its social fabric on which all our futures depend. Making people "more competitive" and increasing their voice on the political stage will not promote the changes we seek unless we all learn to use the power we gain in less selfish and self-centred ways.

The individualism and materialism that characterise globalising capitalism make this exceptionally difficult, for they undermine the co-operative solidarities and institutions we will need to confront the collective problems that will shape the 21st century—trans-boundary pollution, global trade and capital flows, conflict and the mass movement of refugees and displaced persons. It is one of the paradoxes of globalisation that the more we succeed as individuals in the global marketplace, the more we may fail in other areas of our lives and our relationships with others, a failure which destroys the possibilities of similar success for millions of people now and many more in generations still to come. We cannot compete ourselves to a co-operative future, and if the future of the world depends on co-operation then clearly we must try something different.

In fact, "something different" requires a fundamental shift in values; to be sustainable that shift must be freely-chosen; that choice is more likely to be made by human beings who have experienced a transformation of the heart; NGOs have a crucial role to play in fostering those transformations in the 21st century.

The core of our argument is that personal or inner change, and social or outer change, are inseparably linked. This is as obvious as it is neglected in development thinking, including the praxis of most NGOs. We know that this is difficult and sensitive ground on which to tread, and we realise that our arguments are preliminary. However, we are convinced that any realistic vision of sustainable development must tackle the question of personal power relations head-on.

Process of Change

From the perspective of change, all social systems rest on three bases: a set of principles that form an axiomatic basis of ethics and values; a set of processes—the functioning mechanisms and institutions that undergird the system; and the subjective states that constitute our inner being—our personal feelings and intuitions in the deepest sense. The first of these bases of change describes how we understand and rationalise the workings of the social order, while the third describes how we understand ourselves. Some of this understanding revolves around our own place in the social order, but it also concerns the deeper questions we ask ourselves about the meaning of human existence and the nature of reality.

When we explore any episode of historical change, we can identify how these three bases of change have worked together to produce a particular set of power relations. For example, the evolution of capitalism was built on the axiomatic basis that individual self-interest leads—by and large—to collective welfare. Its institutional structures are rooted in private property and market-based incentives. And the subjective state of being most compatible with capitalism is a commitment to individual advancement and competitive behaviour.

The interaction of these three bases of change determines how different forms of power are exercised in society. Economic power is expressed in the distribution of productive assets and the workings of markets and firms; social power is expressed in the status and position awarded to different social groups; and political power defines each person's voice in decision-making in both the private sphere and public affairs. These systems of power combine to produce a "social order", and transforming this social order is the task of social change. The social order that is emerging under globalising capitalism is one which excludes or oppresses certain groups of people, especially those already on the margins, women in labour-rich economies, and those with less access to skills and education wherever they live.

However, the linkages that develop between these different bases of change are not immutable. Considerable room-to-manoeuvre exists to alter the ways in which they interact, in order to produce a different framework of power relations, a better set of outcomes, and a new social order. It is this room-to-manoeuvre that NGOs are trying to exploit in their work, though they rarely do so consciously. For example, people may rebel against the subjective state that is promoted by a particular set of social transformations, as they have always done in relation to capitalism and the selfish values it breeds. Or, working from a different subjective or axiomatic base, they may experiment with new processes and institutions that try to produce the same economic outcomes with fewer social and political costs - much as NGOs are doing today in their work with multi-national corporations and corporate codes of conduct. The point about these experiments is not that they generate ready-made answers to questions of economic and social life, but that they consolidate a new bottom line of values, principles and/or personal behaviour from which better models may evolve in different ways in different contexts. Any relationship that is truly principled will lead towards a more fulfilling conclusion, even though we can never be sure what it will look like at any level of detail.

Our conclusion from this section is that social change requires a recognition and conscious integration—of all three bases of change, and each of these systems of power. The problem is that few theoretical systems acknowledge this, and even fewer institutions use it as a framework to guide their practice. For example, social theories generally emphasise the axiomatic and institutional aspects of change, assuming that the related subjective states are simply universal descriptions of human nature, or that changes in subjective states follow automatically from changes in institutions and incentives.

At the opposite extreme, many of the world's religions focus on the subjective states of persons and their transformation, and attach less importance to the institutional basis of social change. Of course, not all religions are identical in this regard. Some assign more importance to outer behaviour; others to the inner motivations that lie behind it. But, the tendency to privilege one category over another remains, condemning both social theories and religious teachings to a partial approach that downgrades the links between social change and personal transformation. A fresh look at the links between value systems, institutional processes, and subjective states is therefore essential, especially at a time when the processes of globalisation are altering each of these things and their relationships with each other.

Importance of Integration

Against this background, it is clear that social change requires us to adopt an integrated approach that looks for positive synergies between different bases of change and different systems of power. When change in one area supports change in another, there is more of a chance that the outcome will be sustainable, as when ethics of co-operation are matched by institutions through which they can be expressed, and the deeper personal commitment required to put those ethics into practice. Such self-reinforcing cycles of co-operation, sharing and stewardship are the key to a social order that enables all people to meet their basic needs for security, voice and equality of rights, with less of a risk that in doing so they will deny others the same opportunities for a fulfilling life.

It is important to recognise that integration is an exercise in re-balancing, not the wholesale replacement of one rationality by another. Not all competition generates overweening selfishness, nor do markets always exploit the poor or powerless. There are many examples that show how well-regulated markets and open trade can benefit the poor, and how economic growth can contribute to poverty-eradication, the improved provision of social goods, and the conservation of natural and social capital (Edwards 1999). If it is unrealistic to focus on economic systems to the exclusion of personal change, it is equally unacceptable to call for inner transformation unless we can show how material needs will be met in less damaging ways.

However, the general point we wish to make remains valid: the emergence of a new social order requires those who gain power to make room for those with less; and all to use the power they gain in more responsible ways—not submerging their own self-interest entirely, but modulating it so that individual advancement is not bought at the cost of the broader conditions required for a secure and prosperous world. This may sound highly abstract, but as we shall see in Section 5 there are already concrete examples to draw on.

History offers us at least some examples of such an integrated approach to social change, notably the Indian nationalist movement under Mahatma Gandhi. There, a powerful underpinning of personal belief in the power of universal love and non-violence energised and sustained large numbers of ordinary Indians in the movement's tumultuous struggle for political independence. The testimony of those who participated in this movement suggests that ordinary people not only behaved and believed differently, but that they were different in a more fundamental sense. The failure of Indian politics and society to sustain these transformations in the post-Independence era suggests that the process of integration was far from complete, but it does not invalidate the basic principles involved.

Indeed, there are many more examples of incomplete integration which show why social change is so hard to achieve even when many of its component parts are in place. We have chosen the example of "development-as-empowerment" because such strategies are central to current NGO practice. By doing so we are not suggesting that NGOs are worse offenders in this respect than other institutions—merely that even the socially-committed will be unsuccessful if they ignore the inner basis of change.

Democratising the ownership of productive assets, capacities and opportunities continues to be a priority under globalisation, even if the nature of these things is changing (Edwards, Hulme and Wallace 1999). NGOs have been enthusiastic advocates of this form of empowerment for a decade and more, yet rarely do they question how people use the power they gain. The assumption is that greater material security, organisational capacity and political voice will be used to promote the common interest as well as the advancement of those individuals who benefit directly. Is this true?

In industrial societies, we know that rising wealth and democratic strength tend to produce a "culture of contentment", or the ebbing away of the "habits of the heart". In these circumstances, rising incomes may act as a block against more fundamental changes which are necessary for the rest of the population to attain the same level of satisfaction of their basic needs. The same pattern is evident from many Third World communities, though it is often mediated by cultures which do encourage sharing and co-operation, especially in times of crisis. All over the world, broader economic participation breeds selfish and competitive behaviour unless it is accompanied by a deeper shift in values, and by new institutions which allow those values to be expressed in collective action. This is especially true in a world of integrated markets where the temptation to cut costs and "race each-other to the bottom" is particularly strong (Korten 1995). Even when successful, economic empowerment may leave the structures of social power untouched, or even reinforce them, especially discrimination based on gender and age. Equally, social advancement may be unsustainable unless political power is also re-distributed to the benefit of those who have less voice. Rarely do empowerment strategies make the links that could generate shifts in inner values strong enough to ensure that improvements in one area are not bought at the cost of damage done elsewhere.

Need for Personal Change

Generalising from a theoretical situation like this is clearly dangerous, but the problem it describes is familiar: change at the subjective level is exceptionally difficult to achieve. It is rarely possible to generate sustainable changes in human behaviour simply by altering the rules and institutions that govern our lives. The missing ingredient is personal change, which acts as the wellspring of change in all other areas. Why?

A common lesson of experience is that processes of social change can easily lose touch with the values and principles that originally motivated and sustained them in the rough and tumble of the struggle. As a result, attempts to generate a new social order can unwittingly be poisoned by the "thieves of the heart"—the negative feelings of personal ego, jealousy and fear that destroy one's inner tranquillity. If people are not caring and compassionate in their personal behaviour they are unlikely to work effectively for a caring and compassionate society. Resisting these feelings, and developing the inner security required for a lifetime of co-operative endeavour, requires a disciplined process of self-reflection and contemplation about the values and purposes of our lives, and the desire and willingness to change ourselves. Undertaking this inner journey with courage can reward one with inner peace, greater energy and more effectiveness in one's actions, an expansive compassion in our attitudes towards others, and a tenderness of the heart that, on a mass scale, can have profound social implications.

We are not so naïve as to believe that a simple recognition of such things will change people's behaviour. But, acknowledging the fact that the absence of personal change can impede the social transformations we are searching for can be salutary in the search for a more integrated approach. Nor are we speaking of social indoctrination under duress, exemplified by the Chinese Cultural Revolution or Maoist self-criticism sessions. Inner change cannot be forced by the self-righteous; when hearts and minds are brutalised into submission or silence there will be little energy left for social engagement. Our vision is a positive one: the energies unleashed by serious and deep-rooted personal transformation can fuel the search for more humane social and economic systems as little else can.

What kind of personal changes could energise the move towards an economic order which re-balances competitive and co-operative rationalities, a politics of dialogue rather than unrepresentative democracy, and a social policy that works against marginalisation and values the care and nurture of all human beings? The first principles for such change lie at the heart of the teachings of all the great religions—"Love thy neighbour as thyself" in the Judaeo-Christian tradition, "See God in each other" in Sanskrit. It is fascinating to recognise that the core of religious teaching concerns our feelings towards each other—a deeply social statement as much as it is profoundly personal. But, to love our neighbours as ourselves, we must come to understand our own inner being—to recognise that in our deepest essence we are compassionate, capable of giving love, and worthy of receiving it.

Even when imperfectly established in this positive self-knowledge, we can identify more easily with the same inner being in other people—what the Hindu Vedanta calls "unity-consciousness." It then becomes easier to empathise with what it means to be the "other" from whom we usually distance ourselves in subtle or overt ways. That shift is crucial because it provides the foundation for personal behaviour which is more expansive and less damaging to others—for why would we damage the life-chances of someone who is as much a part of our Selves? The irony of today's globalised world is that, as knowledge about each-other grows, so do the criteria of "otherness" that breed selfishness, greed, anger and hatred—the fault-lines of race, ethnicity, gender, sexual orientation, caste, class, nationality, region, and economic blocs.

One question that often comes up in this context is whether more attention to inner transformation will divert one's energy away from social change. A related question is whether greater personal tranquillity will sap the angry energy needed to struggle against injustice. Anger is certainly a powerful form of energy that can be harnessed, particularly in the struggles of the socially oppressed. But, over time it can be corrosive of those who use it, becoming a deadly and increasingly-uncontrolled weapon. Inner centredness, on the other hand, can take more controllable but no less powerful forms. Those who have espoused non-violence, in India, South Africa, the USA and elsewhere, have not been weak. Their courage and energy have often been startling, and their example has sometimes and unexpectedly catalysed a process of transformation in their opponents. Inner-centredness can release enormous energy for the struggle against social injustice without having to draw upon the destructive legacy of anger or hatred.

Are there other dangers in the call to link social to personal change? Throughout the ages, organised religions have often spawned fundamentalist bigotry and a narrowing of the realm of personal beliefs to accord with what is considered by some to be "moral" conduct. Our own age shows us the dangers that religious fundamentalism brings to social institutions when it spills over from the private to the public realm. Social conservatism is rarely more dangerous than when it cloaks itself in religious garb that cannot adequately be challenged by rationalist arguments for social justice because it assumes an other-worldly authority. The rising tide of religious bigotry across the world in recent decades is one of the reasons why space for serious discussion of the links between social and personal change has been so narrow. The other is a woolly-headed and self-indulgent "new ageism" that confuses material detachment with a wholesale retreat from social engagement.

However, disciplined self-enquiry of the kind we have described provides a way out of this impasse, by constantly exposing attitudes and behaviours that masquerade as compassionate or detached. Paradoxically, the expansive compassion and tenderness of heart of which we speak calls for all the toughness of mind, courage and flexibility that are also required in the outer struggle for social change. Our conclusion then is clear: personal transformation is essential if we are to see society change in the directions we espouse. Confronting this challenge squarely and with honesty is the need of the hour.

Role of NGOs in Promoting Personal Change?

NGOs are unlikely vehicles for the direct transformation of the individual, though the best traditions of the sector—like selfless service among volunteers and the courage to undertake the seemingly-impossible -sometimes generate experiences that come close to the spiritual realm. However, the model of social change we have described makes it clear that there are many indirect ways to encourage the transformation of people's subjective states, so long as our approach to processes and institutions is properly-integrated—in other words, that the goal of personal change is a conscious and explicit element in all that we do. Most of us know that our true Self is loving and compassionate, but feel we must disguise it in the street-fighting of everyday life. However, when we consciously create more institutional spaces for inner transformation, we can begin to exercise our economic, social and political responsibilities in ways which both draw from and encourage the personal changes we are looking for. It may sound romantic to call for an economics or politics that is loving and compassionate, but this is exactly what we can shape through conscious action.

We want to look briefly at three areas in which NGOs have a crucial role to play in fostering these integrated changes: their programme activities (the work they support in the field, directly or through others); their fund-raising and constituency-building work; and their own organisational praxis—the ways in which values are expressed in structures, systems and management. Constraints of space mean that we can only mention a small number of examples.

Programme Activities

The overriding challenge for NGOs in the 21st century will be to help re-balance the competitive and co-operative forces that motivate each one of us, whether in economics, politics or social life. They can do this by regulating—and ultimately re-constructing—all systems of power in ways which achieve three things: a more equal distribution of what they deliver, less costly ways of producing it, and more co-operative values and behaviour among those involved as producers or consumers. When we talk of "costs", we explicitly include damage done to ourselves, the social fabric that sustains us as fully-human beings, and the environment we all depend on for our future.

Although, NGOs rarely see their work in this way, there are plenty of experiments already underway which show how such integrated transformations might work at a much larger scale:

- In economics, for example, new forms of enterprise are competing effectively in open markets but distributing work and profits with a social purpose, backed up by codes of conduct to level up working conditions and supported by a growing movement for "ethical consumption." The links that are developing between peasant production systems in Latin America and supermarket campaigns in industrialised countries provide a good example of this wave of the future. The best NGO credit schemes provide another.

- In politics, Latin American municipalities are inventing new forms of "dialogic democracy" in which representatives from civil society and business share in decision-making with local government. Similar experiments are underway in other parts of the world—like India's "Panchayati Raj" system of decentralised governance—and around Agenda-21 planning, post-conflict re-construction, and the elaboration of national development strategies. These innovations give everyone a voice in decision-making and reduce the dangers of "elected dictatorships" which favour the interests of the rich. At the same time, they build new capacities for dialogue and co-operation across old institutional boundaries.
- In the area of social policy, organisations like SEWA in India and the Grameen Bank in Bangladesh are promoting different ways of sharing the costs and responsibilities of child-care so that women can increase their incomes and assets without sacrificing their own health and welfare to the interests of their children. These innovations achieve a better set of trade-offs between social and economic outcomes, challenging the structures of social power in the process and building the material security people need to participate in dialogic politics.

Although, personal change is rarely an explicit element in these experiments, there is a clear linkage between the processes and institutions they foster, and the subjective states they grow from and reinforce. Ethical production systems are not viable without ethical consumers, for example; equitable social policies are impossible if men and women are unwilling to share the burden of paid and unpaid work. Such experiments can consolidate their gains by making personal change a more explicit part of their agenda, so that new, more co-operative institutions can be backed up by corresponding innovations in values and behaviour.

Mainstreaming these experiences will require pioneers in all walks of life, but government and business are unlikely to spearhead moves for radical changes which involve reduced consumption or the ceding of authority to non-state actors. The major pressure must come from those parts of civil society who are committed to new social and economic models. It is NGOs and other civic groups that are already lobbying corporations to be more responsible, organising collective approaches to welfare, and acting as a counterweight to vested interests in decentralised politics. We believe that these activities will dominate civic action in the next fifty years.

Constituency building

Although, there are many interesting experiments like these to report on, they do not add up to much when compared to the forces that really drive change in the contemporary world. What are missing are scale, depth and sustainability—to make these innovations the norm rather than the exception. Achieving those goals requires a mass base to support radical change, and that in turn requires an inner transformation on a scale not realised in any period in history. Motivating large numbers of people to shift to more co-operative behaviour and persuade those in power to create more inclusive institutions goes against the heart of the current socio-economic order. Without personal change towards more caring and compassionate ways of being and dealing with each other, it will be very hard to generate the momentum to bring about such a shift.

At first sight this might appear to be the job of the churches and other faith-based groups in civil society, not of development NGOs. It is no accident that dissatisfaction with current models of development and foreign aid has coincided with a resurgence of interest in the developmental role of the Faiths, even in such non-spiritual organisations as the World Bank. However, there are a number of reasons for thinking that development NGOs also have a crucial role to play, not least because the established religions so often fail to live up to their theology. More broadly, it is the secular world of environmental and social activism that forms at least as powerful a connection in most people's lives between the "personal and the political." We no longer reserve our moral expressions for church on Sunday; indeed, the increasing diffusion of moral action through civil society and beyond is one of the most heartening developments of the late-20th century.

Development NGOs have been an important part of this expanding moral space, but they have never fulfilled their potential as constituency-builders on the wider stage. In contrast to environmental NGOs, they rarely use their high levels of public trust and extended fund-raising networks as channels for personal transformation and lifestyle change, and their membership of civil society (both domestic and international) is increasingly called into question. Consequently, we still lack institutional expression for the exercise of conscience on the scale that would be necessary to resolve world poverty or intervene against fundamental abuses of human rights. Without such mass-based institutional pressure, there will be another Rwanda, and then another.

One of the key problems here takes us back to the discussion of "unity-consciousness". This is that traditional fund-raising images—and the paternalistic cloak of foreign aid—elicit sympathy, but not solidarity. Under the guise of bringing people closer together they force them further apart, increasing the psychological distance between donor and recipient, and reinforcing the conviction of separateness that lies at the root of our failure to act. "Caught in the models of the limited self, we end up by diminishing one-another. The more you think of yourself as a philanthropist, the more someone else feels compelled to be a supplicant", and the less inclination they both have to co-operate together as equal partners. Fifty years of foreign aid have left us ill-prepared to face a co-operative future.

Paradoxically, therefore, the decline of foreign aid provides a window of opportunity to advance a transformative agenda, by re-focusing attention on international co-operation and the values that make co-operation work. There won't be a constituency for international co-operation, unless there is a commitment to co-operative living generally, for why should people co-operate with distant strangers if they do not do so with their neighbours? Global regimes impose clear limitations on personal autonomy, so it won't be the United Nations that will solve global warming, but you and us—by reducing the energy we use in our homes, cars and factories. Co-operation requires the constant exercise of co-operative values, rather than the peddling of stereotypes about other people who need a "sponsor" to "save" them. This implies relationships among equals, and the acceptance of responsibility to put our own house in order. And at root, that is always a matter of personal change.

Organisational Praxis

The claim that development NGOs are explicitly "values-based" organisations is something of an article of faith these days. There is less evidence that NGOs put these values into practice in their organisational structures and behaviour, or even that they are clear what their core values are. This is a major weakness, because it is the link between values and actions that is crucial in generating legitimacy when arguing the case for change. Institutions must be seen to implement values as the bottom line in their own practice if they are to build a coalition in support of those values on the wider stage. The best way NGOs can help to foster the mass movement that has been missing from the field of international development since the end of the Cold War is for them to be exemplars of the society they want to create—to show that it is possible to be an effective organisation which values its employees as it does its partners, fights discrimination, practices internal democracy, and always uses the organisational power it has in liberating ways.

Unfortunately, few development NGOs have done this. For one thing, high levels of dependence on foreign aid and the limitations of contractual relationships make it very difficult to expand into real values-based action -there are simply too many compromises that have to be made. For another, NGOs are not immune to class, race, and gender problems, nor the oppression and sexual exploitation they breed. Behind the screen of progressive attitudes toward social change in the world outside, the world inside the organisation can be an ethical morass. Such organisations cannot be the basis of far-reaching social change.

Fortunately, this point is beginning to be taken to heart in many NGOs. The link between personal change and organisational effectiveness is increasingly being recognised, even though its practical application remains weak. These pioneers stress that is certainly possible to help others effectively, but only if we realise that in doing so they help us to grow to a fuller, more independent knowledge of ourselves—closing the circle once more between personal change and change in the wider world. If our own practice is autocratic, closed, and chauvinist it is unlikely that we will be able to encourage others to be democratic, open and egalitarian.

What remains is for NGOs to experiment more seriously with management practices, organisational structures, and personnel policies that create the feedback loops we are looking for between personal change, institutional performance, and wider impact. A start has been made in this direction, but a huge area remains unexplored (Fowler 1997). Perhaps a re-visioning of NGO strategy around values-based action in programme work, constituency-building and organisational praxis would be a useful place to start.

CONCLUSION

This study is only a beginning in our exploration of what are clearly some complex and personally-demanding questions. However, we are convinced that the journey is the right one, and that the responsibility to undertake it is inescapable. Although, questions of personal transformation and spirituality may appear threatening to mainstream NGO activity, the roles and relationships we have sketched out above constitute an exciting agenda for civic action in the 21st century. Transforming systems of power is the key to a sustainable future in which all people can live in dignity and fulfilment, but it is impossible unless we ourselves are also transformed. Such an agenda would simultaneously help NGOs to make a reality of their stated mission for social change; provide a clear focus for civic action in a world where foreign aid looks set to decline still further; and establish a genuine leadership role in society at large. It would, therefore, meet both the "institutional and the developmental imperatives" that all NGOs must manage.

In a profession that talks constantly about results, the importance of personal accountability is often forgotten. Yet, as we have argued in this chapter, the willingness to confront the shadow of the Self is the secret of all sustainable progress.

NOTES AND REFERENCES

Bellah, R. (1985) *Habits of the Heart: Individualism and Commitment in American Life*, Berkeley, CA: University of California Press.

Chambers, R. (1996) *Challenging the Professions,* London: Intermediate Technology Publications.

Dass, R. and P.Gorman (1988) *How Can I Help? Stories and Reflections on Service,* New York: Knopf.

Edwards, M. (1996) *International Development NGOs: Legitimacy, Accountability, Regulation and Roles,* London: Commission on the Future of the Voluntary Sector.

Edwards, M. (1998) NGOs as Values-Based Organisations, in: D.Lewis (ed.) *International Perspectives on Voluntary Action: Rethinking the Third Sector,* London: Earthscan.

Edwards, M. (1999) *Future Positive: International Co-operation in the 21st Century,* London: Earthscan.

Gailbraith, J. K. (1992) The Culture of Contentment, London: Sinclair-Stevenson.

Kaplan, A (1997) *The Development Practitioners Handbook,* London: Pluto Press.

Korten, D (1995) *When Corporations Rule the World,* West Hartford, Conn: Kumarian Press.

7

MODERNISATION IN INDIA

While it is, strongly affected by this global background, the history of modernisation studies in India is also rather distinctive. Unlike in most other Third World countries, American modernisation theory did not dominate the study of social change in India, although it was a prominent and influential presence in the realm of state policy. This difference is due to the combined effect of three factors: the prior involvement of other Western scholarly traditions; the presence of a small but relatively well-developed indigenous research establishment; and the hegemonic influence exerted by a long-standing nationalist movement.

As an ancient civilisation with a living Great Tradition (rather than a 'decapitated' one, to use Robert Redfield's starkly evocative term), India was no *tabula rasa* for Western scholars. The production of systematic knowledge on Indian society of a recognizably modern kind developed very rapidly from 1760 onward, based on the pioneering work of Orientalist Indologists, colonial administrators and missionaries, as Bernard Cohn has shown. By the early decades of the twentieth century, these varied traditions had already produced a considerable body of works on the arts, sciences and cultural-religious practices of classical Hinduism; the cultural coherence of Indian/Hindu or aboriginal communities; and regional inventories of castes and tribes detailing their 'customs and manners'. To this must be added the later work of Western and Indian scholars trained mainly in the British tradition of social anthropology, as well as some American anthropologists, consisting largely of ethnographic monographs on village, caste or tribal communities.

However, this diverse body of largely anthropological work on India did not show any deep or sustained interest in social *change,* except in the form of enquiries into the decay or degeneration of traditional practices, institutions and communities. With independence, of course, the search for social change became an important item on the agenda of social anthropology in India — so much so, in fact, that some scholars worried that it would eclipse other issues. But, even when it did get taken up, this search was conducted largely independently of American modernisation theory as such, in keeping, perhaps, with the relative indifference towards this theme in anthropology.

The second and third reasons for the Indian difference have to be viewed together: the hegemonic status of nationalism in the 1950s, and the existence of institutions that could give intellectual expression to this hegemony. In India, as in most of the non-Western world, the themes of modernisation, development, growth and progress were part of the much wider canvas of the colonial encounter, particularly since the latter half of the nineteenth century. They were woven into colonialist narratives of the white man's burden and the *mission civilisatrice* — and also into emergent nationalist narratives of the desire for development thwarted by colonial oppression and economic drain.

In the heady aftermath of Indian independence, the idea of modernisation took on the dimensions of a national mission; it became an integral part of the Nehruvian 'tryst with destiny' that the nation had pledged to keep. While Indian nationalism in itself was hardly an aberration (though older than most others in the Third World), India's colonial inheritance of a viable nucleus of Western-style academic institutions was unusual, possibly even unique. Like other social institutions of the time, Indian universities and research institutes were also eager to participate in the agendas of the nationalist state, and provided another site for the emergence of modernisation studies in India, one marked by an ambivalent attitude towards Western scholars and institutions, and by a bias against basic research and towards policy-oriented studies.

Survey of Literature

Given the peculiarities of its long pre-history, the study of societal change in India evolved into a much more diverse field of enquiry than that suggested by American modernisation theory. The central fact here is the relativisation of modernisation studies as one paradigm among others speculating on the consequences of the interface between the West and India. Some measure of the extent of this relativisation is provided in the distinctive stance of Orientalist Indology, the first Western scholarly tradition to address Indian society and culture in the late-eighteenth and early-nineteenth centuries. While it was surely less than egalitarian, this stance still entertained the possibility of a reciprocal relationship, something unthinkable in later models of modernisation. However, by the latter half of the nineteenth century and certainly in the twentieth, the Indologists' perspective had been sidelined, and questions of societal change could only be framed within — or against — a firmly Eurocentric intellectual horizon. Nevertheless, the larger question of India's response to Western modernity continued to be asked and answered in ways that could not simply be reduced to speculations about the manner in which tradition would be superseded.

T.N. Madan has suggested that in Indian sociology and social anthropology, the question of modernity is posed in three major forms. It first appears in the 1930s as opposition to the Weberian thesis of the other-worldly orientation of Hinduism and its consequent lack of affinity for modern materialist modes of thought, when scholars like Benoy Kumar Sarkar and Brajendranath Seal attempt to foreground the positivistic tendencies in Hindu thought by proposing a 'Hindu sociology'. The second occasion is the public controversy over the policy to be adopted towards tribal communities — whether they ought to be modernised and 'mainstreamed' or protected and 'preserved'. This debate involved not only the well-known exchanges between Verrier Elwin and G.S.Ghurye, but also engagements with contemporary notions of 'progress' by scholars like D.P.Mukerji and D.N. Majumdar. The third recurrence of this question is, of course, in the post-independence context of development — an ideology that dominated world history for several decades.

While these three episodes offer a useful entry point into the history of scholarly engagement with modernity, they are not as helpful in ordering the literature on modernisation because the hegemonic sway of the idea of development is such that it dwarfs or subsumes the other two instances. Indeed, if we revert from the broader question of the India-West interface to the more conventional meaning attached to modernisation, then the entire literature on the subject— certainly everything written after 1947—is directly or indirectly influenced by the notion of national development.

Given a strong and enduring but not necessarily unchanging traditional social system, the modernisation question seems to allow for only three elementary outcomes: (a) tradition prevails over modernity, absorbing or obstructing it successfully; (b) modernity triumphs over tradition, undermining and eventually supplanting it; or (c) tradition and modernity coexist in some fashion. One could therefore categorise the literature in terms of these outcomes, and there have been attempts to do so. However, this categorisation also proves to be lop-sided because the first two possibilities were very quickly marginalised in post-independence India: the massive impact of modernity could not be ignored, nor could the continuing resilience of tradition. The bulk of the Indian literature on modernisation, is thus, concerned with characterising the nature of the interaction between tradition and modernity, and the long term trend of this relationship.

Since there is no obvious classificatory scheme available, the following survey of literature is based on an eclectic mix of criteria such as disciplinary location, theoretical perspective, and value orientation. Even so, the field to be covered is vast, given the variety of disciplines (including social anthropology, sociology, social psychology, politics, political economy and area studies) and theoretical perspectives (such as structural-functionalism, behaviourism, structuralism, Marxism or evolutionism, not to speak of combinations of these) represented. Moreover, modernisation is such a broad theme that almost every author and every work on Indian society can be seen as addressing it in some sense or the other. This overview is therefore limited only to work in and around sociology and anthropology that has had a significant influence on the analysis of social change in post-independence India — somewhat imprecise and arbitrary criteria, but unavoidably so.

Social Anthropological Perspectives: Though he refuses the term 'modernisation', M.N. Srinivas is among the first and easily the most influential scholar to have written extensively on the question. The *locus classicus* of Srinivas' approach is his book *Social Change in Modern India,* published in 1966, although the major concepts in it had already found mention in his 1952 work on Coorg. Acknowledging the enormity of the enterprise, Srinivas deliberately takes an 'all-India' view of social change, though he relies heavily on the insights garnered during his own field work in Coorg (1940-42) and Mysore (1947-48). For Srinivas, change takes two major forms: first, various forms of mobility within the caste system (captured by the concepts of Sanskritisation and dominant caste); and second the wide-ranging process of Westernisation. (He also adds a chapter on secularisation, but the weight of his analysis is undoubtedly borne by the first two areas.)

As is well known, Sanskritisation refers to a process that 'seems to have occurred throughout Indian history and still continues to occur' by which 'a 'low' Hindu caste, or tribal or other group, changes its customs, ritual, ideology, and way of life in the direction of a high, and frequently, 'twice-born' caste' with a view to claiming a higher position in the caste hierarchy. Such claims may, over 'a generation or two', result in some upward mobility, but mobility may also occur without Sanskritisation and vice versa. However, the mobility associated with Sanskritisation results only in *positional changes* in the system and does not lead to any *structural change.* That is, a caste moves up, above its neighbours, and another comes down, but all this takes place in an essentially stable hierarchical order. The system itself does not change.

The concept of a dominant caste, on the other hand, is an attempt to capture the change in the status of some relatively high touchable castes as a result of their numerical strength, predominant position in the agricultural economy (mainly land ownership), and, over time, accumulation of 'Western' criteria such as education and government jobs. In other words, this concept points to the rise in secular status, political power (following adult franchise) and economic power (following land reforms) of some caste groups who have benefited from the social changes introduced since independence.

Westernisation refers to the 'changes introduced into Indian society during British rule and which continue, in some cases with added momentum, in independent India'. Despite being a relatively recent influence, Westernisation is recognised as 'an inclusive, complex, and many-layered concept' ranging 'from Western technology at one end to the experimental method of modern science and modern historiography at the other', and its different aspects 'sometimes combine to strengthen a particular process, sometimes work at cross-purposes, and are occasionally mutually discrete'. Though the upper castes have been particularly active in mediating it, all castes are affected by Westernisation, which brings about 'radical and lasting changes in Indian society and culture' based on a very wide range of causal factors, including 'new technology, institutions, knowledge, beliefs and values'. The changes it effects can often be counter-intuitive, as indicated by the fact that it 'has given birth not only to nationalism but also to revivalism, communalism, 'casteism', heightened linguistic consciousness, and regionalism' or that it is linked to Sanskritisation in a 'complex and intricate interrelation'.

Srinivas' early work on Coorg attracted considerable attention because it was the first social-anthropological study of a complex society with 'high' cultural traditions (as different from the 'simple' or 'primitive' societies that social-anthropologists had studied until then). Srinivas' notion of Sanskritisation, and his innovative spatial hierarchy of local, regional and 'all-India' Hinduism, seemed to offer novel ways of theorising the relationship between the 'great' and 'little' traditions posited by the University of Chicago anthropologist, Robert Redfield, and this is how his associates McKim Marriott and Milton Singer came to study India in the early 1950s.

Singer's main work on modernisation is based on innovative fieldwork — done in three stints in 1954-55, 1960-61 and 1964, in middle and upper-class *urban* settings in south India, mainly Madras — and helps complement rural-based perceptions on social change.

He focuses on the specific strategies used by urban Indians to manage the simultaneous presence of tradition and modernity in their everyday lives. Thus, *compartmentalisation* refers to the strict spatial and temporal segregation of traditional and modern contexts/ institutions; *ritual neutralisation* is a sort of prophylactic gesture to contain the threat of pollution or other forms of transgression of traditional values in modern contexts such as the workplace; and *vicarious ritualisation* is a kind of division of labour in which householders unable to perform religious rituals (because of conflicts with their modern occupations) get their wives or professional priest to perform them on their behalf.

The main contributions of Marriott relevant here are two concepts developed from field work in a north Indian village, namely, *'parochialisation'* and *'universalisation'*. The latter is a process whereby elements of the 'little' tradition (customs, deities and rites) circulate upward to enter the 'great' tradition and thus acquire a more universal status, while the former refers to the opposite process of elements from the 'great' tradition becoming confined to particular local 'little' traditions.

The core of the specifically social-anthropological work on the theme of modernisation consists basically of the 'Srinivas-Chicago' body of work and its many critics, elaborators and interlocutors. Sanskritisation in particular has generated a large literature and is the most prominent (some would say the only) concept from the Indian literature to have made an impact on the larger discipline. Numerous studies have appreciated, extended or criticised the concept, mooted the notions of re- or de-Sanskritisation, or examined its regional spread. Similarly, the notions of 'great' and 'little' traditions have also elicited further transformations on the basic model, the most important being the presence of multiple traditions whose importance and modes of inter-articulation are context dependent.

Tradition-Identified Perspectives: While the Srinivasian position has attempted to remain neutral about the valuation to be placed on the modernisation process, a significant minority tendency has not only strongly identified with Indian tradition in a personal-existential sense, but has gone on to fashion a disciplinary agenda sharply critical of the process of modernisation and especially Westernised modes of studying it. The best known representatives of this tendency are D.P. Mukerji and A.K. Saran, both of the Lucknow 'school' of Indian sociology, who arrive at this position by very different routes — the former through long engagement with Marxist materialism and its inadequacies, and the latter by way of Hindu religion and metaphysics.

Mukerji's priorities are forthrightly stated in his famous Presidential Address to the first meeting of the Indian Sociological Society in 1955: 'the study of Indian traditions' is the 'first and immediate duty of the Indian sociologist'. Indeed, he goes further: 'it is not enough for the Indian sociologist to be a sociologist. He must be an Indian first, that is, he is to share in the folk-ways, mores, customs and traditions for the purpose of understanding his social system and what lies beneath it and beyond it'. Mukerji argues for indigenous modes of analysis because Western concepts fail to capture the complex particularity of Indian society, which 'requires a different approach to sociology because of its special traditions, its special symbols and its special pattern of culture and social actions'. It is only 'thereafter' that there can be a case for studying change, because 'the thing changing is more real and objective than change per se'. According to T.N. Madan, Mukerji viewed modernisation as 'at once an expansion, an elevation, a deepening and a revitalisation' of traditional values and cultural patterns — that is, as a kind of self-conscious synthesisation of modernity by tradition.

However, this synthesis and the derivation of indigenous concepts from Hindu philosophy, the life of Mahatma Gandhi and so on is never pursued systematically, but remains at the level of suggestive claims and passing examples, evidence perhaps of the 'self-cancellation' and 'reluctance' attributed to Mukerji. A.K. Saran appears to have moved in the direction of Hindu religion and philosophy with a view to exploring their potential for Indian sociology. But, again there is a lack of substantial texts where this position is spelt out adequately, and even as sympathetic a commentator as Veena Das is constrained to note that Saran's attitude towards tradition ultimately lapses into nostalgia.

This broad position—defined by the triad of tradition-identification, anti-modernism, and theoretical indigenism—has exerted a disproportionate influence despite its lack of dominance. Though its intellectual reach has always exceeded its scholarly grasp, this tendency continues to attract adherents to its general vicinity, albeit with differing emphases on its three planks. Early exponents include the controversial figure of Verrier Elwin, famous as the anthropologist gone native, while more contemporary versions of different sorts are to be found in the work of Tariq Banuri, T.N. Madan, McKim Marriott, J.P.S Uberoi, Shiv Visvanathan, or Claude Alvares and especially Ashis Nandy.

Synthetic Overviews: Among the various attempts to synthesise different perspectives on modernisation in India, the most comprehensive and best known is Yogendra Singh's *Modernisation of Indian Tradition.* Singh's ambitious theoretical project is to overcome the 'partial focus on social processes' and the 'limitations of the analytical categories used' in previous treatments of change in India, which have rendered them 'narrow and inadequate'. He identifies commonalties in the earlier perspectives and uses them to fashion his own overarching taxonomic synthesis based on 'unilinear evolutionism in the long run' which distinguishes: (a) the micro and macro contexts in which change-producing processes begin and materialize; (b) internal (orthogenetic) and external (heterogenetic) sources of change; and (c) the structural and cultural substantive domains in which phenomena are undergoing change. This is said to yield a 'comprehensive as well as theoretically consistent' synthetic theory into which social change in India from Vedic times to the present can be fitted, including such major epochal changes as the advent of Muslim rule, British colonialism, or independence.

S.C. Dube's general survey is notable for bringing together the literatures on modernisation and development, and for the fact that it was written well after disillusionment with modernisation had set in. Dube's emphasis is on 'the search for alternative paradigms' (the subtitle of his book), among which he includes 'conscientisation', 'affirmative action' and 'institution building'. His survey is oriented towards the practical issues of social policy, like his two earlier works relevant here, namely the famous 1955 book *Indian Village* (although it does not explicitly address modernisation) and the later edited collection *India's Changing Villages*, both significant studies of social change in rural India.

Gunnar Myrdal's well-known 'institutional approach' to the problem of development in South Asia bases itself on the premise that not only is the social and institutional structure different from the one that has evolved in Western countries, but, more important, the problem of development in South Asia is one calling for induced changes in that social and institutional structure, as it hinders economic development and as it does not change spontaneously, or, to any very large extent, in response to policies restricted to the "economic" sphere.. Easily the largest single work on the subject, *Asian Drama* was based on a decade-long pioneering effort to collect, evaluate and synthesize secondary material from a vast variety of sources on the political economy of India. Myrdal's overall conclusions were pessimistic because he saw resilient traditional institutions and values as an insurmountable obstacle to modernisation. In contrast, the institutions of modernity in India — most notably the state — tended to be 'soft', and would therefore be unable to pursue a modern agenda effectively unless traditional blockages were comprehensively destroyed. However, a contemporary review by a social anthropologist notes that Myrdal's social institutions remain under-specified, caste being the only one discussed at some length, though even here the treatment ignores literature offering contrary evidence.

David Mandelbaum's vast and copiously referenced survey of scholarship on Indian society provides a compendium of early work on the theme of change, especially in terms of caste mobility, and religious and tribal movements. Also well known is two volume collection on the theme of modernisation of underdeveloped societies edited by A.R. Desai. The collection contains more than sixty articles (mostly previously published) by scholars from across the world writing from diverse perspectives; there are also a few articles written for the collection, among which Inkeles' paper on the problems of field work in Third World countries and Srinivas' brief queries on modernisation are particularly interesting. Myron Weiner's popular collection (originally a series of radio talks on the Voice of America) has also been influential as nine out of his twenty-five contributors have worked on India.

Social-Psychological Perspectives: Perhaps, the most typical example of American modernisation studies in India is the study by Alex Inkeles and David Smith that examines how 'people move from being traditional to becoming more modern personalities' in six developing countries: Argentina, Chile, India, Israel, Nigeria and East Pakistan. Distinctive in looking for attributes of modernity among individuals, the study was based on intensive interviews with a stratified sample of 1,000 males in each country, whose responses were measured for their degree of modernisation on a composite attitudinal scale developed by the authors. The main findings confirmed the existence of a 'psycho-social syndrome' of modernity as internalised values and attitudes, and manifested in behaviour demonstrating a feeling of personal efficacy, autonomy from 'traditional sources of influence', and openness towards 'new experiences and ideas'. The most important causal factor was education, followed by occupation and exposure to mass-media, but urbanisation was found to be unimportant.

David McClelland and David Winter's study took the form of a training programme (conducted by the government Small Industries Extension Training Institute, Hyderabad) for small businessmen from the south Indian towns of Kakinada and Vellore. Based on McClelland's earlier research on the psychology of motivation, the study sought to identify the determinants of the 'need to achieve' with a view to (in the words of their subtitle) 'accelerating economic development through psychological training'.

Other Disciplines and Perspectives: Political science has perhaps been the most active discipline in modernisation theory (along with rural sociology) and has produced numerous studies on 'political development' around the world, largely in response to the intense interest in the politics of Third World countries during the cold war. In India, the best known examples (from the perspective of sociology and social anthropology) would be Rajni Kothari and Lloyd and Susanne Rudolph. Kothari's classic work adopts a functional approach towards modernisation and focuses on the mutual interaction of tradition and modernity, the specifics of their relationship, the process that it is part of, and their functionality for each other. The Rudolphs famous study attempts to show how modernisation in Indian politics changes traditional institutions such that they begin to take on modern roles, the most prominent case being that of caste.

Political economy and Marxism would be next in importance from a sociological perspective. But, the work here is very diverse, ranging from the historical emphasis of Daniel Thorner, through the economics-oriented overview by Pranab Bardhan to the political theory of Kaviraj's essay on the 'passive revolution'. But, the most important marxist work on the theme of modernisation — theorised, however, in terms of the transition from a pre-capitalist to a capitalist mode of production — is that stimulated by the 'mode of production' debate, which tried to ascertain whether and to what extent Indian agrarian relations were capitalist in nature. The decade-long debate produced very sophisticated discussions on the conceptual categorisation of 'aberrant' social formations such as India — neither capitalist, nor feudal, but with the strong presence of elements of both. Some of the theoretical options advocated included semi-feudalism, semi-capitalism, a 'colonial mode of production' and characterisations based on the distinction between formal and real subsumption of labour by capital. Given the valuable contributions that marxist scholars have made to Indian historiography and political economy, it is a pity that they have, by and large, not ventured very far onto the sociological terrain of modernisation.

Finally, looking at the sponsoring institutions involved in research around the theme of modernisation gives us another perspective on the field. Different kinds of institutional and financial support has been provided to researchers by Indian and especially foreign universities: Harvard, Chicago, Berkeley, Cornell and Stanford have been particularly important, but Oxford, the London School of Economics, Stockholm and McGill have also been involved in facilitating fieldwork or publications. American private foundations have been very active, led by the Ford Foundation, which has invested heavily in research on change, development and planning in India but the Rockefeller Foundation has also been involved in the early stages, as have the Twentieth Century Fund (Myrdal) and the

Carnegie Corporation. Government sources in India have included the Small Industries Extension Training Institute, the National Service Extension Programme, the Community Development Programme and the Planning Commission. Various organs of the US government have also supported modernisation research, including the State Department (which controlled the PL 480 counterpart funds in India and other countries receiving US aid), the US Agency for International Development, and, in at least one instance, even the US Air Force (through its Office of Scientific Research which helped with the Inkeles and Smith study.

'We may have become weary of the concept of modernisation,' writes T.N. Madan, 'but the important question is, have we carefully formulated the reasons for this weariness?' Indian sociology does seem to be weary of modernisation, not only in the sense of being bored or disenchanted with this theme, but also in the sense of having been exhausted by it—one of the reasons, perhaps, why sociology in India has sometimes looked like a tired discipline. Why has the conceptual pursuit of modernisation been so debilitating? Among the better known answers is the conceptual dead-end of dualism; less well-known are the peculiar disciplinary location of Indian sociology, and the problems posed by the abstract generality of the term 'modernisation'.

Dualism and its Discontents

The dominant view among students of modern India held that neither tradition nor modernity would be strong enough to completely erase the other. This meant that the search for an adequate summary-description of Indian society was transposed into the problem of defining dualism—or characterising the nature of the relationship between tradition and modernity.

There is, of course, nothing exceptional in this, for dualism is the presiding deity in the conceptual pantheon of modernisation not just in India but everywhere in the 'non-West'. Consider, for example, one of the most famous vignettes in modernisation studies—the story of 'The Grocer and the Chief'—with which David Lerner begins his classic work on *The Passing of Traditional Society*. Presented as 'the parable of modern Turkey', this story contrasts two main characters who stand for modernity and tradition. The chief is a 'virtuoso of the traditional style'. A prosperous farmer and an imposing personality, he has no unfulfilled ambitions, loves to expound on the values of 'obedience, courage, loyalty', and responds to persistent enquiries about where else he would like to live with a firm 'nowhere'. Balgat's only grocer is described by his interviewer as an 'unimpressive type' giving 'the impression of a fat shadow', whom the villagers consider to be 'even less than the least farmer'. But, the grocer visits Ankara frequently, is fascinated by Hollywood movies, would like to own 'a *real* grocery store' with floor-to-ceiling shelves, and is eager to live in America because it offers 'possibilities to be rich even for the simplest persons'. As if to underline the centrality of this dichotomous model for modernisation theory, Alex Inkeles and David Smith present an identical contrast between Ahmadullah, a 'traditional' illiterate farmer from Comilla, and Nuril, a 'modern' metal worker in a Dacca factory, who enact Lerner's Turkish parable all over again—sixteen years later, in Bangladesh..

The point of recalling these emblematic figures is not to claim that they are absent in India—how could they be?— but to highlight the fact that the *dominant* descriptions of dualism in the Indian literature are different. Simply put, Indian descriptions of dualism seem discrepant because they are relatively more sophisticated than those elsewhere, at least in the early period of modernisation studies. The precociously complex analyses of influential scholars like M.N. Srinivas minimises the impact of the cruder models of dualism, even though they are as common in India as elsewhere in the Third World. On the other hand, this means that the aporias of dualism are reached sooner in India, and that more time is wasted in conceptual wheel-spinning because the tradition-modernity dichotomy fails to get a grip on Indian social reality.

The most obvious differences in Indian accounts of dualism have to do with the social units in which tradition and modernity are located, and their reciprocal articulation. Thus, tradition and modernity are not only segregated into two separate personalities as in the Bangladeshi or Turkish tale, but are also apt to occur, in comparable Indian accounts, as integral parts of *the same personality.*

For example, M.N. Srinivas mentions meeting the 'driver of a government bulldozer' in his field village of Rampura in 1952, barely two years after Tosun B. met with the Turkish grocer and chief on Daniel Lerner's behalf. The bulldozer driver, a Tamil-speaker from Bangalore, was skilled enough to operate his machine and also to 'do minor repairs; but he was not only traditional in his religious beliefs, he had even picked up some black magic, a knowledge usually confined to small groups'. Srinivas reports that 'he saw no inconsistency between driving a bulldozer for his livelihood and indulging in displays of black magic for his pleasure', the 'two sectors being kept completely "discrete"'.

But, if such descriptions are more believable and complex than the caricatures of crude dualism, they also place the Indian personality under permanent suspicion of schizophrenia. Here is Srinivas again, speaking this time of the first generation of his own community, South Indian Brahmins, who took to English education in considerable numbers and entered the professions and government service at all levels. In the first phase of their Westernisation, their professional life was lived in the Western world while their home life continued to be largely traditional. The term 'cultural schizophrenia' comes to mind, but a caution must be uttered against viewing it as pathological. The theme of the coexistence of 'discrete' sectors in a single person, family or other social group is a common one in the literature on modernisation in India, and, indeed, in the conversational anecdotes of everyday life. The dualistic-but-unified personality may be described in a wide range of registers—from pathos through pathology to pride. But, whatever the tenor of the description, and regardless of the attitude of the person being described, the describer — especially the professional social scientist — is unable to shake off a sense of incongruity which invariably inflects the description. Nevertheless, in the Indian literature, the choice between tradition and modernity is rarely presented as a mutually exclusive 'either-or', though it is often seen as a morally charged one.

In Lerner's description, tradition has no value whatsoever for the grocer, who wishes only to escape from its parochial constraints; and the chief, though forced to acknowledge the impact of modernity, remains thoroughly immune to it morally. In this parable, 'modern Turkey' is the only transcendent entity capable of subsuming these contrary worldviews, while in the Indian literature the burden of subsumption is felt by social units all along the scale from the national to the individual.

But, too much must not be made of such differences. After all, they hold only for the early stage of modernisation studies up to the 1960s; there is every reason to presume that anthropological accounts of Third World modernisation grew in sophistication over time. Moreover, comparisons of this sort need to consider carefully further questions of detail: Are the Lerner or Inkeles-Smith type of multi-country survey-based studies really comparable with Srinivas' soloethnography? Is each really representative of the sociological or anthropological work done on the respective field areas? and so on.

However, there is another difference that does seem important: the prominence *of Indian* scholars in the social anthropology of India. In India, the Western anthropologist encountered not only natives and 'local counterparts' but also his/her own *'double'*, the native anthropologist with comparable Western training. Such an early and sizeable presence of local scholars is quite unusual among Third World countries, and may well be unique. Whatever the reasons responsible, the crucial question is whether the presence of Indian researchers made any difference to the *descriptions produced.* Returning to the comparisons between modernisation in Lerner's Turkey and Srinivas' India, a striking difference is now visible. Tosun B., the Turkish graduate student whose field notes caught Lerner's attention and helped produce the parable, is himself outside the frame of reference, or, at best, at its edges. In contrast, Srinivas, the anthropologist with an Oxford degree, is never allowed to forget his Indianness, and is constantly being pulled into the frame of the picture he is painting. Perhaps, it is this sustained incitement to self-reflexivity that makes Indian accounts of dualism precociously complex. Indian anthropologists are acutely aware that modernisation is happening not just 'elsewhere' but in the 'here and now' that they themselves inhabit.

Whatever the truth of their claim to greater sophistication, Indian accounts of dualism cannot escape the limitations of this mode of theorising. Modernisation—even in its minimalist version of an ongoing interaction of some sort between tradition and modernity—proves to be a conceptual dead end because there is, literally, no exit. A modernising society is always only a modernising society: it can no longer call itself traditional, and its modernity is never quite the real thing. In a strange twist on the 'allochronism' that anthropology is accused of, the modernisation paradigm evacuates the contemporaneity of such societies, robbing the present of its immediacy and constricting its relations with the past and the future into narratives of loss or inadequacy. It is truly remarkable how this motif of a society, a culture, a history, a politics or even a personality permanently in a state of inbetween-ness—a double-edged failure—recurs across disciplinary contexts.

For example, in anthropology, the 'developing societies' become 'deceived societies as they have had their present transformed into a permanent transition', 'an endless pause'. In marxist political economy, (as Mihir Shah puts it in his requiem for the mode of production debate), 'Indian agrarian relations are perhaps destined forever to remaining semi-capitalist'. And Ranajit Guha inaugurates the 'Subaltern Studies' initiative with the announcement that the 'central problematic' of historiography is the 'failure of the nation to come into its own'. All the various avatars of this theme — whether in the garb of a search for modernity, democracy, capitalism, or development — are marked by the anxiety of striving for a norm that is, so to speak, unattainable *ab initio.*

Ambiguous Inheritance of Indian Sociology

Apart from its difficulties with the barrenness of dualism (which it shared with its siblings in other disciplines), the social-anthropological search for modernisation suffered from certain other disabilities peculiarly its own. These had to do with the public image and perceived concerns of social anthropology before and after independence, and how its disciplinary location differed from that of its neighbours in the social sciences.

The pre-independence reputation of Indian social anthropology was an ambiguous one. On the one hand, sections of the nationalist elite approved of orientalist Indology and enthusiastically participated in its celebration of classical Indian/Hindu achievements in literature, philosophy and the arts. Indeed, Indian-Hindu religio-spiritual traditions and culture were the crucial fulcrum on which nationalist ideology leveraged itself: asserting India's cultural-spiritual superiority enabled the acceptance of undeniable Western economic-material superiority and paved the way to the forging of a nationalist agenda for fusing the best of both worlds. But, on the other hand, colonialist anthropology met with hostility and resentment because it was perceived as deliberately highlighting the 'barbarity' of Indian culture and its 'customs and manners'. What this means from the specific standpoint of modernisation studies is that the 'passing of traditional society' was apt to be viewed with mixed feelings, unlike, say, the transformation of the economy or polity, where the past could in principle be left behind without much soul searching because there was nothing much there worth salvaging. 'Tradition' was an area of considerable ambivalence because, on the one hand, it contained the wellsprings of nationalist ideology, social solidarity and cultural distinctiveness; but, on the other hand, it was also the source of embarrassing 'social evils', 'superstitions' and other signs of backwardness.

Finally, another aspect of disciplinary location, namely, the internal composition of Indian social anthropology was also relevant. In Indian social anthropology, the distinction between sociology and anthropology has been refused at least since Srinivas (that is, since the mid-fifties or so). This is an unexceptionable refusal in so far as the convention of the former studying 'complex' and the latter 'simple' societies could not really be followed in India and is no longer the rule elsewhere either. However, the well-established Indian practice of referring interchangeably to sociology and anthropology hides the fact that the latter is much better developed here than the former. Because the social anthropology of India was heavily oriented towards 'tradition'—that is, towards institutions like caste, tribe, kinship and religion, and towards rural rather than urban society—modernisation studies here were also biased in this direction. Had urban sociology, economic sociology, social history or political sociology been better developed, the content of modernisation studies may have been more balanced, with the new and emergent getting as much attention as the old and traditional.

Most studies of modernisation in India located themselves in the world of tradition and looked out upon modernity from that vantage point, with its attendant strengths and weaknesses. Indian social anthropology failed to cultivate intensively those methods (such as survey research or quantitative techniques) and research areas (like industry, the media or the class structure) of sociology proper which fell outside its usual zone of intersection with anthropology. This in turn affected the manner in which the discipline dealt with the question of modernisation, particularly since this question privileges generalisation from a macro perspective, something which anthropology is neither theoretically inclined towards nor methodologically equipped for.

Catholicity of the Concept

Finally, at least part of the difficulty that Indian sociology has had with the theme of modernisation has to do with the nature of the term itself, and uncertainties as to what was or was not included within its ambit. It is pertinent to recall here that modernisation was introduced into social theory as a very broad, catch-all concept that was considered 'useful despite its vagueness because it tends to evoke similar associations in contemporary readers'. As Dean Tipps has written in an important critique already twenty-five years old:

> The popularity of the notion of modernisation must be sought not in its clarity and precision as a vehicle of scholarly communication, but rather in its ability to evoke vague and generalised images which serve to summarise all the various transformations of social life attendant upon the rise of industrialisation and the nation-state in the late eighteenth and nineteenth centuries. These images have proved so powerful, indeed, that the existence of some phenomenon usefully termed 'modernisation' has gone virtually unchallenged. This may sound somewhat excessive in the Indian context — the momentous and swift transformations taking place here clearly amounted to more than just 'some phenomenon'. But, the question of whether 'modernisation' was a useful conceptual basket into which all these varied changes could be thrown did bother Indian scholars sensitive to the 'messiness' of the process. The fact that in modernisation theory, this process is 'defined in terms of the goals towards which it is moving' is particularly problematic not only because the directionality of change is difficult to gauge in unilinear terms, but also because this telos is intertwined with conflicting ethical-

moral values and claims. The sensitive scholar's instinctive distrust of such treacherous terrain is seen in Srinivas' doubts and queries, expressed in the second epigraph to this essay: Is all social change to be called modernisation? Is modernisation the same as Westernisation? Similar instances can be found in the work of most scholars, and the very existence of many different viewpoints shows that these doubts are not easily settled.

CHALLENGES AND PROSPECTS

Looking back at the modernisation literature at the turn of the century, we cannot but be impressed by the central contradiction that frames it—the remarkable longevity of the theme and its conceptual paraphernalia despite the very early onset of doubts and disillusionment. What needs did it fulfil, what core concerns did it address that allowed it to live so much of its life on borrowed time? What was *at stake* in the question of modernisation? To answer these questions, we must return to the beginning, the word.

Etymological History

The English word 'modernisation' inherits the semantic legacy of its ancient Latin root-word, modern, which has been used in two conceptually distinct but commonly conflated senses: as a generic term that characterises the *distinctiveness of any contemporary era;* and as an abbreviation for a *specific period in the history of Western civilisation* and the values and institutions associated with it.

In pre-nineteenth century usage, 'modern' appears to have been a pejorative term with strong negative connotations, and we are told that 'Shakespeare invariably used the term in this sense'. However, as Raymond Williams points out, 'through the nineteenth century and very markedly in the twentieth century there was a strong movement the other way, until *modern* became virtually equivalent to improved or satisfactory or efficient' Although, 'modern' still retains its comparative-temporal sense of something close to or part of the present, it is interesting to note that, in the last decades of the twentieth century, this sense has been yielding ground to words like 'contemporary' or to neologisms prefixed by 'post', and that the word is no longer unequivocally positive in its connotations.

These recent developments in the career of the word point to a complicated and unequal relationship between its two meanings: the generic one has generally been subordinated, whether surreptitiously or openly, to the specific meaning. The consequences of the ascendancy of the sense connoting Western European modernity are acutely felt when we shift from the relatively static noun-form to the more dynamic and processual verb-form. *Modernisation* entered the English lexicon during the eighteenth century when the reversal of the pejorative connotations of the noun-form had already begun. By the twentieth century, the word had become increasingly common and was 'normally used to indicate something unquestionably favourable or desirable'. This general connotation of a process of *positive change or improvement* (particularly with reference to machinery or technology) was inflected — especially when speaking at the macro-level about institutions or societies — by the suggestion of a more closed-ended teleological movement towards the *European Enlightenment model of modernity.* It is in this latter sense that the word enters the discipline of sociology — and vice versa.

Shadow of the West

The social sciences especially sociology are themselves products of and responses to *modernity* in the specific sense of 'modern' that invokes the era inaugurated by the Enlightenment in seventeenth century Western Europe. Unlike other attempts to distinguish a modern present from its pasts, modernity is not content with establishing a merely relativistic difference but claims fundamental superiority. Once claimed, such normative privileges pre-position modernity in a profoundly asymmetrical relationship to all other epochs and cultures.

These claims have, of course, been much more than abstract assertions, having had the status of self-evident truths for most of mainstream social science. Whether in terms of a contrast with the world of *tradition* (another critical keyword of modern times), or in terms of the coherence of its own multifaceted achievements, there is a formidable array of evidence proclaiming the uniqueness of post-Enlightenment Western-European modernity. Some of this evidence is eloquently recounted by the Rudolphs in the first epigraph to this essay, and forms a long list including: the transformation of the human relationship to the natural world; the supremacy of universalistic, utilitarian, scientific-technological rationality; the rise of the individual as the normative agent of social action; the subordination of ascriptive, affect-based communities to impersonal, voluntary associations; the emergence of urban, industrial society and the bureaucratisation of social institutions; the revolutionising of modes of governance with the emergence of democracy, the modern nation-state and its institutional apparatus; and the onset of new and intensified forms of temporality. Also relevant, at a somewhat different level, are the supplanting of God and Nature by Man and Reason as foundational categories, and the consequent predilection for metanarratives of various kinds, most notably that of Progress.

It hardly needs emphasising that the ideas and institutions of modernity have wielded enormous material and moral power. Like all other social systems, modernity too has been historically and culturally specific; but it is perhaps the only social system in human history that has had the technological capability, the social organisation and the systemic will-to-power to make so comprehensive an attempt to reshape the entire world in its own image. Colonisation is only the starkest form taken by this attempt, beginning with pre-modern Europe itself, through the de-population and re-settlement of the New World, to the direct or indirect colonial subjugation of the rest of the globe. The mental-moral forms of colonisation have been even more profound in their effects: whatever be our attitude towards it, modernity has shaped to an extraordinary degree the ideological frameworks we inhabit, the intellectual tools we use and the values that we hold dear.

This overgeneral sketch must immediately be qualified and complicated in a number of ways. Despite the remarkably convergent forces and processes it has unleashed across the globe, modernity has hardly been a single unified entity. Indeed, it is only at the highest level of abstraction that one can speak of something simply called 'modernity'. Not only have disparate, even incompatible perspectives been produced within its ambit, but modernity has itself spawned oppositional philosophies of various kinds (such as the romanticism of a Rousseau or the nihilism of a Nietzsche). And though it is true that modernity's attempts to colonise the world have been largely successful, this has usually meant not the simple erasure of other cultures or social systems but rather their subjection to sustained pressure. At the same time, modernity has legitimated itself well enough to have transcended to a significant degree its early image of an alien imposition and has acquired, in a wide variety of social contexts, the status of a freely chosen material and moral goal.

It is only against this 'deep background' that one can appreciate the full significance of the idea of modernity outside the West, especially after the birth of modernisation theory in the 1950s context of decolonisation.

Non-Western Dilemmas

The stakes in modernisation are raised enormously in non-Western countries who encounter it as a sort of secular 'theory of salvation'. The defining condition of non-Western engagements with the idea of modernity is, of course, the fact that it is an idea which 'always-already' bears the signs of a prior Western presence. Given that even the most amicable routes to decolonisation involved some sort of adversarial relationship with the West, this immediately sets up a tension, a predicament. Modernity is the object of intense desire, at the very least because it promises resources with which the marks of colonial subjugation may be erased and equality claimed with the erstwhile masters. It is also the source of extreme anxiety because it seems to threaten any distinctive (non-Western) identity — which alone would be the proof of true equality rather than mere mimicry. Matters are made worse by two further factors: first, the sense of urgency associated with modernisation and change both as a response to late-comer status and because of the release of nationalist energies and aspirations after independence; second, the realisation that most of the intellectual resources with which questions of this sort may be tackled are themselves inseparable from Western modernity.

It is this combination of circumstances that produces the long interregnum of scholarly ambivalence and anxiety around the question of modernisation. But, the transformations initiated by the process of modernisation outflank the scholarly mode of posing the question: social history overtakes social philosophy.

Modernisation has been an omnibus concept, a sort of summary description of epochal dimensions based on an underlying dichotomy between tradition and modernity. If there ever was a time when such an abstract, generalised dichotomy was conceptually useful, it is surely gone now. All the common uses to which it was put — to indicate a division of global society into different spheres, to refer to a similar division within a given society, or to distinguish between past and present — are no longer viable because, today, there are as many similarities as differences across the divide.

'Most societies today possess the means for the local production of modernity,' as Appadurai and Breckenridge point out, 'thus making even the paradigmatic modernity of the United States and Western Europe (itself not an unproblematic assumption) no more pristine.' To continue to refer to non-Western or Third World societies as simply 'traditional' is therefore seriously misleading. Similarly, if one were to believe, with Robert Redfield, that ' the word "tradition" connotes the act of handing down and what is handed down from one generation to another' and that it therefore 'means both process and product' then it is clear that no sharp division can be made between tradition and modernity in the long term. On the one hand, what is modern for one generation will perforce become part of tradition for the next; on the other hand, the product that is passed on cannot possibly exclude the modern. Analytically, it seems futile to think of 'tradition' and 'modernity' as though they were the names of distinct pre-existing objects or fields of some kind; it is more fruitful to think of them as value-laden labels which people wish to attach to particular portions of what they inherit or bequeath. Descriptively, no purpose is served by this contrast after the thorough diffusion and domestication of modernity across every conceivable area of tradition.

However, it would seem that this very ubiquity of modernity has created a new use for 'tradition'—not as a descriptive term, but rather as a 'space-clearing' or 'distinction-creating gesture'. Tradition of this sort—that is, invoked as a sort of claim-to-difference—is itself a product of modernity, and forms part of the reservoir of resources with which modern adversaries fight each other. Thus, in a very general sense, everything and everyone is modern today, the Taliban as much as Microsoft, velcro and vibhuti as much as dowry and debentures. This does not mean, of course, that everyone and everything is *the same*—just that the traditional-modern axis is unable to tell us anything useful about the very important differences that distinguish contexts, institutions, processes or relationships.

Another angle on the non-viability of the high level of abstraction at which terms like tradition, modernity and modernisation have been pitched is offered by recent attempts to re-examine the self-evident unitary status of most objects to which these terms used to be applied. The nation-state is an obvious example: 'fragmentary' perspectives may have their own problems, but it cannot be denied that the taken-for-granted status of entities like 'India' or 'the nation' has suffered serious damage. This break down of its objects of reference also serves to evict the concept of modernisation from its high perch.

Current Trends

If 'modernisation' has lost its analytical-heuristic value as a summary-description of epochal sweep, this is as much due to the internal collapse of the tradition-modernity dichotomy as to the external attacks by dependency theory and world systems theory. But, there are as yet no obvious successors, though terms like 'post-colonial', 'post-modern', and lately, 'globalisation' have been hovering in the wings. However, the most noticeable change in Indian social theory today is the marked increase in confidence *vis-à-vis* the West. (In this, theory seems to have followed social life rather than the other way around, but that is another story.) While such self-assurance was not exactly unknown before, it is probably more widespread and sophisticated, and certainly more ambitious now. Contemporary responses to the demise of the modernisation paradigm could take four broad routes.

Downsising and Avoidance: The most common response has been to avoid the term—modernisation is no longer invoked in the grand theory mode. If it is used at all, the scope of the term has been scaled down, and it seems to be returning to the specific technical sense in which it first entered the English language. Since it is only at very high levels of abstraction and generalisation that the term has proved extravagant, it may still be serviceable in restricted contexts with clear referents, as for example, in the modernisation of libraries or irrigation systems. However, this does amount to banishing the term from social theory.

Reclaiming the Present: The previous response simply rejects one of the main functions of modernisation as a summary-description —a name—for an epoch in which societies previously described as 'traditional' begin to experience rapid change. What gets obscured, however, is that this epoch is a contemporary one, that it constitutes the present of the societies undergoing modernisation: the teleological orientation is so strong that descriptions of the journey are overwritten by descriptions of the destination. If modernisation studies in general tend to 'evacuate' the present, those within social anthropology are doubly affected because of the discipline's old habit of constructing an 'ethnographic present' in which other cultures are 'distanced in special, almost always past and passing, times'. It is not surprising, therefore, that some recent initiatives in this discipline have concentrated precisely on the recovery and reconceptualisation of contemporaneity.

Thus, for example, Veena Das undertakes an anthropology of 'critical events' explicitly in order 'to reflect on the nature of contemporaneity and its implications for the writing of ethnography'; Geeta Kapur confronts the problem of identifying the 'founding equation between history and subject' that might help define the contemporary moment in cultural practice; Madhav Prasad seeks to go 'back to the present' to signal not 'the nation's arrival at some pre-determined telos, but *arrival as such,* arrival in the present as the place from which to find our way forward' and Vivek Dhareshwar asks what it means to be modern if 'our time' is one where the conditions of intelligibility of 'the key words of our cultural and political self-understanding' no longer hold. More generally, these and other such attempts are part of an effort to pay rigorous attention to the historicity of the present without allowing this historicity to be hijacked by the teleology of notions like modernisation. As D.P.

Mukerji reminds us, it is more important to understand 'the thing changing' rather than 'change per se'.

Exploring Emergent Locations: Indian social anthropology has until recently been concerned mainly with tradition and how it copes with modernity. This has meant that modernity has been viewed through the frameworks of tradition and has been looked for in its 'traditional' sites, so to speak. These, of course, are not the only or necessarily the most important ones where it is to be found—indeed, it is one of the hallmarks of the contemporary era that eruptions or claims of modernity may take place in the most unexpected locations. For example, the last epigraph to this essay, the slogan painted on a bus—'They should realise that we too are modern'—is also the punch line of a mid-1980s television ad for sanitary napkins. It is spoken by a mother as she hands a package of napkins to her daughter (who is returning to her in-laws), the connotation being that the napkins will prove to the 'boy's side' that the girl comes from a 'modern' family. That a television advertisement would self-reflexively foreground menstruation in this manner can hardly be anticipated by conventional notions of the 'inner/outer' and 'private/public' domains. Examples of scholarly attempts to explore systematically such unconventional sites where the peculiarities of Indian modernity find expression include recent studies on social aspects of the film-form in India and new work on the domain of sexuality and its linkages to such varied institutions as the state, the media, the law, and academic disciplines such as demography or anthropology.

Comparisons across Third World Contexts: For both obvious and less obvious reasons, the lateral contacts among sociologists of non-Western countries have been few and largely under the auspices of Western institutions. Unfortunately, what Srinivas and Panini said a quarter century ago still remains true, including especially their concluding observation:

> Paradoxical as it may seem, the very need to understand Indian society requires from Indian sociologists a commitment to a comparative approach in which the problems, processes and institutions of their society are systematically compared with those of neighbouring countries in the first instance, and later with other

developing countries. So far such a comparative approach has been conspicuous by its absence.

Though some Indian sociologists have, indeed, worked on other Third World countries (Ramakrishna Mukherjee on Uganda; Satish Saberwal on Kenya and J.P.S. Uberoi on Afghanistan, for example, not to mention T.N.Madan's comparative essay on Japan), the impact on the discipline at large has been negligible. Third World countries have always only provided the non-Western empirical grist for Western theoretical mills, as the Brazilian sociologist Mariza Peirano points out: 'the moment we leave behind the frontiers of the country, what here was a theoretical discussion, almost immediately becomes merely regional ethnography'. It is only through this kind of cross-cultural comparative work in Third World contexts that we can move beyond tiresome lamentations of Western intellectual hegemony to a situation where the specificities of Indian, Turkish, Indonesian or Brazilian society can finally refuse to be merely 'local colour' and aspire to be part of 'global theory'.

Theory in this sense has long evaded us. Perhaps, the story of our long struggle with the theme of modernisation will manage to interrupt this evasion.

NOTES AND REFERENCES

Abercrombie, Nicholas, Stephen Hill and Bryan S. Turner 1988. *The Penguin Dictionary of Sociology.* (2nd ed). Harmondsworth, England: Penguin.

Appadurai, Arjun 1997. *Modernity at Large: Cultural Dimensions of Globalisation.* Delhi: Oxford University Press.

Breckenridge (ed). *Consuming Modernity: Public Culture in Contemporary India.* Delhi: Oxford University Press. pp.1-20.

Banuri, Tariq 1990. 'Development and the Politics of Knowledge: A Critical Interpretation of the Social Role of Modernisation'; and 'Modernisation and its Discontents: A Cultural Perspective on Theories of Development'. In Stephen Marglin and Frederique Apfel Marglin (eds). *Dominating Knowledge: Development, Culture and Resistance.* Oxford: Clarendon Press. pp.29-101.

Bardhan, Pranab 1984. *The Political Economy of Development.* Delhi: Oxford University Press.

Bendix, Reinhard 1967. 'Tradition and modernity reconsidered'. *Comparative Studies in Society and History.* V.9. (April). pp. 292-346.

Béteille, André 1991. *Society and Politics in India: Essays in a Comparative Perspective.* Delhi: Oxford University Press.

Black, Cyril E. 1966. *The Dynamics of Modernisation: A Study in Comparative History.* New York: Harper and Row.

Burghart, Richard 1990. 'Ethnographers and their local counterparts in India'. In R.Fardon (ed). *Localising Strategies: Regional Traditions of Ethnographic Writings.* Edinburgh: Scottish Academic Press. pp.260-78.

Cartier-Bresson, Henri. 1987. *Henri Cartier-Bresson: India.* (tr. by Paula Clifford). Ahmedabad: Mapin.

Chakrabarty, Dipesh 1992. 'Postcoloniality and the Artifice of History: Who Speaks for Indian Pasts?'. *Representations.* n.37. (Winter). pp.1-26.

Charsley, Simon 1998. 'Sanskritisation: The career of an anthropological theory'. *Contributions to Indian Sociology.* V.32. N.2. pp.527-49.

Chatterjee, Partha 1986. *Nationalism and the Third World: A Derivative Discourse?* London: Zed Books.

__ 1994. *The Nation and its Fragments: Colonial and Postcolonial Histories.* Delhi: Oxford University Press.

Clifford, James 1986. 'Introduction: Partial Truths'. In J.Clifford and G.E.Marcus (eds). *Writing Culture: The Poetics and Politics of Ethnography.* Berkeley: University of California Press. pp.1-26.

Cohn, Bernard 1987. *An Anthropologist Among the Historians and Other Essays.* Delhi: Oxford University Press.

Das, Veena 1995. *Critical Events: An Anthropological Perspective on Contemporary India.* Delhi: Oxford University Press.

Datta, Ratna 1971. *Values in Models of Modernisation.* Delhi: Vikas Publications.

Desai, A.R. (ed) 1971. *Essays on Modernisation of Underdeveloped Societies.* (2 vols.) Bombay: Thacker & Co..

Deshpande, Satish 1994. 'The Crisis in Sociology: A Tired Discipline?'. *Economic and Political Weekly*, V.29. N.10. pp.575-6.

Dhareshwar, Vivek 1995a. '"Our Time": History, Sovereignty and Politics'. *Economic and Political Weekly.* V.30. N.6. pp.317-24.

—, 1995b. 'Postcolonial in the Postmodern; or the Political After Modernity'. *Economic and Political Weekly.* (Review of Political Economy) V.30. N.30. pp.PE104-PE112.

—, 1998. 'Valorizing the Present: Orientalism, Postcoloniality and the Human Sciences'. *Cultural Dynamics.* V.10. N.2. July. pp.211-31.

Dube, S.C. 1955. *Indian Village.* London: Routledge and Kegan Paul.

—, 1958. *India's Changing Villages: Human Factors in Community Development.* London: Routledge and Kegan Paul.

—, 1988. *Modernisation and Development: The Search for Alternative Paradigms.* New Delhi: Vistaar Publications & Tokyo: The United Nations University.

Dumont, Louis 1964. 'Introductory Note: Change, Interaction and Comparison'. *Contributions to Indian Sociology* VII. (old series). (March). pp.7-17.

Fabian, Johannes 1983. *Time and the Other: How Anthropology Makes its Object.* New York: Columbia University Press.

Friedland, William H. 1989. 'Considerations on the new political economy of advanced capitalist agriculture'. (mss.) Santa Cruz: University of California.

Gendzier, Irene 1985. *Managing Political Change: Social Scientists and the Third World.* Boulder, Colorado: Westview Press.

Guha, Ramachandra 1999. *Savaging the Civilised: Verrier Elwin, His Tribals and India.* Delhi: Oxford University Press.

Guha, Ranajit (ed) 1982. *Subaltern Studies I: Writings on South Asian history and society.* Delhi: Oxford University Press.

Gusfield, Joseph 1967. 'Tradition and modernity: Misplaced polarities in the study of social change'. *American Journal of Sociology.* V.72. N.4. (January). pp.351-62.

Hawthorn, Geoffrey 1987. *Enlightenment and Despair: A History of Social Theory.* (2nd edition). Cambridge (UK):Cambridge University Press.

Inkeles, Alex 1971. 'Fieldwork Problems in Comparative Research on Modernisation'. In A.R. Desai (ed) 1971. *Essays on Modernisation of Underdeveloped Societies.* Bombay: Thacker & Co.. Vol. 2, pp. 20-76.

Inkeles, Alex and David H. Smith 1974. *Becoming Modern: Individual Change in Six Developing Countries.* London: Heinemann.

John, Mary and Janaki Nair (eds) 1998. *A Question of Silence? The Sexual Economies of Modern India.* New Delhi: Kali for Women.

Kapur, Geeta 1991. 'Place of the Modern in Indian Cultural Practice'. *Economic and Political Weekly.* V.26. N.49. pp.2803-6.

Kaviraj, Sudipta 1988. 'A Critique of the Passive Revolution'. *Economic and Political Weekly.* (Special Number). V.23. N.27. pp.2429-2443.

Kopf, David 1969. *British Orientalism and the Bengal Renaissance: The Dynamics of Indian Modernisation, 1773-1835.* Berkeley: University of California Press.

Kothari, Rajni 1970. *Politics in India.* Delhi: Orient Longman.

Lele, Jayant 1994. 'Orientalism and the Social Sciences'. In C.A. Breckenridge and P. van der Veer (eds). *Orientalism and the Postcolonial Predicament.* Delhi: Oxford University Press. pp. 45-75.

Lerner, Daniel 1958. *The Passing of Traditional Society: Modernising the Middle East.* Glencoe (Illinois): Free Press.

Madan, T.N. 1969. 'Caste and Development'. (Review of Myrdal's *Asian Drama*). *Economic and Political Weekly.* V.4. N.5. pp.285-90.

—, 1995. *Pathways: Approaches to the Study of Society in India.* Delhi: Oxford University Press.

Mandelbaum, David 1970. *Society in India* (2 vols). Berkeley: University of California Press.

Marriott, McKim (ed) 1955. *Village India: Studies in the little community.* Chicago: University of Chicago Press.

Mayo Katherine 1927. *Mother India.* London: Jonathan Cape.

McClelland, David C. and David G. Winter 1969. *Motivating Economic Achievement.* New York: Free Press.

Mukerji, D.P. 1955. 'Indian Tradition and Social Change'. (Presidential Address to the first meeting of the Indian Sociological Society). In T.K. Oommen and Partha

Mukherji (eds). *Indian Sociology: Reflections and Introspections.* Bombay: Popular Prakashan. 1988. pp.1-15.

Mukherjee, Ramakrishna 1979. *Sociology of Indian Sociology.* Bombay: Allied Publishers.

Myrdal, Gunnar 1968. *Asian Drama: An Enquiry into the Poverty of Nations.* (3 vols.) London: Allen Lane/Penguin Press.

—, 1970. *An Approach to the Asian Drama: Methodological and Theoretical.* New York: Vintage Books.

Pandey, Gyanendra 1991. 'In Defence of the Fragment: Writing About Hindu-Muslim Riots in India Today'. *Economic and Political Weekly.* (Annual Number). V.26. Nos.11-12. pp.559-572.

Patnaik, Utsa (ed) 1990. *Agrarian Relations and Accumulation: The 'Mode of Production' Debate in India.* Bombay: Sameeksha Trust and Oxford University Press.

Peirano, Mariza G.S. 1991. 'For a Sociology of India: Some Comments From Brazil'.*Contributions to Indian Sociology.* (n.s.). V.25. N.2. pp.321-7.

Prasad, Madhav 1998a. *The Ideology of Hindi Cinema: A Historical Construction.* Delhi: Oxford University Press.

—, 1998b. 'Back to the Present'. *Cultural Dynamics.* V.10. N.2 (July). pp.123-131.

Raj, K.N. 1997. 'Planning: Getting the Economy on Track'. In *India* (special supplement to *The Hindu* on the 50th anniversary of independence). August. pp.107-9.

Rajadhyaksha, Ashish 1993. 'The Phalke Era: Conflict of Traditional Form and Modern Technology'. In Tejaswini Niranjana, P. Sudhir and Vivek Dhareshwar (eds). *Interrogating Modernity: Culture and Colonialism in India.* Calcutta: Seagull Books. pp.47-82.

Ray, Rabindra 1990. 'And Why an Indian Sociology?'. *Contributions to Indian Sociology.* (n.s.). V.24. N.2. pp.265-75.

Rosen, George 1985. *Western Economists and Eastern Societies: Agents of Change in South Asia, 1950-1970.* Delhi: Oxford University Press.

Rostow, Walt W. 1960. *The stages of economic growth: A non-communist manifesto*. Cambridge (UK): Cambridge University Press.

Rudolph, Lloyd I., and Susanne Hoeber Rudolph 1967. *The Modernity of Tradition: Political Development in India.* Chicago: University of Chicago Press.

Saberwal, Satish 1982. 'Uncertain Transplants: Anthropology and Sociology in India', in T.K. Oommen and Partha Mukherji (eds). *Indian Sociology: Reflections and Introspections.* Bombay: Popular Prakashan. 1986. pp. 214-232.

Saran, A.K. 1958. 'India'. In J.S. Roucek (ed). *Contemporary Sociology.* New York: Philosophical Library. pp.1013-34.

—, 1962. Review of '*Contributions to Indian Sociology* No. IV'. *Eastern Anthropologist.* V. 15. N.1. (Jan-Apr). pp. 53-68.

Sarkar, Benoy Kumar 1985. *The Positive Background of Hindu Sociology.* (Reprinted). Delhi: Motilal Banarasidas.

Seal, Brajendranath 1985. *The Positive Sciences of the Ancient Hindus.* (Reprinted) Delhi: Motilal Banarasidas.

Shah, Mihir 1985. 'The Kaniatchi Form of Labour'. *Economic and Political Weekly.* (Review of Political Economy). V.20. N.30. pp. PE65-PE78.

Shils, Edward 1961. 'The Intellectual Between Tradition and Modernity: The Indian Situation'. *Comparative Studies in Society and History.* Supplement 1. pp.1-120.

Singer, Milton 1972. *When A Great Tradition Modernises: An Anthropological Approach to Indian Civilisation.* New York: Praeger.

— (ed), 1975. *Traditional India: Structure and Change.* Jaipur: Rawat.

Singh, Yogendra 1973. *Modernisation of Indian Tradition.* (2nd printing 1977). Faridabad, Haryana: Thompson Press.

Srinivas, M.N. 1971a. *Social Change in Modern India.* Berkeley: University of California Press. (First published 1966, fifth printing).

—, 1971b. 'Modernisation: A Few Queries'. In A.R. Desai (ed). *Essays on Modernisation of Underdeveloped Societies.* Bombay: Thacker & Co..V.1. pp.149-58.

—, 1992. *On Living in a Revolution and other Essays*, Delhi: Oxford University Press.

—, 1994. *The Dominant Caste and Other Essays.* (Revised and enlarged Oxford India Paperbacks edition). Delhi: Oxford University Press.

—, 1996. 'Indian anthropologists and the study of Indian society'. *Economic and Political Weekly.* V.31. N.11. pp.656-657.

Srinivas, M.N. and M.N. Panini 1973: 'The Development of Sociology and Social Anthropology in India'. In T.K.Oommen and Partha Mukherji (eds) *Indian Sociology: Reflections and Introspections.* Bombay: Popular Prakashan.1986. pp.16-55.

Srivatsan, R. 1993. 'Cartier-Bresson and the Birth of Modern India'. *Journal of Arts and Ideas.* Nos.25-26. (December). pp.37-54.

Thorner, Alice 1982. 'Semi-Feudalism or Capitalism? Contemporary Debate on Classes and Modes of Production in India'. *Economic and Political Weekly.* V.17. N.49, pp.1961-78; N.50, pp.1993-99; and N.51, pp. 2061-66.

Thorner, Daniel 1980. *The Shaping of Modern India.* New Delhi: Sameeksha Trust and Allied Publishers.

Tipps, Dean C. 1973. 'Modernisation Theory and the Comparative Study of Societies: A Critical Perspective'. *Comparative Studies in Society and History.* V.15. (March). pp.199-226.

Trautmann, Thomas R. 1997. *Aryans and British India.* Berkeley: University of California Press.

Uberoi, Patricia (ed.) 1996. *Social Reform, Sexuality and the State.* New Delhi: Sage Publications.

Weiner, Myron (ed.) 1966. *Modernisation: The Dynamics of Growth.* New York: Basic Books.

Williams, Raymond 1983. *Keywords: A Vocabulary of Culture and Society.* (Revised edition). New York: Oxford University Press.

—, 1989. *The Politics of Modernism: Against the New Conformists.* London: Verso.

8

INDIAN DEMOCRACY AND SOCIAL CHANGE

Democracy: Ideals, Institutions, and Implementations

In assessing the past achievements and future potential of Indian democracy, it is useful to distinguish between democratic *ideals,* democratic *institutions,* and democratic *practice.* Democratic ideals represent various aspects of the broad idea of "government of the people, by the people and for the people." They include political characteristics that can be seen to be intrinsically important in terms of the objective of democratic social living, such as freedom of expression, participation of the people in deciding on the factors governing their lives, public accountability of leaders, and an equitable distribution of power. Democratic institutions go beyond these basic intents, and include such instrumental arrangements as constitutional rights, effective courts, responsive electoral systems, functioning parliaments and assemblies, open and free media, and participatory institutions of local governance.

While democratic institutions provide opportunities for achieving democratic ideals, how these opportunities are realised is a matter of democratic practice. The latter depends among other things, on the extent of political participation, the awareness of the public, the vigour of the opposition, the nature of political parties and popular organisations, and various determinants of the distribution of power.

Both democratic institutions and democratic practice are important in achieving democracy in the fuller sense, but the presence of the former does not guarantee the latter.

Democratic Institutions

In terms of democratic institutions, India has done reasonably well, and this may look particularly impressive in the international perspective, given the failure of many countries to secure even the most elementary constituents of a democratic institutional structure. Earlier democratic institutions in India-often stretching back in history-were decisively consolidated within the constitutional framework soon after independence in 1947. It is often forgotten how radical the Indian constitution was in those days, especially in light of the limited reach of democracy elsewhere in the world. It is not just that most other developing countries were still under the yoke of colonialism and authoritarianism at that time.

Even economically advanced countries still lacked the political freedoms guaranteed by the Indian constitution in many cases. In 1947, when India achieved independence, women were still deprived of universal and equal voting rights in many "developed" countries.[1] In Switzerland, women were twenty-four years away from the right to vote. In the United States, African Americans too were effectively deprived of equal voting rights (through systematic denial of the opportunity to register and vote), and state-sponsored racial discrimination (e.g., the prohibition of interracial marriages as well as racial segregation in public places) was widespread; it took a protracted civil rights movement, lasting until the late 1960s, to overcome these suppressions of basic democratic freedoms. In other countries of Western Europe and North America, elected parliaments often coexisted uncomfortably with lingering monarchies and also conceded temporal powers to church authorities. These "irregularities" (in terms of democratic norms) continue to this day in many cases, in contrast to India where the constitution made a clean sweep of feudalism and laid solid foundations for a modern secular democracy.

India was also among the first countries to include legislation aimed at affirmative action to combat the lasting influence of past social inequalities. The "reservations" and other priorities for scheduled castes (formerly, the "untouchables") and scheduled tribes expanded the horizon of legal support for social equity, no matter how we judge the exact achievements and failures of this early departure. Affirmative action would not become a serious possibility in the United States for many years after the Indian constitution (which had many affirmative provisions) came into effect in 1950.

What is more, India's democratic institutions have-on the whole-stood the test of time and popular support. In the early stages of Indian independence, there was widespread scepticism about the ability of democratic institutions to survive, let alone flourish, in a poverty-stricken and inequality-ridden country. There was also much pessimism about the potential for democracy in the "third world" as a whole. In both respects, the outlook is much brighter today. India's democratic institutions have proved quite robust (even surviving major challenges such as the imposition of "emergency" in 1975 to 1977, which was reversed by a popular electoral vote), and enjoy wide legitimacy among most sections of the population.[2] The healthy survival of Indian democracy has also given a major boost to the spread of democracy elsewhere in the world.

Furthermore, the institutional basis of democracy in India has retained some dynamism, particularly reflected in the fact that emendations and extensions have been instituted with some regularity. Since the constitution came into effect in 1950, various constitutional amendments have further enlarged the scope of democratic freedoms. For instance, the 73rd and 74th constitutional amendments (the "*panchayati raj*" amendments), which came into effect in 1993, have consolidated the foundations for local democracy.

Much, of course, remains to be done, and there is scope for further institutional democratisation in the future. The right to information, for instance, remains severely restricted, and greater accessibility of official records is a needed step for fuller public accountability. Similarly, provisions for a better political representation of women are needed to address today's blatant male domination of many democratic institutions, from parliament to *panchayat* (village council).[3] There is also much scope for more equitable electoral rules, better safeguards against human rights violations, more decentralised governance, and so on.

Indian Democracy in Practice

The *main* limitations of Indian democracy do not, however, relate so much to democratic institutions as to democratic practice. The performance of democratic institutions is contingent on a wide range of social conditions, from educational levels and political traditions to the nature of social inequalities and popular organisations. Democratic practice in India has often been deeply compromised by a variety of social limitations inherited from the past. To illustrate, consider one of the most basic democratic freedoms-the right to vote. India has an impressive electoral system (monitored by an independent Election Commission), which has proved its credibility and resilience on numerous occasions since independence. Voter turnouts in India are also quite respectable by international standards, especially among underprivileged groups. However, the right to vote is not a momentous freedom when voters are so poorly informed that they are unable to distinguish between different political parties, as is still the case in some areas today. Similarly, while Indian elections are formally "free and fair" in most cases, their effective fairness has been compromised by nepotism, the criminalisation of politics, and pervasive inequalities in electoral opportunities as a result of disparities in economic wealth and social privileges.[4]

Another example concerns the legal system. An impartial and efficient judiciary is indispensable for genuine democracy. India's legal system has sound institutional foundations, which incorporate basic democratic principles such as impartiality, secularism, and equality before the law. In practice, however, its functioning is, in many ways, at variance with democratic ideals. For one thing, the legal system is virtually paralysed by a backlog of millions of "pending cases"—about 30 million according to one estimate.[5] Legal proceedings can take years (if not decades) to be completed, and are often far from intelligible for the average citizen. For this and other reasons, legal protection tends to remain beyond the effective reach of most, especially the poor. In fact, the legal system can also be used as an instrument of harassment (rather than as an efficient means of dispensing justice). Those at the receiving end of the system can end up suffering terrible injustice. For instance, undertrial prisoners (there are some 250,000 of them in India at this time, according to the Home Ministry) often languish in prison for years without any legal recourse.

Similar points can be made about many other components of the democratic institutional structure.[6] The Indian press has much to offer in terms of quality and pluralism, but with less than 10 percent of all households subscribing to a daily newspaper, its contribution to political awareness and public debate remains much below potential. In some states, the legislatures are packed with criminals.[7] Village panchayats are often controlled by the local elite. There are many other failures of democratic practice.

Scope for Improvement

On the positive side, it can indeed be said that there is enormous scope for improving the quality of democracy in India through better democratic practice, and also, to some extent, through expanding democratic institutions. Indeed, democratic practice constantly evolves, as new constituencies are mobilised, new issues come under public scrutiny, and new organisational skills are developed. To illustrate, until recently corruption was not much of a political issue in India. It was accepted as a familiar feature of public life, about which little could be done. In the 1990s, however, corruption became a matter of widespread concern and discussion after a wave of high-profile scams were exposed. Innovative campaigns for public accountability and the right to information sprung up in various parts of the country (Rajasthan, Maharashtra, Kerala, Madhya Pradesh, Orissa, among others), and have gradually developed into a major social movement. This has not, of course, led to an automatic eradication of corruption, but the issue is at least on the political agenda and there is much scope for securing practical results through harnessing this process. These campaigns, with their innovative focus and techniques (from public hearing to social audit), also signal a transformation of political culture, with much potential in other contexts as well. These developments would have seemed quite unlikely even ten years ago. The nineties have witnessed many other political developments of a similar nature, from pioneering experiments with decentralised planning in Kerala to the growing participation of women in local politics across the country.

As the recent developments show, in various ways, the reach of democratic practice can be radically enhanced in India. But, the first step is to see the need for democratic practice as a distinct issue from the existence of democratic institutions. The sense of satisfaction at securing democratic institutions-justified within its context-must not be an excuse for failing to pursue vigorously the strengthening of democratic practice. The great accomplishments in the former do not obviate the need for vigilant pursuit of the latter. There is much scope for making institutionally democratic India more effectively democratic.

Inequality and Empowerment

It is useful to distinguish between different causes of the limitation of democratic practice. Given the democratic institutions, the practice of democracy may be limited for at least three distinct reasons. First, democratic institutions may become dysfunctional due to, say, corruption or inefficiency. Examples include electoral fraud and the paralysis of the legal system through case overload. Second, there may be inadequate use of functional democratic institutions on the part of concerned persons or groups, often due to limited understanding or skill, and sometimes even lack of motivation. Low electoral participation, and the powerlessness of the public in the face of complex legal proceedings, are some illustrations, among many others.

We have already commented briefly on these two deficiencies. We have also touched on the third reason for the failure of democratic practice, viz. the reach and power of antecedent social inequalities, but we must discuss it more. Democratic practice may indeed be thoroughly undermined by social inequalities, even when democratic institutions are all in place. For instance, even if elections are technically free and fair, their effective fairness may be compromised by the role of money and influence in the electoral process. This also applies to the legal system, which is often far from impartial between different classes (even in the absence of any corruption), if only because richer people can afford better lawyers.

At the risk of some over-simplification, the foundations of democratic practice may, thus, be described as *facility* (functional democratic institutions), *involvement* (informed public engagement with these institutions), and *equity* (a fair distribution of power). The central relevance of equity arises from the fact that a fair distribution of power is a basic-indeed fundamental-requirement of democracy. A government "by the people" must ultimately include all the people in a symmetric way, and this is essential also to enable the government to become "of the people and for the people." This is not, of course, a question of the "yes or no" type. In most societies, it is the case that a person's ability to use electoral rights, to obtain legal protection, to express oneself in public, and to take advantage of democratic institutions in general tends to vary with class, education, gender, and related characteristics. In striving for democratic ideals, reducing the asymmetries of power associated with these social inequalities is one of the central challenges of democratic practice in every institutionally democratic country in the world. That challenge is particularly exacting in India, given its historical economic and social inequalities.

It is, however, important to see the reach of inequality in adequately broad terms. The relevant inequalities can be of very different types. In economic analysis, the lion's share of attention tends to go to the inequality of individual income levels. This is indeed an important part of economic inequality. However, economic inequality is a more inclusive-far larger-concept than mere income inequality, and inequality in the fuller sense goes even beyond economic inequality, no matter how broadly the latter may be defined. There are many economic determinants, other than income, of well-being, freedom, and power, and there are social factors-distinct from purely economic ones-that influence inequality between persons and groups.[8]

There has been much discussion in recent years on the discrepancy between measures of income inequality and a broader understanding of the multidimensional nature of economic and social inequality.[9] The contrast can be illustrated through inter-regional comparisons of social inequality in India. For example, the Gini coefficient of the distribution of per-capita expenditures indicates that there is *more* inequality in Kerala than in, say, Bihar or Uttar Pradesh. In fact, Kerala turns out to be one of the most unequal states in this respect, while Bihar is one of the least unequal.[10] The figures may well be correct as far as they go (even though many conceptual and practical difficulties arise in the computation of these coefficients). But, if we were to rely on them for an overall assessment of social disparities in different states, we would be deeply misled.

The broader picture of social and economic inequality must also note, *inter alia,* the fact that Kerala has (1) comparatively low levels of basic gender inequality (reflected, for instance, in a high female-male ratio), (2) relatively equitable educational opportunities (indeed near-universal literacy, especially among the young), (3) extensive social security arrangements (e.g., broad-based entitlements to homestead land, old-age pensions and the public distribution system), (4) limited incidence of caste oppression (e.g., few violent crimes against scheduled castes), and (5) low rural-urban disparities.[11] In all these respects, Kerala does radically better than Bihar and Uttar Pradesh, which are ridden with inequalities between women and men, between child labourers and school-going children, between low castes and high castes, and so on. And yet these states do better than Kerala in terms of indicators of income inequality seen as a factor on its own. As this example illustrates, there is much need for a broad understanding of economic and social inequality.

These distinctions are particularly important in understanding the nature of inequality and also the problems of democratic practice in India. Indeed, indicators of income inequality, seen on their own, can be a very deceptive basis for grasping the far-reaching consequences of inequality on Indian lives and democratic practice. They can also hide the diverse ways in which more equity can be pursued through state policy and public action.

Consider, for instance, the pattern of inequality in Indian society during the last forty years or so. Judging from standard indices of income distribution, there has been little change. The Gini coefficient of per-capita expenditure, for instance, has remained fairly close to

.30 in rural areas and .35 in urban areas throughout that period.[12] This is, however, deceptive as a guide to inequality for two distinct reasons.

First, it overlooks the new developments of inequality that have added to the burden of the older, pre-existing ones. For example, the hold of the newly prosperous and socially influential middle classes escapes notice in the constancy of the Gini coefficient of income distribution. Through dominance over the media, political pressure groups and even instruments of knowledge, this flourishing, vocal and (in absolute numbers) fairly large class enjoys new powers that very few groups could have had in the past, in using the levers of democratic politics. The world has been changing, even if the Gini has not.

Second, the remarkable stickiness of the measures of income inequality over a long period suggests a kind of inescapable immutability of inequality which hides the possibility of change and progress through public policy and social action. Indeed, the stationarity of income inequality is often invoked to argue that attempts to achieve greater equality are likely to be futile, and that economic growth (increasing the size of the pie, rather than altering the shares) is the only effective way of raising living standards. But, neither the pessimism about altering inequality, nor the faith in economic growth as the only effective means of improving the lot of the deprived, is entailed by the empirical picture of income distribution.

Indeed, even in terms of India's actual experience, the constancy of income inequality indicators during the post-independence period has gone hand in hand with some fairly major changes-often with much positive achievement-in other kinds of economic and social disparities. For instance, upper-caste dominance in the rural economy and society has been decisively challenged with the abolition of zamindari, the introduction of adult franchise, economic progress among the cultivating castes, and various political movements. Correspondingly, there has been a major rise in the economic and political power of the so-called "backward castes" and, to a lesser extent, of scheduled castes.[13] Similarly, the slow but steady march towards universal elementary education has eroded one of the crucial bases of social stratification in India, namely the exclusion of disadvantaged classes and castes from the schooling system.

Even in terms of gender relations (perhaps one of the more resilient domains of social inequality in India), there have been some major developments in recent years, involving for instance the emergence of a female advantage in life expectancy (overturning a long history of superior male longevity), a radical diminution of oppressive practices such as child marriage, and growing participation of women in local politics.[14] Other ongoing changes, such as the steady decline of fertility, the accelerated increase in female literacy, and new constitutional provisions for the political representation of women, are likely to facilitate further progress towards more equal gender relations.

No less eminent a sociologist as M.N. Srinivas has even suggested that we are "living in a revolution". Even if we do not accept such optimism about the recent changes (there are fields of stationarity as well as transformation), the last fifty years have certainly been a time of significant change in India's social structure. There is nothing in the record of India's last half a century that would vindicate the thesis of the futility of changing the hold of antecedent economic and social inequalities in India.[15] The rejection of social fatalism and the cynicism that it generates can be extremely important for motivating attempts to work against pre-existing inequalities and for the enhancement of democratic practice.

One crucial implication of this broader perspective on economic and social inequality is that it points to many different ways of countering inequalities in Indian society. The reduction of income inequality is a difficult challenge in India as elsewhere, partly due to incentive problems (e.g., the possible need for a link between productivity and reward), and partly because of the resistance of privileged classes. But, there is no corresponding reason to tolerate widespread gender discrimination, the continued oppression of disadvantaged castes, the persistent divide between the literates and the non-literates, and other destructive economic and social inequalities. Indeed, the dilemmas that arise in reducing economic inequality in particular, possible conflicts between efficiency and equity often have little force in addressing these inequalities. In fact, in many circumstances, distributional concerns are *highly congruent* with other social objectives, including economic efficiency.[16] Reduced gender discrimination, for instance, expands the scope of women's agency, which is an important factor of social change and economic success.[17] The congruence between distributional concerns and other social objectives is also striking in the context of basic education. Indeed, the universalisation of elementary education in India would not only reduce educational disparities (and other social inequalities associated with these disparities), but also contribute to a wide range of other economic and social objectives, given the diverse personal and social roles of education.[18]

Achieving greater equity in Indian society depends crucially on political action and the practice of democracy. Indeed, a reduction of inequality both contributes to democratic practice and is strengthened by successful practice of democratic freedoms. There is, in fact, a "virtuous circle" here, the nature of which has to be more adequately reflected in policy analysis and social action in India. There have been, as was noted earlier, significant gains in that respect during the last fifty years, and while reductions of inequality have strengthened the reach of democratic practice, they have often been achieved through determined use of the democratic opportunities that were already available. Indeed, the achievements discussed earlier were often the result, at least in part, of democratic political action.

In some cases, these achievements have been facilitated by economic change. For instance, the rise of the "backward castes" has something to do with their growing economic prosperity, linked *inter alia* with the "green revolution" (and, before that, the abolition of zamindari).[19] But, even here, political action has played an important role, for instance, through farmers' movements as well as direct political participation.

In other cases, political action has succeeded in empowering disadvantaged social groups even in the absence of any significant economic improvement (sometimes even in the face of growing impoverishment). Not so long ago, for instance, tribal communities were routinely displaced by dams and other large projects without any compensation. The situation has radically changed over time, as displaced tribal communities learnt to organise against forced displacement even though they have not invariably succeeded in changing public policy. Today, this movement is among the most politically active and best organised in India, and is also a source of much inspiration elsewhere in the world.[20] Whatever position one may take on the projects in question, the force of this movement cannot leave any impartial observer without a major recognition of the power and vigour of organised popular resistance.

Decentralisation and Local Democracy

The interconnections between democratic practice and social equity have a strong bearing on recent initiatives to promote local democracy in India. These initiatives have taken place in the framework of the 73rd and 74th constitutional amendments (the *"panchayati raj"* amendments), which require all the state governments to introduce certain legislative measures geared to the revitalisation of local representative institutions. These measures include mandatory elections at regular intervals, reservation of seats in village panchayats for women and members of scheduled castes or tribes, and substantial devolution of government responsibilities to local authorities. The panchayati raj amendments, which took effect in 1993, have led to a range of interesting initiatives in different parts of the country, undertaken not only by state governments but also by political parties, NGOs, grassroots organisations, women's groups, and other activist formations. There is a great deal to learn from recent developments associated with these initiatives.

Achieving greater democracy at the local level must be a crucial component of the broader task of transforming the practice and quality of democracy in India. Indeed, local democracy represents one means of participation in the larger democratic system, which is relatively accessible to the disadvantaged, and can be potentially a stepping-stone towards other forms of democratic participation. Local democracy is also essential as a basis of public accountability, particularly in the context of the need for effective and equitable management of local public services. These services-from schools and health centres to fair price shops and drinking-water facilities-are often crucial for the quality of life. Their effective functioning, however, depends a great deal on the responsiveness of the concerned authorities to popular demands. To illustrate, it is difficult to see how the endemic problem of teacher absenteeism in rural India can be successfully tackled without involving the proximate and informed agency of village communities in general and parental groups in particular. As things stand, there is no mechanism to ensure any kind of accountability of village teachers to the local community or to the parents in large parts of India, and this is an important factor in the persistence of endemic dereliction of duty.[21]

The importance of local democracy is not confined, of course, to these and other instrumental roles of participatory politics. Participation can also be seen to have intrinsic value for the quality of life. Indeed, being able to do something through political action-for oneself and for others-is one of the elementary freedoms that people have reason to value. The popular appeal of many social movements in India confirms that this basic capability is highly valued even among people who lead very deprived lives in material terms.

Local democracy is sometimes treated as synonymous with "decentralisation," but the two are in fact quite distinct. In particular, decentralisation is not necessarily conducive to local democracy. In fact, in situations of sharp local inequalities, decentralisation sometimes heightens the concentration of power, and discourages rather than fosters participation among the underprivileged. To illustrate, in some tribal areas where upper-caste landlords and traders dominate village affairs, the devolution of power associated with the panchayati raj amendments has consolidated their hold and reinforced existing biases in the local power structure.[22]

Similarly, top-down decentralisation sometimes undermines local democracy by destabilising traditional institutions of governance and fostering corruption. An interesting example comes from a recent case study of two villages of Uttarakhand, the hill region of Uttar Pradesh (now Uttaranchal, a separate state). The study villages earlier had fairly democratic traditional institutions of local governance, based among other things on consensus decision-making and egalitarian contributions to village funds. Then came state-sponsored panchayat elections and "decentralised" development programmes, one effect of which was the integration of these villages into a wider system of prevailing corruption, in which these programmes are embedded. This process undermined local democracy and also created sharp social divisions in the villages studied.

Recognition of these dangers should not be seen as an overall indictment of decentralisation. There is undoubtedly much need for decentralised governance in India, especially in relation to the management of local public services, where responsiveness to local conditions is paramount. But, we must also recognise that the effects of decentralisation are highly context-dependent and circumstance-specific, and that its success depends on decentralisation being integrated with other aspects of local democracy. A similar observation applies to the panchayati raj amendments. These amendments, like other democratic institutions, have provided a great opportunity to expand the scope of democracy in Indian society, but their practical results have varied a great deal depending on the extent to which institutional reform has been combined with other types of public action.

Recent studies of the developments associated with the panchayati raj amendments in different parts of the country throw much light and these and related issues.[23] It is, first and foremost, very encouraging to find plentiful evidence of active engagement with the new possibilities of local democracy on the part of the Indian public. By all accounts, panchayat elections elicit keen public interest. Voter turnout rates have been high in most states (even higher than in parliamentary or assembly elections), including among underprivileged groups. This is a sea of change from the days when members of the lower castes were prevented from voting, or when women were not expected to cast an independent vote. Beyond electoral participation, public interest and involvement in local governance has risen markedly during the last few years, even in areas where apathy used to be widespread.

However, the experience so far confirms that the results of state initiatives to promote local democracy are highly contingent on the social context. Indeed, the reforms associated with the panchayati raj amendments have followed very different courses in different states. At one extreme, Bihar has barely reached the stage of organising panchayat elections. Kerala, on the other hand, has gone far beyond the constitutional requirements and initiated a visionary campaign of "decentralised planning" through panchayati raj institutions.[24] Even among states that have followed a similar course in terms of legislative reform, the practical results have varied a great deal depending on the extent of social preparedness in terms of educational levels, political mobilisation, and social equity. The issue of social preparedness has emerged quite clearly in states like Madhya Pradesh, where (unlike Bihar) the state has been constructively active in legislative reforms, yet the practical results have been held back by the antecedent social inequalities, educational backwardness and other barriers inherited from the past.[25]

The panchayati raj experience highlights the importance of social equity for local democracy, and also the interactive relationship between the two. This can be seen particularly clearly in connection with the issue of political representation of women and disadvantaged castes at the panchayat level. The 73rd amendment stipulates that one-third of all panchayat seats are "reserved" for women, with a similar (overlapping) provision for scheduled castes and tribes.[26] In north India, where caste and gender inequalities are particularly resilient, the local elites have tended to adapt to this requirement by putting up "proxy" candidates from the required group, and continuing to wield power through them.[27] In south and western India, the overall picture is quite different in this respect, with greater success in terms of independent political representation of women and scheduled castes. It must, however, be noted that even in north India, there is considerable evidence that the prevailing patterns of social discrimination and political mar-ginalisation are far from immutable. Local politics, and the different forms of political mobilisation and social activism associated with panchayati raj (for example, training programmes for female candidates and political assertion of the scheduled castes), have provided new avenues through which traditional inequalities can be challenged. The fact that these challenges have often been met with violent repression (including even cases of rape of assertive female sarpanchs) is both a telling reminder of the survival of extreme inequality and oppression in Indian society, and an indication that the politics of panchayati raj are perceived as a serious threat by dominant groups. Over the time, the forces of repression seem to be losing some ground, with good prospects of further advance in the direction of both greater social equity and more vibrant local democracy in the near future.[28]

These developments illustrate a crucial feature of local democracy, indeed of democracy in general, namely that it involves a certain amount of "learning by doing."[29] Other aspects of this process include the influence of role models (for example, of a successful female sarpanch), the spread of various skills involved in local governance (e.g., the ability to hold orderly meetings or to deal with the bureaucracy), the evolution of a culture of political participation, the creation of new forms of social mobilisation, and even changes in public perceptions of the need for as well as scope for foundational change. Given the dynamism of learning by doing, it is important to resist the pessimism arising from observing particular limitations in the current practice of local democracy. The constructive possibilities over time have to be recognised.

In the light of these learning possibilities, the first wave of social change associated with the panchayati raj amendments warrants cautious optimism about the potential for local democracy in India. There are, of course, also matters of concern. These include the frequent derailing of local democracy by social inequality, the limited participation of the public in local governance on a day-today basis, the dormant condition of *gram sabhas* (village assemblies) in many states, the lack of significant devolution of powers in many fields, and-last but not least-the widespread embezzlement of public resources associated with local development programmes under panchayat auspices. Nevertheless, there are clear signs of a sustained expansion of democratic space at the local level, and also of local politics being an important arena of positive social change. The limitations are best addressed through democratic practice itself, and as far as the potential for the latter is concerned, there is much ground for hope.

Transparency and Corruption

One of the major challenges that democratic practice has to face in India is to eradicate corruption in different fields of civic administration and public life. Among its many terrible consequences, rampant corruption erodes and undermines democratic institutions. Indeed, democratic institutions cannot perform their role adequately if the actions of political leaders, civil servants, police officers, judges and others can be mobilised in defence of private and special interests through illegal inducements. The effect of corruption on ethical codes and social norms also tends to be antithetical to democratic values. And yet democracy itself can be seen as a possible means to fight corruption that can be-and must be-used more effectively. Democratic ideals include the need for transparency and accountability, which are ultimately the principal methods of restraining and dislodging corrupt practices. There is, thus, a two-way relationship between the practice of democracy and the eradication of corruption. The former can help the latter, but the latter, in its turn, can be of great value in extending the force and effectiveness of the former.

In India, the adverse effects of corruption on democracy have come into sharp focus in recent years in connection with issues of local governance and village politics. While there have been promising steps towards local democracy in the nineties, one of the major barriers against further progress has been the prevalence of widespread corruption, particularly related to development programmes and electoral processes. To illustrate, consider the issue of panchayat elections. In most states the main responsibility of a sarpanch (village head) is to oversee various development programmes, such as the Jawahar Rozgar Yojana (local public works) and the Indira Awas Yojana (a subsidised housing scheme). Attached to these schemes, in many cases, is an organised system of loot of public resources, which requires the *sarpanch* to "redistribute" some of the development funds to various officials, varying from the *"gram sevak"* (village-level worker) to the Junior Engineer, Block Development Officer, and others at different steps of the ladder. Often the shares are pre-spec-ified.[30] The sarpanch himself or herself, of course, tends to be one of the principal beneficiaries. The post of village head can be, under these circumstances, highly lucrative. This is one reason why large sums of money are spent in panchayat election campaigns. Where these patterns apply, local electoral politics are thus integrally linked with various development rackets, and can even generate what might be called "competitive corruption."

This nexus undermines local democracy in several ways. First, it raises the up-front cost of election campaigns, making it more difficult for poor candidates to participate. Second, this situation can make it very difficult for an honest person motivated by social concerns to contest panchayat elections. Indeed, unlike candidates geared to corruption, an aspiring candidate who wants to forgo the opportunity of replenishing his or her coffers after a successful election is financially at a disadvantage in the electoral competition. In addition, honest candidates often face the prospect of official harassment for refusing to cooperate with the system of corruption.[31] Third, the task of plundering public resources, distributing commissions and avoiding scrutiny distracts the panchayats from their primary purpose of working for the public good in the area under their jurisdiction. A sarpanch, for example, often has far more to gain from awarding Indira Awas Yojana subsidies to the highest bidders than from responding to the social need for an electricity connection for the village, or from organising a school enrolment drive.

The "systemic" nature of the corruption arrangements associated with local development is one reason why they are difficult to eradicate: even if one individual culprit is disciplined and punished, another tends to step into his or her shoes. Another barrier to their eradication relates to the fact that the embezzlers (e.g., the sarpanch and private contractor who collude to build a school at half the official cost and pocket the difference) tend to gain at the expense of the public at large. It has been argued, not without reason, that in such situations (known in the economic literature by the somewhat puzzling name of "corruption with theft") corruption may be particularly hard to eradicate.[32] Indeed, since the losing group consists of a diffuse and typically unorganised collectivity, the losers may find it difficult to take joint action with adequate effectiveness. Vigilance may, of course, be entrusted to a public agency on the basis of crosschecks, inspections, audits, and so on, but that supervising agency may often have little incentive to dig deep, which can be bothersome and even dangerous, given the power of the private gainers, compared with the often-inert mass of public losers.

But, this is exactly where the remedial use of democracy can be important. The losers may be inactive and hard to mobilise, but once mobilised, the weight of numbers as well as the force of public opinion and open criticism can be quite effective. The practical possibility of such mobilisation has been demonstrated in many actual cases. A good illustration comes from the work of such organisations as Mazdoor Kisan Shakti Sangathan (MKSS) in Rajasthan.[33] The movement began in 1987 by organising underpaid labourers working on drought relief programmes (who can be seen as victims of "corruption without theft," and were to that extent comparatively easy to mobilise). Following this early success, MKSS started mobilising village communities against the private appropriation of local development funds (corruption with theft), using means such as public hearings and social audits. The organisation has considerable popular support and has achieved some striking successes, involving for instance the restitution of embezzled funds. Over the time, it has inspired many similar initiatives elsewhere, from a campaign to expose corruption in the public distribution system in Surguja (Madhya Pradesh) to recent protests against police harassment of rickshaw-pullers and hawkers in Indian cities. A nation-wide "campaign for the people's right to information," which includes lobbying for adequate legislative reform in this field, has also emerged from these initiatives.

The significance of these movements goes well beyond specific victories such as the restitution of embezzled funds in a particular village, or the introduction of new legislation in a specific state. The demonstration effects can have a much wider reach. Even in areas where no such organisations existed earlier, public initiatives to expose corruption have begun to spread in recent years, with significant results. It has been noted, for instance, that drought relief programmes in Rajasthan in 2000 to 2001 have been remarkably "corruption-free" (at least in comparison with the situation that prevailed in earlier droughts), largely due to greater public vigilance as well as to the improved accessibility of official records-both of which are closely related to the "right to information" movement. This is a major achievement, especially in the light of widespread scepticism about the possibility of eradicating corruption in India, and there is a major lesson here about the possibility of achieving wider changes in social norms through local action. In all this, there is reason for hope, since there is some prospect that public vigilance may become an integral part of the political culture in many Indian villages.[34]

Accountability and Countervailing Power

The importance of public vigilance at the village level in curbing corruption, discussed in the last section, is just one example of the general role of vigilance, which can operate at different levels not just related to local governance, and can be aimed at many different objectives (not just the prevention of corruption). Indeed, even in curbing corruption, vigilance is needed at other levels as well, including non-local politics (involving the operation of organised parties), broader cooperative activities (involving grassroots initiatives), appropriate state policies (involving incentives, monitoring, sanctions, etc.), and so on. Vigilance is crucial to accountability, which in its turn is central to efficiency and equity of public policies in different spheres.

The improvement of living conditions in developing countries depends a great deal on constructive public policies in various fields (basic education, health care, social security, nutritional support, environmental protection, gender equality, among others).[35] And yet there are well-recognised inadequacies from which state actions tend systematically to suffer, as has been noted widely across the world. One problem is, often enough, the presence of persistent inefficiency, reflected in such phenomena as bureaucratic delay, breakdown of public services, lack of timeliness and certainty of delivery, and unusually high costs of operation. Inefficiency, in turn, has much to do with the lack of accountability in the public sector.

If, for example, a public health centre is closed on a work day, the patients may not have any simple means of taking remedial action. Of course, instruments of protest and censure do exist, at least in principle, such as sending a complaint to the local newspaper, or organising a demonstration, or voting for a rival political party to the one in office, or perhaps even seeking redress from the courts. These means can be widely used, as they indeed are in some parts of India, for example in states such as Kerala (with high levels of education and a long tradition of public activism). But, traditions are not easy to establish when they are not already there, and they certainly require a good deal of initiative and acumen.

The need for accountability has tended to be substantially ignored in Indian institutional reforms. Indeed, the debates on the pros and cons of "liberalisation" have tended to add, to some extent, to the neglect of this problem. There is, in fact, an odd meeting ground here between the advocates and opponents of liberalisation. The *advocates* of liberalisation have tended to concentrate on privatisation, and correspondingly, they have taken little interest in the possibility of improving the performance of the public sector. The *opponents* of liberalisation, on the other side, have tended to downplay the inefficiencies of the public sector, in their effort to resist privatisation. In the process, the crucial issues of accountability and public sector reform have tended to be highly neglected.

There is perhaps something curious in the fact that accountability levels are so low in India, despite the country's strong democratic tradition. Indeed, democracy is intrinsically concerned with the accountability of political leaders and government officials to the general public. In principle, the contestability of public office in a democracy provides a potential basis for accountability in the public sector. If, for example, plague breaks out somewhere in India, the health officials involved may have to face severe censure and even the Health Minister may have to resign, and these punitive possibilities give those in charge a strong incentive to prevent disasters of this kind. But, accountability is much easier to guarantee in cases of this kind (such as an outbreak of plague), in which a sensational failure receives widespread attention, and where large sections of the population (including privileged classes) have a combined stake in seeking effective action. In many other situations, however, the accountability mechanisms are likely to be much weaker, and this is especially so when the failures harm only small groups of less vocal people and those affected happen to be politically marginalised or powerless.

Further, in some cases, other institutions that are themselves part of the democratic system may actually contribute to sheltering the government officers and employees from public scrutiny and censure. For instance, some trade unions in the public sector have tended to block pressures for public scrutiny and sometimes have even helped to dismantle whatever little mechanisms of accountability were in place earlier. This process is one of the chief causes of low accountability in the schooling system, which has played a major part in depriving millions of children of basic education.[36] In other spheres of the public sector, too, low standards are often blamed on the fact that government employees have permanent jobs and earn salaries unrelated to performance, and have been comfortably sheltered from any pressure to work, no matter how dissatisfied the public might be.

The solution of this problem cannot, obviously, lie in the dismantling-or even undermining-of trade unions, since they have their legitimate functions as well. Indeed, trade unions constitute a necessary part of a decent society, as the dreadful work conditions of non-unionised workers in India bring out. Rather, the remedy must lie in developing and reinforcing the countervailing institutions that can give greater "voice" to those who have a stake in the efficient provision of public services.

The importance of countervailing power has been particularly emphasised by John Kenneth Galbraith (1952) in a classic work in institutional economics. The effectiveness of institutions has to be assessed in terms of the power they have over each other to moderate their respective influences. Asymmetric power in one domain can be checked by a different configuration of forces in another domain. For example, applying this institutional logic to the regressive influence of teachers' unions on the management of schools, it can be argued that the effective way of altering this handicap may have to lie in the development of other-countervailing-institutions, such as parental organisations and gram sab-has, which have a natural interest in enhancing the efficiency of schools.

Similar countervailing institutions can be built up in other fields, involving, for instance, the users of particular public services (such as health centres or ration shops) and even the public at large (based for instance on a general need for protection from police harassment or abuses of power). It is important to note that this need not be done on a case-by-case basis, as if (say) every individual school or health centre needed its own "watchdog" in order to function effectively. In fact, as mentioned earlier with reference to the eradication of corruption, local demonstrations of vigilance can have wider effects, *inter alia* by influencing social norms and the political culture. This link between local action and social norms is one important basis for confidence in the possibility of radical change through democratic practice.

Human Rights and Democracy

The effective practice of democracy also involves the acknowledgement and use of the rights of citizens. The rhetoric of rights is omnipresent in the contemporary world. The concept is persistently invoked in many different contexts: political rights in demanding basic participatory freedoms, personal rights to privacy and liberty in defending elementary autonomies in private life, civil rights in protesting against authoritarianism, gay and lesbian rights to safeguard freedoms to pursue minority lifestyles, and so on. While many of these rights have legal recognition, others-even some extremely important ones-are not matters of legal rights at all. If a government is accused of violating some "human right" such as the right of free speech, that accusation cannot really be answered simply by pointing out that there is no legal entitlement to free speech in that country. What may be at issue in such cases is not whether the established legal rights have been violated, but (1) whether the scope of these established legal rights should be extended to encompass the demands in question, and (2) whether the claim of people to have those freedoms (such as free speech) should be accepted even in the absence of legal entitlements.

Human rights are rights that relate not to citizenship, but to what is taken to be the entitlement of any human being, no matter of which country he or she is a citizen and no matter what the legal system of that country does or does not guarantee. In fact, it may not even be appropriate to define human rights simply as rights that ideally should be legally recognised. A human right can be invoked in many contexts even when its *legal* enforcement-as opposed to giving it general support-would be inappropriate and unhelpful. For example, the human right of a wife to participate fully, as an equal, in serious family decisions (no matter how chauvinist her husband is) may be widely acknowledged as a human right even by many people who would nevertheless not want this requirement to be legalised and enforced by the police. Similarly, the "right to respect" is another example where legalisation and attempted enforcement would be problematic, even bewilderingly so. Human rights have their own domain, and while their legalizable components can be sensibly used for fresh legislation (or judicial rein-terpretation), these rights may also be seen, in other cases, as general demands on individuals and institutions.

Reasoning based on human rights has been used quite effectively in many countries, and this applies to India as well. Such reasoning can be particularly effective in dealing with violations of political liberties and autonomies, even when the legal rights are somewhat ambiguous. It can also be used to demand public action in support of such rudimentary necessities as elementary school education, basic health care, and so on. Indeed, the trend towards acknowledging the right to elementary education as a "fundamental right" in India has closely followed the human-rights-based defence of that putative right as something that children *should* have.

It must, however, be acknowledged that there is still quite a distance to go in the general acceptance in India of a broad band of human rights, including personal liberties and basic civil rights. India is not ordinarily thought of as a major perpetrator of human rights violations, and its international rating in that respect is by no means dismal. Yet, major human rights violations do take place in various forms, deeply compromising the integrity of Indian democracy. This applies first and foremost in areas of violent conflict such as Kashmir, the North-East, and parts of Bihar and Andhra Pradesh, where human rights have been extensively abused by military and para-military forces as well as by insurgent groups. In addition, human rights violations of a more "routine" nature do take place on a substantial scale in other areas as well. Torture in police custody, for instance, is "pervasive and a daily routine in every one of India's 25 states," according to Amnesty International.[37] Apart from these instances of brutality on the part of state authorities, there are also other human rights violations to consider, ranging from the practice of bonded labour to the victimisation of AIDS patients.

The protection of human rights is a prime example of a cause on which democratic practice has a major bearing. This is because formal legal protection and the related constitutional rights are largely in place, and they can be put more into practice, along with broadening their domain through wider recognition of basic human rights. While there is also much scope for better legal safeguards especially in relation to human rights violations by the Armed Forces, which are sheltered by extensive provisions of immunity,[38] much can be done even within the existing legal framework.

Unfortunately, the protection of human rights in India has been a much neglected field of public activism. Indeed, it is sobering to find that, until recently, comprehensive reports on human rights violations in India were compiled mainly by foreign or international agencies (from Amnesty International to the U.S. Embassy). Domestic efforts tended to be confined to relatively unambitious "fact-finding reports" on specific cases of human rights violations. The mainstream press, for its part, has paid very little attention to these matters. This is a field where there is enormous scope for more active and ambitious campaigning and organising, drawing on India's strong tradition of investigative reporting. There have indeed been important initiatives in that direction in recent years.

There are at least three plausible reasons why violations of basic civil liberties have tended to remain out of focus for a long time. First, the tolerance of human rights violations is often assumed to be an essential (if "regrettable") condition of effective "counter-insurgency" operations in border areas (mainly in Kashmir, Punjab, and the North-East). Criticism of these operations, no matter how brutal or illegal, tends to be branded as "anti-national." This, combined with lack of public awareness of the facts in many cases (itself related to failures of transparency and accountability), has led to a remarkable tolerance for the infringement of human rights not only in those areas but also-through emulation-in other parts of the country.

Second, the Indian military seems to have a large domain of license in violating the rights of citizens on grounds of security. As discussed elsewhere, militarism has tended to have many adverse effects on democracy around the world, and while this problem is perhaps less serious in India than in many other countries, there are reasons for concern about the anti-democratic influences of military expansion in the region, particularly since the nuclear tests of May 1998.[39]

The adverse effects of militarism on democracy in India relate in particular to (1) displacement of developmental concerns by security concerns, (2) concealment of military activities behind a veil of secrecy, (3) the use of propaganda to rally the public behind prevailing security policies and programmes, (4) the powerful lobbying activities of military commanders, arms dealers, strategic think-tanks, scientific organisations involved in defence-oriented research, and other parts (or close correlates) of the military establishment, and (5) the consolidation of authoritarian tendencies in the society at large, particularly but not only during periods of active conflict. Each of these adverse influences of militarism has tended to undermine the guaranteeing of civil and human rights in the democratic polity of India.

Third, human rights violations have a strong class dimension. A well-educated, middle-class person in India does not have much to fear by way of physical harassment from the police or para-military forces. By contrast, underprivileged sections of the population often live in terror of arbitrary repression. The class differentials also make it more difficult to bring human rights issues within the scope of mainstream politics. These perceptions are in need of drastic change, since the Indian public at large has a stake in the integrity of democracy, which can be deeply threatened by widespread human rights violations.

Democracy and Participation

India took a radical step towards the realisation of democratic ideals in 1950, when the constitution came into effect. Aside from laying the foundations of India's democratic institutions, the constitution addressed the need to promote a wide range of social opportunities. In particular, it defined the "fundamental rights" of all citizens, which include equality before the law, freedom of speech and association, the right to personal liberty, and protection against exploitation. In fact, the "directive principles of state policy," which supplement hard legislation, go much further than the strict legal provisions. For instance, they urge the state "to secure a social order for the promotion of welfare of the people" as well as to uphold a range of more specific entitlements, from "the right to an adequate means of livelihood" and "free legal aid" to "free and compulsory education for all children" and "the right to work."

However, Dr. Ambedkar, the chairman of the Constituent Assembly's Drafting Committee and essentially the "author" of the Indian constitution, concluded his work with a profound warning:

> On the 26th January 1950, we are going to enter into a life of contradictions. In politics, we will have equality and in social and economic life we will have inequality.

This basic tension lives with us to this day, and recognising the tensions involved is, in fact, quite central in understanding the nature of contemporary India.

The contrast at which Dr. Ambedkar pointed could be expected to have one of two possible consequences. The first possibility was that the inequalities of social and economic opportunities could undermine democracy altogether, and thus leave India with no political equality either. The second possibility was the continuation of the sharp dichotomy, with the survival of democracy, but also of the manifest economic and social inequalities, in an uneasy equilibrium. Dr. Ambedkar's immediate preoccupation was with the first possibility, and he feared that the "contradiction" that he had identified would undermine democracy itself: "We must remove this contradiction at the earliest possible moment or else those who suffer from inequality will blow up the structure of political democracy which this Assembly has so laboriously built up". Fifty years after Dr. Ambedkar's warning, Indian democracy is alive and-on the whole-well. It is the second scenario that we see in India today, with a surviving democracy which is deeply compromised by the tension highlighted by Dr. Ambedkar.

It should be observed clearly that not only does there remain remarkable economic and social inequalities, but also as a consequence there are major asymmetries in the opportunities that different sections of the population have to participate in democratic institutions. Corresponding to this uneven distribution of power and influence are systematic biases in public priorities and policy. Elitist biases can be found, for instance, in the orientation of the news media (dominated by middle class concerns), parliamentary debates (now heavily geared to business-oriented legislative reforms), the legal system (far from impartial between different classes), foreign policy (strongly influenced by the superpower aspirations of the Indian elite), and so on.

The low priority attached to basic needs fits into this general pattern. While "lack of political will" is often invoked in this context, it is important to go beyond this black box and to relate policy priorities to the political practice of India's democracy. To illustrate, India has world-class institutions of higher education (especially in fields such as management and engineering) side by side with ramshackle primary schools in disadvantaged areas. This contrasting pattern has much to do with the disproportionate influence of privileged classes on public policy. Similarly, the fact that the government spends about three times as much on "defence" as on health care is not unrelated to the lobbying powers of the military establishment, especially in comparison with those of underprivileged hospital patients.

The limitations of India's democracy sometimes provoke calls for a more authoritarian system of governance, insulated from pressure-group politics. Development, so goes the argument, requires order and discipline. The fact that trains (supposedly) ran on time during the Emergency in 1975 to 1977, is seen by some as definitive proof of this proposition. On a less superficial note, authoritarianism is often said to have contributed to rapid development in various countries of east Asia as well as China.

These examples, however, are highly selective. An impartial comparison of development in democratic and authoritarian countries should not be restricted to the more successful countries in the latter group, which also includes Afghanistan, Congo, pre-Aristide Haiti, and North Korea, to cite a few cases where the blessings of authoritarianism have been less transparent. Even in the more successful countries in the authoritarian group, such as China, the suppression of political freedoms has often exacted a heavy price.[40]

Taking the world picture as a whole, there is no evidence of a positive association between authoritarianism and development, even if development is narrowly interpreted in terms of economic growth.[41] Furthermore, a broader understanding of development, incorporating the expansion of freedom and social opportunities, points to the wide-ranging complementarities between development and democracy.[42]

As far as, India is concerned, the basic problem of political marginalisation of the underprivileged can hardly be solved by marginalising them *even more* by further concentration of political power. The challenge, rather, is to expand the scope of democracy and address the tension identified by Ambedkar through political action and democratic practice.

In some respects, the challenge of expanding democracy has grown taller in the 1990s. The economic reforms, focused as they are on the promotion of private enterprise and foreign investment, have consolidated the elitist mindset in economic policy and the political influence of the corporate sector. The nuclear tests of May 1998 and the Kargil conflict in 1999 have strengthened the influence of the security establishment, with its considerable demands on public resources and political energies. There has also been an ominous expansion of communal and authoritarian tendencies, marked for instance by the demolition of the Babri Masjid in December 1992 and the recent wave of violent attacks on Christian "missionaries."

The picture is not, however, uniformly bleak. The eighties and nineties have also seen some decisive expansion of the practice of democracy. The decentralised planning experiment in Kerala, the participatory successes of the Bargadar movement and other advancements of land reform in West Bengal, the anti-arrack campaign in Andhra Pradesh, the schooling revolution in Himachal Pradesh, the right to information movement in Rajasthan, and the gradual expansion of the reach of local democracy in many parts of India, are some striking illustrations-among others-of the possibility of defeating the elitist biases of public policy and expanding the horizons of democracy in India.[43] There are no particular reasons for smugness in recording and appreciating these achievements, but they also indicate that things can change and that the practice of democracy is not necessarily doomed in India.

It has sometimes been claimed that democracy being a majoritarian system cannot really provide an effective voice to the underdogs of society when they happen to be a minority as, for example, is the case with those in extreme poverty.[44] It is easy to see why this scepticism about the reach of democracy would appear to be plausible. How, it is asked, can the power of the majority protect the interests of a minority (perhaps even a relatively small minority)? This is a good line of challenge, but it is ultimately too mechanical a line of reasoning and significantly negligent of the participatory basis of the practice of democracy. For one thing, democracy is not the same thing as majority rule, since democratic rights include the protection of freedom of speech and other forms of participation as well as the safeguarding of minority rights. But, going beyond that, it is worth noting that the process of public discussion and participatory interaction can make citizens take an interest in the lives of each other.

Indeed, even the fact that democracies tend to be very effective in preventing famines cannot be explained by any mechanical application of majority rule, since the proportion of people who are threatened by a famine is never very large (in fact, typically far less than ten percent of the population and most often less than five percent).[45] Similarly, it is hard to explain how cases of rape or torture, when publicised, can become politically explosive issues, even when the number of victims-actual or potential-is relatively small. As has been said, democracy is "government by discussion" and the political salience of selective misery depends not only on the specific number of sufferers, but also on the effectiveness of public discussions that politicise the sufferings involved.

It is for these reasons that further progress of democratic practice in India must be seen to be crucially dependent on enriching the participatory processes. We have identified some successes as well as some failures in the participatory basis of Indian democracy. Much will depend on the possibility of enhancing public participation much more widely in India. In the multi-institutional format of the process of development (incorporating markets as well as the government, the media, popular organisations, and other enabling institutions), public participation has a crucial role to play in the expansion of the reach and effectiveness of each of these institutions as well as in the integration of their joint functions. India's record in all this is one of limited success, but a critical examination of this record also indicates how the limitations can be overcome and the successes enhanced and secured. In this study, we have tried to clarify how the further advancement of development and democracy in India can most effectively proceed. There are reasons here for hopeful engagement.

NOTES AND REFERENCES

1. See the comparative international data on "women's political participation" presented in Human Development Report (2001: 226-9).
2. On the latter point, see particularly Yadav and Singh (1997), Pushpendra (1999) and Yadav (2000).
3. How this is best brought about is a subject of active debate at this time in India. For example, see Kishwar (1996) and Omvedt (2000); also Menon (2000) and earlier contributions cited there.
4. Bhatia (2000). The author describes the predicament of under privileged women during the 1995 Assembly elections in central Bihar as fol lows: "Most of the women I interviewed had never voted before, nor did they understand the meaning or significance of chunav (elections), vote or parties. While some of them were able to recognise some party symbols, they were often unable to relate the symbol to the party, and none of them could relate it to a particular candidate or programme" (p. 120).
5. Debroy (2000) adds: "On an average, it takes twenty years for a dispute to be resolved, unless real estate or land is involved, in which case it takes longer. The Thorat case in Pune took 761 years to be settled, it was started in 1205 and ended in 1966. If present rates of disposal continue and there are absolutely no new cases, it will take 324 years for us to clear the present backlog. The conviction rate is only around 6 percent" (p.201).

6. "For diverse assessments of the nature, achievements, and limitations of Indian democracy, see Jayal (1999a), Blomkvist (2000a, 2000b), Frankel et al. (2000), Heller (2000a), Varshney (2000), and the earlier literature cited in these studies.
7. In Uttar Pradesh, for instance, 22 Cabinet Ministers are known to have "criminal antecedents" (Chari 2000).
8. These distinctions have been discussed further in Sen (1992). Also important in some contexts is the question of how different types of inequality relate to each other, for example, how gender or class inequalities interact with the caste hierarchy. For instance, in understanding the historical roots of social oppression in north India, it is important to note the particularly powerful way in which caste and class inequalities have tended to reinforce each other in that region; on this see Drèze and Gazdar (1996).
9. Sen (1992, 1997, 2000a).
10. Datt (1997, 1999b). Note that the available Gini coefficients are sector-specific (i.e., rural or urban); rural-urban disparities, for their part, are comparatively low in Kerala.
11. Relevant indicators are presented in Drèze and Sen (forthcoming, see Statistical Appendix).
12. Datt (1999a, 1999b).
13. Drèze (1997) and Jayaraman and Lanjouw (1999), and the literature cited there.
14. There have also been some adverse trends, such as the spread of the practice of dowry, which tends to cause daughters to be seen as an economic burden, and also, in the 1990s, the spread of sex-selective abortion. Here as with other aspects of social inequality, the possibility of negative as well as positive change has to be borne in mind.
15. On "futility" arguments as an aspect of the "rhetoric of reaction," see Hirschman (1991).
16. Even in the case of income inequality, there is an important area of congruence between equity and efficiency concerns. For instance, while income redistribution may well raise incentive problems in many cases, asset redistribution (e.g., land reform) is often conducive

not only to equity but also to efficiency. On these issues, see Bardhan, Bowles and Gintis (2000), and the literature cited there; also Sen (1992).

17. Drèze and Sen Ch. 7.

18. Drèze and Sen (1995:13-16, 96-7); also Probe Team (1999, Ch. 1).

19. In some cases, economic empowerment has also contributed to the emancipation of the "scheduled castes"; see, for example, Sudha Pai's (2001) analysis of the economic antecedents of "Dalit assertion" in Uttar Pradesh.

20. Drèze, Samson and Singh (1997), Roy (1999), and the literature cited there.

21. For a detailed case study of this process, focusing on Uttar Pradesh, see Drèze and Gazdar (1996); also Probe Team (1999).

22. Shah et al. (1998:289-93). The recent Panchayati Raj (Extension to Scheduled Areas) Act, which combines further devolution of power with provisions for the empowerment of tribal communities, was introduced partly to address this problem.

23. A wealth of field-based studies are available; see Lieten (1996a, 1996b), Mathew and Nayak (1996), Mayaram and Pal (1996), Bhatia and Drèze (1998), Crook and Manor (1998), Pai (1998, 2001), Raj and Mathias (1998), Institute of Social Sciences (1999), Powis (1999), Vyasulu and Vyasulu (1999), Ghatak and Ghatak (2000), Menon (2000), Mullen (fortcoming), among many others; also the monthly Panchayati Raj Update published by the Institute of Social Sciences, New Delhi, and the periodical Grassroots.

24. Isaac and Harilal (1997), Powis (1999), Heller (2000b). West Bengal has also been active, for a long time, in making constructive use of local democracy to raise the political profile of the underprivileged, and to carry out economic and social reforms, including land redistribution. For different perspectives on West Bengal's experience, see Kohli (1987), Lieten (1996a), Sengupta and Gazdar (1996), Ghatak and Ghatak (2000), Mullen (forthcoming), among others.

25. For insightful case studies of the subversion of local democracy by dominant classes and castes in Madhya Pradesh, see Mathew and Nayak (1996).

26. As mentioned earlier, separate legislation was introduced later for the "scheduled areas," with further provisions for the representation and empowerment of dis- advantaged groups (especially the "scheduled tribes").

27. For a striking case study of this process, see Mander (2001:137-48). For other examples, see Lieten (1996b), Mathew and Nayak (1996), Drèze and Sharma (1998), Pai (1998), among others. Cases of "proxy" members have also been reported in south India, especially in the early years of panchayati raj (see Vyasulu and Vyasulu 1999, and Menon 2000), but they are not the dominant pattern, as seems to be the case in much of north India.

28. The use of "proxy candidates," for one, seems to be declining with each panchayat election, and today there are even cases of members of "reserved" cate gories contesting non-reserved seats (see Menon 2000).

29. On this point, see particularly Mullen; also Mayaram and Pal (1996), especially with reference to the participation of women in panchayat institutions.

30. Jayal (1999b), who reports that in Uttar Pradesh "the percentages due to various officials and elected representatives are fixed... the commission amounts are openly announced in the panchayat meetings, and rarely provoke any protest" (p.25).

31. The study cited in the preceding footnote also mentions how a female sarpanch was victimised "f or her refusal to allow district authorities to give her a cheque from which the commissions [had] already been deducted" (Jayal 1999b:26).

32. Shleifer and Vishny (1993), where corruption with theft is contrasted with other situations ("corruption without theft") where one person gains at the expense of some other private individual, as when a railway employee over charges a passenger for a ticket. In such cases, the loser (e.g., the fleeced passenger) has an incentive to blow the whistle, and sometimes this feature can be used to discourage corruption. In the case of "corruption with theft," which involves a private appropriation of public resources, the losers form a more dif fuse group, and may, to that extent, find it harder to take effective action.

33. There have been earlier initiatives of similar inspiration elsewhere (notably the anti-corruption movement initiated by Anna Hazare in Maharashtra), as well as many new offshoots of these pioneering movements in recent years. On the work of MKSS (which involves a great deal more than corruption-related campaigns), see Dey and Roy (2000).
34. Kerala has gone further than most other states in developing what Patrick Heller aptly calls a "culture of whistle-blowing" (Heller 1999:128). In this connection, it is interesting to note that Kerala was ranked as the least corrupt Indian state in a recent opinion poll based on interviews with 1,743 residents of 16 major state capitals (India Today, November 24, 1997). This finding is far from definitive, given the subjective nature of the responses and the ad hoc nature of the sample. Nevertheless, it does point to an interesting pattern that deserves further investigation.
35. The "positive roles" of the state in economic development are examined in Drèze and Sen (1989); see also Drèze and Sen (1995 forthcoming), with specific refer ence to India.
36. Probe Team (1999); also Drèze and Sen (forthcoming, Ch. 5), and the literature cited there.
37. In a survey of Indian Police Service officers conducted by the National Police Academy in March 1997, 17 percent of the respondents were found to support the view that detainees should be "subjected to torture and third degree methods to get to the truth" (Human Rights Features 1999).
38. Under Section 197 of the Code of Criminal Procedure, "no Court shall take cognizance of any offence alleged to have been committed by any member of the Armed Forces of the Union while acting or purporting to act in the discharge of his official duty, except with the previous sanction of the Central Government."
39. Drèze and Sen; also Drèze (2000) and Sen (2000b).
40. Drèze and Sen (forthcoming, Ch. 4). Prominent examples of the adverse social consequences of authoritarianism in China include (1) the monumental famine of 1958-61, (2) the excesses of the "cultural revolution," (3) the negative effects of China's draconian "one-child policy" on gender equity and women's freedoms, (4) the sharp slowdown of mortality decline in the post-reform period,

linked to the drastic reduction of public health services in disadvantaged areas, and (5) the frequent violation of basic human rights.

41. See, among other comparative studies, Przeworski (1995) and Barro (1996).

42. On these and related issues, see Sen (1999).

43. For further discussion of these diverse experiences, see Drèze and Sen.

44. Nandy (2000).

45. Drèze and Sen (1989).

9

CHALLENGES FOR MODERN INDIAN FAMILY SYSTEM

A perusal of varied literature on the Indian society and culture, particularly generated by ethnographers, historians, Christian missionaries and subsequently by anthropologists and sociologists, suggests that the twentieth century recorded certain changes of far reaching importance in the family system under the influence of westernisation, industrialisation, modernisation and greater population mobility across the sub-continent. Ever since then the Indian family has progressively confronted and combated various kinds of problems and challenges, and yet India does not have any family policy per se so far; albeit the Government of India has, indeed, taken several useful legislative measures relating to widow remarriage, women's right to property, practice of child marriage, succession, adoption and maintenance, dowry, dissolution of marriage affecting different communities and most recently domestic violence, which have impacted the Indian family system in more ways than one.

It is, however, recognised that the formulation of a single national policy given the large size and heterogeneity of a society like that of India is really a difficult task. Barriers to the creation of a comprehensive national policy in India are intricate parts of Indian ethos and ideology. This is perhaps the important reason why India has not so far succeeded in evolving a common civil code, despite public demand for it through various social and political fora in the recent past. Muslims, who comprise 12.4 per cent of India's population, are opposed to the idea of a uniform civil code in the country. Anyway, in order to do that one must have a reasonably good understanding of problems that the Indian society has been facing. Here we would like to throw some light on the major problems that confront the Indian society in general and a family in particular. It is really imperative that one should understand the hurdles in promoting social protection and intergenerational solidarity for the well being of family as a social sub-system.

At the outset, let us move a word of caution—it is hazardous to offer a generalised view of the nature and problems of the Indian family system which have persisted over the years, as the subject is quite complicated for the reason that the Indian society is very vast and is characterised by bewildering complexity.

According to the 2001 census, India consists of 192.7 million households spread over 0.59 million villages and about 5,000 towns. The Indian society exhibits considerable variations between regions, between rural and urban areas, between classes, and finally, between different religious, ethnic and caste groups. The Indian society is, in fact, a congeries of micro-regions and sub-cultures and differences between which are quite crucial from sociological angles. Furthermore, the differences are also discernible with respect to the level of female literacy, sex ratio, age at marriage of girls, incidence of dissolution of marriage, household size, female workforce participation rate, marital practices, gender relations and authority structure within the family. Diversities inherent in Indian society are also reflected in the plurality of family types.

It has been observed that the magnitude of changes that the Indian family has experienced over a period of a centaury appears to be far greater than the expectations of Indian sociologists and anthropologists. The virtual disappearance of traditional joint family from the urban scene, increase in the life expectancy of women from 23 years in 1901-10 to 65 years (it is higher than that of men by three years) in 2009, rise in the proportion of female headed households, decrease in the average age of household heads, increase in the incidence of separation and divorce, greater tension and conflicts between wife and husband, parents and sons and between brothers, increased freedom of marital choice, passing of child marriages, shrinking of kinship ties, continuous consultations between sons and parents on familial matters, greater involvement of females in decision making process, increase in the mean age at marriage of female from 13 years in 1901 to 18.3 years in 2001, rise in the level of female education, decline in total fertility rate from 4.9 in 1971 to 2.76 in 2009 are concrete and clinching evidence to suggest a whole range of changes in the family system— its structure, functions, core values and regulative norms. In course of these changes many new problems have surfaced, while some of the old ones, such as dowry, divorce, lack of intergenerational solidarity, discord between siblings and gender violence have got further intensified.

Break-up of the Joint Family System

Since time immemorial, the joint family has been one of the salient features of the Indian society. But, the twentieth century brought enormous changes in the family system. Changes in the traditional family system have been so enormous that it is steadily on the wane from the urban scene. There is absolutely no chance of reversal of this trend. In villages the size of joint family has been substantially reduced or is found in its fragmented form. Some have split into several nuclear families, while others have taken the form of extended or stem families. Extended family is in fact a transitory phase between joint and nuclear family system. The available data suggest that the joint family is on its way out in rural areas too.

The joint family or extended family in rural areas is surviving in its skeleton or nominal form as a kinship group. The adults have migrated to cities either to pursue higher education or to secure more lucrative jobs or to eke out their living outside their traditional callings, ensuing from the availability of better opportunities elsewhere as well as the rising pressure of population on the limited land base. Many of the urban households are really offshoots of rural extended or joint families. A joint family in the native village is the fountainhead of nuclear families in towns. These days in most cases two brothers tend to form two independent households even within the same city owing to the rising spirit of individualism, regardless of similarity in occupation, even when the ancestral property is not formally partitioned at their native place.

The nuclear family, is now the characteristic feature of the Indian society. According to the census of India data, of all the households nuclear family constituted 70 per cent and single member or more than one member households without spouse (or eroded families) comprised about 11 per cent. The extended and joint family or households together claim merely 20 per cent of all households. This is the overall picture about the entire country, whereas in the case of urban areas the proportion of nuclear family is somewhat higher still. The available data from the National Family and Health Survey-1 of 1992-93 suggest that joint family does not make up more than five per cent of all families in urban areas. An extended family, which includes a couple with married sons or daughters and their spouses as well as household head without spouse but with at least two married sons, daughters and their spouses, constitute a little less than one fifth of the total households.

With further industrial development, rural to urban migration, nuclearisation of families and rise of divorce rate and the proportion of single member household is likely to increase steadily on the line of industrial West. This is believed to be so because the states, which have got a higher level of urbanisation, tend to have a higher proportion of single member households. Similarly, about a couple of decades ago almost 20 per cent households contained only one person in the USA. More or less, a similar situation exists in other developed countries as well, and above all, not a single country has recorded decline in the proportion of single member household during the last three decades. In fact, the tendency is more towards increase in the proportion of single member households.

As the process of family formation and dissolution has become relatively faster now than before, households are progressively more headed by relatively younger people. Census data from 1971 onward have clearly borne out that at the national level over three-fifths of the households are headed by persons aged less than 50. There is every reason to believe that proportion of households headed by younger persons is likely to constitute a larger proportion than this in urban areas where the proportion of extended family, not to speak of joint family, is much smaller than that of rural areas.

The emergence of financially independent, career-oriented men and women, who are confident of taking their own decisions and crave to have a sense of individual achievement, has greatly contributed to the disintegration of joint family. Disintegration of joint family has led to closer bonds between spouses, but the reverse is also true in certain cases. For many, nuclear family is a safer matrimonial home to a woman. In bygone days people generally lived in joint families, yet familial discord never escalated into extreme physical violence or death, as we so often come across such instances in our day-to-day life and also know through national dailies, both electronic and print media.

Changes in Authority Structure

Once the authority within the family was primarily in the hands of family elders commonly known as *Karta* in Hindi. The general attitude of members of the family towards the traditional patriarch was mostly one of respect. Loyalty, submissiveness, respect and deference over the household were bestowed on him. These attributes also encompassed other relationships in the family, such as children to their parents, a wife to her husband, and younger brothers to their older brothers. Within a household no one was supposed to flout the will of his elders. The father, or in his absence the eldest brother, was consulted on all important family matters like pursuing litigation in courts of law, building a house, buying and selling of property and arranging marriages, etc. The joint family did not allow the neglect or disregard of elders. The age-grade hierarchy was quite strong. Now, the people of younger generation, particularly those with modern tertiary education, do not seem to show the same reverence which their fathers had for their parents or elders.

Among women, patriarch's wife was the paramount authority. In fact, women's position depended on the position of their husbands in the household. The wife of the household head or mother-in-law was in charge of the household. Her word was law or at least had the same force. Her decisions were made for the entire family and not for the welfare of the individuals in it. Young women in the family were expected to be dutiful and obedient. Self-assertion, even in bringing up their own children, was blasphemy. Widows and those spurned by their husbands were assured of the family roof, though mostly as voiceless members.

With a view to absolving themselves of responsibility now parents cleverly encourage their educated sons and daughters-in-law to take independent decision in a joint and extended family situation, leave aside urban areas, the similar situation has started to emerge in rural areas too. This is not unusual when sons and daughters tend to possess a higher level of education and a greater degree of exposure of the world outside the family than ever before. Now, boys and girls, contrary to the old practice, are beginning to assert their wishes in mate selection. Parental decisions are no more supreme. Changes concerning erosion of authority of old guards, particularly in matters of mate selection, are on gradual decline in rural areas too.

Yet, another interesting fact about the change in authority structure within the family is that about nine per cent of all the households are headed by women, while the NFH Survey-1 gives a slightly higher figure (about 10 per cent). Most of the female household heads are usually independent and gainfully employed. In the absence of their husbands, either because of death, separation, transfer in job or business engagement, women are themselves able to run the affairs of their family. Long distance migration of men for employment is also an important reason for the emergence of such households. The phenomenon of female-headed household assumes significance in the Indian society because in the past when the joint family system was so preponderant that the female-headed household was quite an uncommon phenomenon.

Changes in Marital Practices

The traditional system of values of the Indian society, especially that of Hindus, has been such that it stood for the practice of early as well as universal marriage for females. Child marriage or pre-puberty marriage all through has been an archetypal institution of India. The mean age at marriage was reported to be quite low in the 19th century and so also in earlier days. The mean age at marriage for females was about 13 years between 1901 and 1931 censuses and it did not differ much between different communities. Of all the legal measures, the Child Marriages Restraint Act 1929 happened to be quite effective one. Rise in the age at marriage really became conspicuous during the post independence era, that is, during the period onward 1950. The act was further amended in 1978 wherein boys' marriage age was raised to 21 and girls' age to 18 years.

On the whole, the state level census information for the last one hundred years has revealed a clear rise in the age at marriage for girls. During 1891-1991 the age at marriage increased by 4 to 7 years in different parts of the country. Data from NFHS-2 have shown further increase in the age at marriage of females from 18.5 years to 21.5 years at the national level which greatly destabilised the persistence of high fertility regime in the country (the Census of India, 2001 has estimated a somewhat lower age at marriage). Out-of-wedlock birth is highly unacceptable and hence extremely rare in India.

The law provides certain positive initiatives for the intervention of courts to prevent child marriages through stay orders. In India, the National Family Health Survey-2 found that 65 per cent of girls are married by the time they are eighteen. Child marriages are solemnised during times of festivals such as *Akshaya Tritiya, Akha Teej, Ram Navami, Basant Panchami and Karma Jayanti.* According to UNICEF's 'State of the World's Children-2009' report, 47 per cent of India's women aged 20-24 were married before the legal age of 18, with 56 per cent in rural areas.

Child marriages have been prevalent in many cultures throughout human history, but have gradually diminished since some countries started to urbanise and experience changes in the ways of life for the people of these countries. An increase in the advocacy of human rights, whether as women's rights or as children's rights, has caused the traditions of child marriage to decrease greatly as it was considered unfair and dangerous for the children. Today, child marriage is usually practised in countries where cultural practices and traditions of child marriage still have a strong influence. Although, child marriages have been outlawed a long time ago,

South Asia has currently the highest prevalence of child marriage of any region in the world. India, as noted above, happens to be a forerunner in this regard.

Yet, another important marital practice is consanguineous marriage which has been the notable feature of a large segment of the Indian society since long. Through the ages the system of cross-cousin and cross-uncle niece marriages has been the most favoured kind of marriage in South India. The most desirable mate for a man has been his own sister's daughter or mother's brother's daughter (Driver and Driver 1988; Nair 1978: 121, 131). In the face of rising dowry practices across the country consanguineous marriages have appreciably declined in South India in recent years. However, such marriages have remained tabooed among the vast majority of Hindus of North India. The Hindu Marriage and Divorce Act 1955 prohibits marriage among close relatives— called *sapinda* marriage. The *sapinda* relationship extends as far as the third generation in the line of mother and the fifth in the line of father. In North India only Muslims, certain scheduled castes and scheduled tribes tend to practise consanguineous marriages. has reported that most of the tribal groups practise consanguinity of both types such as marriages with the father's sister's daughter, the mother's brother's daughter and the elder sister's daughter.

The Indian society has been a highly endogamous. Marriage within the same sub-caste has been followed very strictly. The scheduled tribes are also endogamous, but most of the tribal communities practise clan exogamy. Polygamy, more particularly polygyny, has been one of salient features of Indian family. It has been more popular among Muslims than Hindus. Here it is not suggested that the incidence of polygyny is more common than monogamy. The polygamous males often derived support from age-old scriptures and mythological stories. But, mainly those who had no issue from the first wife practised such marriages. With the rise in the level of literacy the incidence of polygyny has receded even among the Muslims despite the fact that such marriages have got full cultural and legal sanction. While monogamy is the predominant form of marriage, there are a large number of tribes practising sororal polygyny and non-sororal polygyny.

Dissolution of Marriage

The dissolution of marriage has been quite uncommon and rare in India for a long time. In case of any crisis or threat to stability of marriage, caste, community, kinsmen, tended to have played a dominant say. People had both respect for and fear of social values and public opinion. Authority of community, though implicit, has been supreme. The system of religious belief has provided enough sustenance to the institution of marriage and family. Individual choice has always been subservient to the communal sentiment or public opinion. Hindu marriage is taken as a life-long union for the couple, as it is a sacrament, rather than a contract between the couple to live in a social union so long as it is cordially feasible. Even in the event of frequent mental and physical torture, most Indian women persist in marriage, since remarriage of divorced or separated women is quite difficult. Morality relating to sex is so highly valued that every male wants to marry a virgin girl only. In the past Hindus demanded pre-nuptial chastity on the part of both, but now it is by and large limited to females. Virginity is regarded as the girls' greatest virtue and a symbol of respectability. Under the circumstances remarriage of women is so difficult that annulment of marriage is a very hard choice or option.

Despite all these there has been a significant change in the views and attitudes towards sanctity of marriage in the recent past, especially in cities. Marriage is no longer held to be a 'divine match' or a 'sacred union'. Now it is more like a transfer of a female from one family to another, or from one kinship group to another. The marriage is no longer sanctified as it was believed in the past, and is viewed only as a bonding and nurturing life-long relationship and friendship. The rather flippant and superficial reasons given by many women and men to break a marriage may not portend well for the future. Indian marriages are still largely resilient and lasting, whereas in many developed countries they seem to break up for seemingly trivial reasons. Marriages are very vulnerable or fragile there. One in every four or five marriages breaks up despite more space and freedom in the West. The longevity of marriage in most developed countries ranges on an average from five to seven years. While in India divorce rates are among the lowest in the world. Only one out of 100 marriages ends up in divorce here. These days divorce rates in India's urban sphere are, however, slowly mounting.

Marriage counsellors, formerly pooh-poohed at, have today assumed a lot of importance in guiding couples through stormy seas and averting the imminent pain of divorce. Today, in cities there is disenchantment with the system of arranged marriages in a large number of cases. The Indian family is faced with a new kind of social and psychological constraints. The women, however, tend to be more concerned about their marriage than men and in case of a problem they are expected to go for counselling. They are expected to take the lead to resolve conflicts and when they give up the effort, the marriage is generally over. In today's shifting values and changing times, there is less reliance on marriage as a definer of sex and living arrangements throughout life.

Today, in cities there is disenchantment with the system of arranged marriages. There is a greater incidence of extra-marital relationships, including open gay and lesbian relationships, a delay in the age at marriage, higher rates of marital disruption and more egalitarian gender-role attitudes among men and women. It is reported that in big metropolises a new system of 'live-in-arrangements' between pairs, particularly in upper stratum of society, is steadily emerging as a new kind of family life. Anyway, a relatively higher divorce rate in cities, *inter alia,* connote that marriage is an institution in trouble, or else expectations are so high that people are no longer willing to put up with the kinds of dissatisfactions and empty-shell marriages that the previous generations tolerated. High rate of remarriages clearly means that people are sacrificing their marriages because of unsatisfactory relationships.

Problems of Dowry

Now, let us come to the rising problem of dowry which has become one of the serious social evils of the Indian society in the recent years. Dowry, or the bridegroom price, refers to a lump sum of money with or without some tangible assets constituting an essential part of the wedding settlement, which is transferred by the bride's household to that of her prospective spouse before the actual solemnisation of marriage. Sometimes dowry also accompanies or follows the marriage of a daughter. The dowry and its cognate problems have become so serious that the marriage of daughters tends to bring in nightmarish experiences for scores of parents these days. The menace of dowry has become so severe over the years that the Government of India had to enact the Dowry Prohibition Act in 1961, which was further amended in1986. But, the legislative measures to do away with this practice have so far proved an ineffective exercise.

The dowry has gained social legitimacy across all communities and regions. Marriage negotiations tend to break down if there is no consensus between the bride's and bridegroom' s families regarding the mode or amount of payment of dowry. Dowry, as said before, has become such an essential consideration for marriage that rarely any marriage can take place without it. It may be regarded as a functional imperative for family formation in contemporary India. In very rare cases demands for dowry are eschewed. If the groom's parents, for instance, sense that they can reap greater economic or personal benefits in modes other than the dowry in a lump cash from bride's parents, dowry is not demanded under the pretext that it is an evil of Indian society.

When the dowry amount is not considered sufficient or the expected demands are not met easily, the bride is often harassed, abused and tortured. The dissatisfied husband takes recourse to violence to show his displeasure with the marriage in order to extract additional transfers from the wife's family by threatening her with separation if new demands are not complied with. The dowry related harassment most likely arises from complete lack of respect for the woman and rapacious avarice for money. The woman, as a bride, is subjected to humiliation and brutal behaviour, because she is the softest and the surest means of extracting maximum amount of money or wealth from her parents to enhance one's economic position in society. Since the bride is helpless in her new home and physically so powerless that she cannot retaliate against the coercive tactics or actions of others. Not many women have enough guts to divorce their husbands on the ground of frequent mental or physical torture, since they have nothing to fall back upon in a traditional and poorly developed country like India.

The disturbing fact about dowry related violence is that it is not confined to any particular group, social stratum, geographical region or even religion. Rather, it is regarded as a universal phenomenon, cutting across all sorts of boundaries, as it has already been stressed before. It is claimed to be on continuous increase in the country. It has been often reported that like clockwork every 12th hour a dowry related death claimed to have taken the lives of over 20,000 women across the country between 1990 and 1993. It has also been reported that at least three girls are burnt for dowry related demands every day in the State of Karnataka. This may be taken as a matter of grave concern, for the incidence of dowry death is one of the typical problems of the Indian society. In view of continuing failure of the state through legal means, the civil societies should come forward to fight the menace of dowry. The crux of the matter is that those who have got sons or more sons than daughters tend to have developed vested interests in the persistence of this practice.

Domestic Violence

Violence within family settings is primarily a male activity. The prime targets are women and children. The women have been victims of humiliation and torture for as long as we have written records of the Indian society. Despite several legislative measures adopted in favour of women during the last 150 years, continuing spread of modern education and women's gradual economic independence, countless women have continued to be victims of discrimination and violence in the country. Increasing family violence in modern times has compelled many social scientists to be apologists for the traditional joint family- as happy and harmonious, a high-voltage emotional setting, imbued with love, affection and tenderness. India's past has been so romanticised by certain scholars that they have regarded the joint family as the best form of family.

There are data showing that in India 40 per cent of women have experienced violence by an intimate partner. These stark figures underline the fact that, although the home and community are places where women provide care for others, they are also places where millions of women experience coercion and abuse. A study of five districts of the State of Uttar Pradesh has revealed that 30 per cent of currently married men acknowledge physically abusing their wives. Similarly, the multi-sectoral survey done by the International Clinical Epidemiologists Network (INCLEN) has reported that two out of every five married women reported being hit, kicked, beaten or slapped by their husbands.

About fifty per cent of the women experiencing physical violence also reported physical abuse during pregnancy. With the rise in the level of education and exposure to mass media, women tend to have greater awareness of the notion of gender equality, faith in the effectiveness of legal action to protect their rights, and confidence in such institutions as family courts and certain voluntary organisations working for women. Yet, there is no sign of abatement in gender related violence. Cases of domestic violence, like wife-battering and forced incest with the women of the household, are so personal and delicate that they are seldom reported to the police or law courts. We are sure that the recent legislation of anti-domestic violence act of 2005 would certainly take care of the problem of gender-based violence of the Indian woman to a very large extent.

There is another side of the story of domestic violence as well which has remained uncovered, particularly by feminist writers. It is roughly estimated that every year more than 58000 educated women are making the life of their husbands hell by misusing anti-dowry law and domestic violence act and under these laws legal terrorism is continuing openly to extort money from the husbands and their families. More than 52000 married men are ending their life due to various type of harassment and domestic violence faced form their beloved wives in the form of verbal abuse, financial abuse, mental abuse, sexual abuse, relationship cheating, etc.

Problems of Child Labour

Children constitute a little over 30 per cent of the total population of the country according to the 2001 Census of India. Evidence suggests that they are quite vulnerable and their exposure to violations of their protection rights remains widespread and multiple in nature. The manifestations of these violations are very varied, ranging from child labour and child trafficking to commercial sexual exploitation and many other forms of violence and abuse. With an estimated

12.6 million children engaged in hazardous occupations for instance, India has the largest number of child labourers under the age of 14 in the world. Although, poverty is often cited as the cause underlying child labour, other factors such as discrimination, social exclusion, as well as the lack of quality education or existing parents' attitudes and perceptions about child labour and the role and value of education need also to be considered.

While systematic data and information on child protection issues are still not always available, evidence suggests that children in need of special protection belong to communities suffering disadvantages and social exclusion such as scheduled castes and scheduled tribes, and the poor. It has been estimated that 46 per cent children from scheduled tribes and 38 per cent from scheduled castes are out of school. The lack of available services as well as the gaps persisting in law enforcement and in rehabilitation schemes also constitute a major cause of concern. The children of poor families, especially those of artists, craftsmen, and other professions are trained by their parents and elders of the family in their vocations such as weaving, tanning, sweeping dyeing, hairdressing, painting, carpentry and agriculture. A vast number of children grow up lending a helping hand to elders in their home-industries. The practice or intergenerational transfer of traditional callings more or less is still continuing. Such kids who lack formal schooling, but working and specialising in some craft or their traditional callings help them build a career.

Indeed, the poverty in India forces many parents to send their children to earn extra money. The employers who hire such children pay them paltry wages. One can see boys of poor families act as vegetable vendors throughout India. Children of construction workers help in bringing water, cleaning vessels or collecting twigs for fuel. Their parents are compelled to come to cities when monsoon fails and they cannot cultivate their lands.

Children are also subjected to gender based discrimination. Discrimination against women in fact starts the day she is born. Sometimes it also starts when she is in her mother's womb as a foetus. The practice of female foeticide, despite being illegal, is vigorously practised in urban India. The girl child's right to survival, health care and nutrition, education, social opportunities and protection has to be recognised and made a social and economic priority. Along with this the basic structural inequalities that cause poverty, malnutrition and the low status of women have to be addressed, if these rights are to be ensured. Within family parents are first to practise gender based discrimination and it is the first school of learning where girls are inculcated the values of their being inferior to their brothers.

Although, India loves their children, still thousands of children roam the streets of major cities around the country and receive neither education, proper food, clothing, or a bed to sleep in at night. Why are these children roaming and begging in the streets? What should be done and who is willing to do something to help these poor children? A mind and heart that cares, awareness presentations through multi-media, contributions, talking and sharing information among friends, education, self-help initiatives and good old fashion kindness are all that is needed to get these kids off the streets. Basically they need five things for their living: food, clothing, shelter, medical assistance and education.

Contrary to the above, there are children who belong to the well-off sections of society, but they are also not free from problems. They are facing a different kind of problem either due to lack of adequate care or attention from their working parents or due to heavy expectation from them by their parents in a fiercely competitive modern world full of uncertainties in life. In cases of working mothers, children are placed in an entirely different situation. The demands of city life are such that both wife and husband tend to remain outside their home for work even at the cost of interests of their children. Working couples are unable to give proper care and affection to their children. Obviously, latchkey children of working couples are strangers to the sense of security enjoyed by their own parents. The system of surrogate mothers or the Montessori and Kindergarten systems of schooling has proved to be a very poor substitute for family as an agent of socialisation.

With the diminished role of family as an agent of socialisation juvenile delinquency is on the increase. In the past children enjoyed security of a kind unknown today. Growing up under the joint care of adults made them feel responsible for all the extended members of the family, besides their own parents. Now children are at greater strain than ever before because in general parents intend to accomplish those things in their life through their children what they themselves could not be able to achieve, no matter how difficult they are. Children are put under great stress and stain to score high marks at schools to be able to meet the ever-increasing challenges of fiercely competitive world of education and employment. In addition to helping their children achieve higher goals of life, women, sometimes both the parents, have to work harder with a view to attaining economic independence and maintaining a higher standard of living of their family.

There has been appreciable decline in fertility over the years. This has not been possible without recording drastic changes in the attitude of people towards the size of family and the value system of patriarchy and patriliny. Based on studies on fertility behaviour and contraceptive practices one can conclusively contend that perhaps no element of the Indian social system has experienced greater changes than the system of family during the post-independent period. This is clearly borne out by various empirical investigations. Despite considerable decline in fertility or lesser burden of children on the family, there is no improvement in the quality of care of children especially in rural areas.

There hardly exists any pre-school or community centre in villages There also does not exist even a basic facility of play ground for children. The older children have to mind the younger children at home and sometimes they are also expected to lend helping hands to their parents in the household chores as and when required. The poor children learn the expected roles of life of their own with the passage of time, while the well-off peasantry send their children to private schools (also called public schools in the Western world) in towns and cities for better schooling.

Indian Scenario

The problem of child labour is quite conspicuous to the naked eyes in India. Its prevalence is clearly evident in the form of high workforce participation rate among children, which is higher than that of any other developing country. Poverty is the prime reason behind child labour in India. Unfortunately enough, whatever the meagre income they are able to generate is absorbed by their families. Child labour is extensive with children under the age of fourteen working in carpet making factories, glass blowing units and making fireworks with bare little hands. There are at least 44 million child labourers in the age group of 5-14. More than 80 per cent of the them in India are employed in the agricultural and non-formal sectors and many are bonded labourers, too. Most of them are either illiterate or dropped out of school after two or three years.

The exploitation of little children for labour is an accepted practice and perceived by many as a necessity to alleviate poverty. Carpet weaving industries pay very low wages to child labourers and make them work for longer hours in unhygienic conditions. Children working in such units are mainly migrant workers, who are shunted here by their families to earn some money and send it back to them. Their families dependence on their income forces them to endure the onerous work conditions in the carpet factories. The situation of child labourers in India is desperate. Children work for eight hours at a stretch with only a small break for meals. The meals are also frugal and the children are ill nourished. Most of the migrant children who cannot go home, sleep at their work place, which is very bad for their health and development. About 70 per cent of India's population still resides in rural areas and are very poor. Children in rural families who are ailing with poverty perceive their children as an income generating resource to supplement the family income. Parents sacrifice their children's education to the growing needs of their younger siblings in such families and view them as bread-winners for the entire family.

Bonded Labour among Children

Children are also compelled to work as bonded labourers. They are trapped to grow in a hostage like condition for years. The importance of formal education is also not realised, as the child can be absorbed in economically beneficial activities at a young age. Moreover, there is no access to proper education in the remote areas of rural India for most people, which leaves the children with no choice. There are thousands of bonded child labourers in India. They are also mostly the children of parents who belong to scheduled castes and tribes. Young children are sold to employers by their parents to pay back small loans that they have borrowed. Such children are made to work for many hours a day over several years. Often, child labour is considered to be a 'necessary evil' in poor countries such as India for the maintenance of the family. In that context, some consider it virtuous to give a job to a child. In fact, some academics and activists campaign not for the reduction of child labour but only for a reduction in the exploitation of children.

Bonded labour or slave labour is one of the worst forms of labour not only for children but also for adults. In India, bonded labour has been declared illegal since 1976, when the Parliament enacted the Bonded Labour System (Abolition) Act. However, the practice is still widespread. Children or adults are bonded in order to pay off debts that they or other members of their families have incurred. They toil all their lives and endure physical attacks that often amount to torture. The Indian government has tried to take some steps to alleviate the problem of child labour in recent years by invoking a law that makes the employment of children below 14 illegal, except in family owned enterprises. However, this law is rarely adhered to due to practical difficulties. Factories usually find loopholes and circumvent the law by declaring that the child labourer is a distant family member. Also in villages, there is no law implementing mechanism, and any punitive actions for commercial enterprises violating these laws is almost non existent.

Problems and Prospects of Elderly

The family has started facing a new kind of problem emanating from a relatively faster pace of demographic transition. The incredible increase in life expectancy may be a big triumph of the 20th century, but it has posed one of the toughest problems before the 21st century India. Census reports have revealed that the Indian population approximately tripled during the last 50 years, but the number of elderly people had in fact increased more than fourfold. Based on the continuation of the trend, the United Nations has predicted in one of its report that the Indian population would again grow by 50 per cent by the middle of this century, whereas the elderly population is likely to have another fourfold increase in its size.

It is estimated the that, during the next five decades the size of the population would grow by about 50 per cent, but the number of older people would increase fourfold. The proportion of older people in the population would grow at a higher pace than the other groups. It is estimated that the elderly people (60+) would constitute 20 per cent of the total population which would be quite huge in terms of absolute number—316 million. The Indian policymakers must take a critical note of the rising trends of incoming age wave of older people and the declining trend of the proportion of younger people. Such developments would cause strain on the resources due to increase in more inactive people.

Indian population would be gradually swinging to a greyer one by the next few decades. It is estimated that the median age of the population would increase gradually from 25 years in 2010 to 31.7 years in 2030 and, finally, to 38.4 years in 2050. Similarly, the old age dependency ratio will climb up from 8 per cent in 2010 to 20 per cent in 2050, while the child dependency ratio is expected to come down from 56 per cent to 27 per cent during this period. Hence, every three working Indians may have to take care of one elderly person by 2050 as compared to about eight working persons at present. It has been estimated that an Indian of age 63 today is likely to survive about a decade more in 2050.

Longer life expectancy and incremental dependency ratio will possibly strain the family and the state support system for the older people. Increase in individuals' age is usually followed by increased prevalence of chronic diseases and disability and hence the elderly population is taken as a big burden for the family, community and ultimately the entire nation. Many young people consider the old member of their family as an obstacle to the advancement of their career as well as an economic burden for their family life, as the older parents become frail due to greater incidence of diseases and disability, eventually becoming bedridden in the family and later forced to stay in nursing homes during the terminal stages of their life. This scenario causes young people to have a negative image of the older people and early in their life they adopt a ageistic outlook towards the older people.

In the past, the joint family system not only provided a suitable umbrella to manage personal risks, such as risks of premature death and excessive longevity, but also laid down the norms of intergenerational relationships as well as the role of each member. The elderly played a significant role in decision making regarding household matters, while the younger people were entrusted with the responsibility of ensuring well-being of their ageing parents. But, these days in smaller families, they are gradually marginalised in the decision-making process. Hence, the family that traditionally took care of the elderly or sick, widows and orphans is beginning to rely on society as a whole. As the number of old persons is rising and the social environment is changing, the proportion of the destitute among them may also be increasing. These factors are also leading to the need for a large number of old-age homes where the old people may enjoy the remaining part of their life in a group of their own.

As a consequence of the breakdown of traditional joint and extended families, the elderly people are being steadily marginalised in society generally. Moreover, due to some habits and unhealthy lifestyles, the elderly people tend to suffer from tuberculosis, asthma, cancer, cardiovascular problems, etc., apart from the other gerontological problems. But, the healthcare facilities for the aged people are not satisfactory. A well-equipped, separate division in Indian hospitals is increasingly required for the comprehensive care of elderly people. Such a facility will not only cure the old physically, but will also ensure their mental well-being. It will simultaneously arrange medical treatment as well as improve their quality of life. The government as well as the private healthcare providers have to build up the necessary infrastructure to meet the healthcare requirements of the increasingly ageing population. It may be further aggravated due to the exponentially increasing healthcare expenses, though neglecting those expenses may worsen their quality of life.

Role of Civil Society and Non-governmental Organisations

Under the prevailing situation, the non-governmental organisations and civil societies are expected to play a central role to help out those ageing people who are destined to lead an uncared and solitary life. At the same time, there may be some amount of solace as well because the kind of problem relating to intergenerational solidarity the Indian society is facing is relatively much less serious compared to the developed world, since a vast majority of the elderly people tend to live with their sons or if not with them for some reasons, their sons or other close kinsmen often remain in constant touch with them to attend any exigency which may arise in their life. It is clearly evident from the NFHS-2 data that over 80 per cent of the elderly people live with their sons, daughters or other kinsmen. An elderly person living alone does not constitute more than five per cent, while the elderly couples living independently of any young person in the household is not more than 10 per cent of the total households at any ages between 60 and 80 years. However, this scenario may not last very long because a similar set of data derived from the NFHS-1 has recorded slightly lower percentages for elderly people living alone or independently of others in a household. It may be pertinent to point out here that from Table 1 one should not try to assume that over 80 per cent of the households are joint families. It has already been observed that the joint and extended families together do not constitute more 20 per cent of all the households in India.

An aged person has the right to decide about personal needs and aspirations, depending upon capacity. Only a sound social security system can protect such rights by assuring regular income during the post-retirement years. But, developing such a system for the Indian population is a quite difficult task, as a majority of them do not currently enjoy any type of old-age income security. Neither the government nor the public sector alone can formulate it; the private sector cannot develop it in isolation either. Joint approaches and strategies will be required to design and build up a robust old-age income security system.

A little over 40 per cent (19.18 million) of salaried employees and 289.59 million are engaged in the unorganised sector (including self-employed professionals, farmers, shopkeepers, taxi drivers, casual labourers, etc.) are deprived of being covered by any compulsory retirement benefit plans. In other words, about 92 per cent of working Indians are not covered under any old-age income security plan. Despite the absence of any regular income, a significant proportion of these people stay well above the poverty line during their working life. But, they are likely to sink below the poverty line in their old age, simply because they could not accumulate adequate amounts of savings while they were in the workforce. The reason behind this trend is because of the non-availability of any suitable framework for savings and investments.

The Planning Commission of India has assessed that about 92 per cent of working Indians do not enjoy any formal old-age income. Consequently, the Project Old Age Social and Income Security (OASIS) Committee projected that these people might sink below the poverty line as a result of the non-availability of adequate post-retirement income. On the other hand, framing suitable policies regarding the availability of the pension plans, allowing the participation of the private players in the pension sector, ensuring the availability of need-based pension products, and increasing the level of consumer awareness about old-age income requirements will help to mobilise a large amount (about Rs. 4,065 billion) of very long-term funds by the year 2025.

The importance of this sector in the Indian economy cannot be overlooked. This informal sector of the Indian economy offers employment opportunities to about 92 per cent of the working people and contributes 59 per cent of the GDP, including reasonable export earnings. Considering the existence of this void, Project OASIS Report warned that the demographic transition coupled with poor coverage by existing provisions suggests that we are inexorably moving towards an India with a gigantic number of destitute elderly. Faced with such huge numbers, a social safety net for the retired workers or a poverty alleviation programme, which aims to pay even a modest subsidy, would require a staggering expenditure—much beyond the capacity of the government. Moreover, the Indian constitution has entrusted some responsibility to the state in relation to the social security of the people. But, the obligation of the state regarding old-age income security of the people is primarily limited to the organised workforce. However, due to irregular incomes, retirement is considered a luxury for people of the unorganised sector. This may be observed from the high level of their participation in the workforce, even beyond the generally accepted age of retirement.

It is high time that the Indian policy makers assess the impact of the forthcoming age wave. The process of pension sector reforms should be accelerated, suitable steps should be undertaken to build the required healthcare facilities and a suitable social security system should also be designed. If change is not effected, the family support system as well as the state-sponsored facilities may crash in the near future, thereby jeopardising the well-being of elderly people. It may cause the emergence of a gigantic number of penniless, sick and elderly people in the streets and public places.

For older persons to remain active as long as possible, the informal sector in the general community has great potentials for possible intergenerational activities such as older workers serving as mentors to their younger co-workers in the workplace. There is also a necessity to create or establish the centres where the elderly and the young can meet, interact and work together. This is necessitated to encourage a communal way of living, promote intergenerational solidarity and help prevent social exclusion of the elderly in the community.

New Challenges for Women

Considerable changes have taken place in the traditional role of women. Once the priority for the young women was the husband, but now it has shifted to their career and in addition deep resentments tend to surface when the husbands are reluctant to take part in the household chores. The urban women are seen in many different roles. With 54 per cent of the level of female literacy rate in India at the 2001 census, though much lower by the standard of developed countries, it is not unusual to see women working as clerks, typists, receptionists, nurses, doctors, school and college teachers, lawyers, police, social workers and social activists. Women can assume still greater public roles in society than what we see today. They tend to show lower workforce participation rate because not many suitable jobs are available for them outside their home (Singh, 1996: 56-70). But, on the contrary, countless people often believe that women inherently tend to have stronger attachments with family and household responsibilities. On the whole, with the rise in education, urbanisation and opportunity to proper employment, women are much freer now to come out of their homes with a view to meeting their family expenses. With the rise in education and economic development, the women would steadily move towards greater economic independence in course of time.

The urban woman is in a position to exercise much greater authority than before. Despite her increased duties, the urban woman seems to have emerged as the stronger partner. It is she who monitors children's homework, tutors them in areas of weakness or laziness. Mothers dropping and picking up children— from school or coaching classes in computer and cricket or tennis— by bus, moped, scooter or car, is a common sight today in Indian cities. Mother has become the primary agent of socialisation. But, all mothers are not equally free to mind their children.

With the rise in modern education, gainful engagement, quality of health condition and a fewer number of children, family life may not be always well. The State of Kerala can be cited as one of the examples. Those who are unhappy with current state of family life are on the gradual increase in the state. It is all the more acute in urban areas where the hold of traditional norms and values has largely dissipated. The consumer culture sweeping the urban society and the breakdown of the extended or joint family system have contributed to this. Reports show that the number of cases pending in the family courts is on the increase. The number of children running away from homes has also gone up. Consumption of alcohol has touched an all time high. Modernisation has created dilemmas for family life. Under the new socio-economic urban milieu there has been a tremendous increase in the family violence. With a view to tackling increasing violence in the family, the Government of India introduced a very useful Domestic Violence Act in 2005. This would certainly go a long way in restraining the incidence of domestic violence in the country.

State, Law and Family

India, does not have any systematic coherent family policy, but the government has always been sensitive to the problems concerning family formation and dissolution, rights of women and children, the practice of child marriages, dowry, domestic violence and so forth. This is apparent from various legislations enacted, amended and implemented by the Government of India as well as the state governments as and when necessitated. They are together called family laws. Family law is that area of law which deals with family-related issues and domestic relations including the nature of marriage, civil unions, and domestic partnerships; issues arising during marriage, including spousal abuse, dowry, legitimacy, adoption, surrogacy, child abuse, and child abduction, the termination of the relationship and ancillary matters including divorce, annulment, property settlements, alimony and parental responsibility orders.

The following legislations are an important part of the Indian family laws: Hindu Widows Remarriage Act, 1856 and 1956; The Converts' Marriage Dissolution Act, 1866; The Indian Christian Marriage Act, 1872; The Kazis Act, 1880; The Anand Marriage Act, 1909; The Child Marriage Restraint Act, 1929 and 1978; The Parsi Marriage and Divorce Act, 1936; The Foreign Marriage Act, 1969; The Hindu Women's Right to Property Act, 1937; The Special Marriage Act, 1954; The Hindu Marriage and Divorce Act, 1955; The Hindu Succession Act, 1956; The Hindu Minority and Guardianship Act, 1956; The Hindu Adoptions and Maintenance Act, 1956; The Suppression of Immoral Traffic in Women and Girls Act, 1956, 1978 and 1886; The Dowry Prohibition Act, 1961 and 1986; The Muslim Women (Protection of Rights on Divorce) Act, 1986; The Child Labour Prohibition and Regulation Act, 1986; and The Domestic Violence Act, 2005.

In addition to these, most states of the Indian Union have got their own family laws more or less on the line of these legislations, considering the significance of local practices and the system of belief. It may, however, be recorded here that though most of these laws have been framed to shield the interests of women, yet in varying degrees the personal laws of different religions subvert women's right to equality guaranteed under the Constitution of India. In the following discussion an effort is made to explain as to how the government has time to time responded to various problems that have been encountered by family in India.

Remarriage of Widows. For long, Hindus believed that Hindu widows once married were incapable of contracting a second valid marriage, and the offspring of such widows by any second marriage were held to be illegitimate and incapable of inheriting property. The Widow Remarriage Act was passed in 1856, prohibiting enforced widowhood practised mainly among Brahmins and a few other castes such as Rajputs, Banias and Kayasthas. The law was also designed as a relief for child widows whose husbands died before consummation. The Act was further amended in 1956 to incorporate certain provisions in favour of second marriage. This was done with a view to promoting good morals and to ensure the public welfare. All rights and interests which any widow may have in her deceased husband's property by way of maintenance, or by inheritance to her husband or to his lineal successors would cease on her re-marriage. Yet, the problem of young widows in India has not vanished. Currently widows account for nine per cent of the female population and only 40 per cent of them are over 50 years of age. This suggests that despite laws 60 per cent of widows do not contract second marriage for one reason or the other. Dreze (1990) has contended that the overall incidence of widow remarriage is as low as 1 in 5 or 6. Chen (2000) has reported that only few widows remarry in India. Within her sample of 562 widows, she has argued that the widow remarriage rate is about nine per cent. The census data, however, have revealed that widow remarriage rate has been on the gradual rise, especially in towns and cities.

Child Marriages. Both during ancient and medieval periods, child marriages were widely prevalent in India. The young girls lived with their parents till they reached puberty. Early marriage led to the problem of early widowhood because of high death rates. Since widow remarriage was not possible among caste Hindus, the child widows were condemned to a life of great agony, shaving heads, living in isolation, and shunned by the society. Hence, the child marriage was outlawed in 1869 through the Indian Penal Code. The first law addressing child marriage was the Native Marriage Act, 1872, which was promulgated by the British colonial regime and fixed 14 as the age of consent to marriage. The Child Marriage Restraint Act, 1929 was passed during the tenure of British rule and in order to incorporate some necessary changes and also to raise the age at marriage to 18 for girls and 21 for boys and it was amended in 1949,1955 and 1978. The object of the Child Marriage Restraint Law of 1929 was to eliminate a practice which was potentially detrimental to the life and health of a girl child. Yet, the child marriages, as said before, are still widely practised in India.

According to the 2001 census, out of 593 districts in the country there are 190 districts where the mean age at marriage of females is less than 18 years. The persistence of child marriages implies that laws prohibiting such marriages are not so effective. The state machinery is not so efficient or successful in tackling such a serious social evil because of poor regard for law generally. According to the 'National Plan of Action for Children 2005' (published by the Department of Women and Child Development, Government of India), a goal has been set to eliminate child marriage completely by 2010. This plan is proving to be successful, though it is still difficult to monitor every child marriage due to the sheer size of India's population.

Dowry. What began as a gift of land to a woman as her inheritance in an essentially agricultural economy today has degenerated into gifts of gold, clothes, consumer durables and large sums of cash, which sometimes entails the impoverishment and heavy indebtedness of poor families. In the course of time dowry has become a widespread evil and it has now assumed menacing proportions. Surprisingly it has spread to different communities across the country, which were traditionally non-dowry taking communities. With the increasing greed for the easy inflow of money on account of a bride the chilling stories of bride burning started coming to light.

With a view to eradicating the rampant social evil of dowry from the Indian society, the Parliament passed the Dowry Prohibition Act in 1961 which applies not merely to Hindus but to all communities like— Muslims, Sikhs, Christians and others. Giving, taking and demanding dowry is a criminal offence under the Dowry Protection Act and the Indian Penal Code. Under the Dowry Prohibition Act only Metropolitan Magistrate or the Magistrate of the first class is competent to try these offences. Where any person is prosecuted for taking or abetting the taking of any dowry or the demanding of dowry, the burden of proving that he has not committed an offence shall be on him. The giving, taking or even abetting to give or take dowry amounts to an offence punishable with imprisonment for not less than 5 years and with fine which shall not be less than Rs. 15,000/- or the amount of value of the dowry, which ever is more. If any person demands directly or indirectly, from the parents or other relatives of a bride or bridegroom, as the case may be, any dowry, he shall be punishable with an imprisonment for a term which shall not be less than six months but which may extend to two years and with fine which may extend to Rs. 10,000.

The Indian Penal Code provides that where any women dies an unnatural death within seven years of her marriage and it is shown that she was harassed or subjected to cruelty by her husband or his relative for dowry, such death shall be called a dowry death. The husband or the relative shall be deemed to have caused the death of the women. The offence is punishable with imprisonment of not less than seven years. Whoever, being a husband or relative of the husband subjects such women to cruelty shall be punished with imprisonment for a term of three years. Despite such stringent laws dowry is being increasingly practised throughout the country. It has assumed such an alarming proportion that the number of cases of bride-burning and bride-torture, both mental and physical, in law courts is rising, and the media are agog with ever-increasing number of such instances. This is a reflection of a very serious kind of lapse on the part of the state machinery.

Divorce. As per the ancient Hindu laws, there was no place for divorce and it was with the codification of Hindu law that the first grounds for the new age laws were laid down. All major religions have their own laws which govern divorces within their own community, and separate regulations exist regarding divorce in inter-faith marriages. Hindus, including Buddhists, Sikhs and Jains, are governed by the Hindu Marriage Act, 1955; Christians by the Indian Divorce Act, 1869; Parsis by the Parsi Marriage and Divorce Act, 1936; and Muslims by the Dissolution of Muslim Marriages Act, 1939, which provides the grounds on which women can obtain a divorce, and the uncodified civil law. Civil marriages and inter-community marriages and divorces are governed by the Special Marriage Act, 1956. Other community specific legislation includes the Native Converts' Marriage Dissolution Act, 1866 that allows a Hindu to appeal for a divorce if a spouse converts to Christianity.

In most Western nations, there are approximately 16 distinct reasons for which divorces are granted. In India, however, only five main reasons are generally accepted as sufficient grounds for divorce: (1) Adultery, (2) Desertion, (3) Cruelty, (4) Impotency, and (5) Chronic Disease.

The women, having being given in marriage by her father or other guardian before she attained the age of 15 years, repudiated the marriage before attaining the age of 18. The Muslim Marriage Act, 1939 restricts Muslim women's right to seek divorce by placing conditions that did not exist in Islamic law and are difficult to prove, such as cruelty and impotency. But, a Muslim man has the right to unilateral divorce of triple *talaq*. Polygamy among Muslims continues to remain an issue. While under the Hindu Marriage Act, 1955, polygamy has been declared illegal. Muslim personal law makes the man the sole guardian of a child.

While the Indian intelligentsia often feel that one should have the right to divorce, it is still a highly stigmatising action. Women are looked upon more harshly than men in this regard. There continue to be segments of Indian society that feel divorce is never a right option, regardless of how abusive or adulterous the husband may be which adds to the greater disapproval for women. A divorced woman often can return to her family, but may not be wholeheartedly welcomed. There is also the risk that a divorced woman's presence would ward off possible marriages for other daughters within the household. Unavoidably, the overall status of the family and household are lowered by having a divorcee living with amongst them. A woman's class and caste are a major factor in her acceptance back into society. Women from higher classes tend to have an easier time than middle or lower class women in returning to the social order after a divorce. An exception to this model is the extreme bottom of the society who have experienced little rebuff from peers after a divorce. This results from their already atypical status in society. For these reasons, among some other factors, the divorce rate is less than one per cent here according to the 2001 Census of India.

Succession and Right to Property. As India has been a highly patriarchal and patrilineal society since ancient days, the Indian women, same as men, never enjoyed the right to be a coparcener in the property of an undivided family or had no right to succession. In order to enhance the position of women in society and extend a sense of dignity in their life, the necessity for laws relating to succession was realised, though the realisation was quite late. Under the Indian Succession Act, 1925, everyone was entitled to equal inheritance, except Hindus, Sikhs, Jains, Buddhists and Muslims. For these communities, excluding the Muslims, a separate legislation known as the Hindu Succession Act, 1925 was introduced. In view of certain shortcomings or limitations it was amended in 1956 and 1991. Under this Act the Hindu women, along with women of some other communities, had an equal right to parental property in the absence of a will; but the women tended to forgo their right at the time of marriage possibly accepting dowry as a compensation for a share. Women were also reluctant to exercise their right for fear of causing a breakdown in the relations with their natal family.

The Hindu Succession Act, however, makes provision for a Hindu undivided family to ensure that property remains with the male line of descent. A son gets a share equal to that of his father; a daughter gets only a share in her father's share. She cannot reside in the family home unless she is single or divorced, and cannot claim her share of property as long as the men of the family continue to live in it. And a Hindu woman has no right to her matrimonial home, unless she can prove that it was purchased with her earnings. However, this law could not do the needful as there was another law, the Mitakshara coparcenaries (Hindu Law) that had an overriding effect on entitlement of women. According to Mitakshara coparcenaries, in a joint family, a daughter had a much smaller share of property compared to the son. If the family owned a dwelling house, then the daughter's right was confined only to the right of residence and not possession or ownership.

Some Muslim laws have been nominally codified in the Shariat Act, 1937, the Dissolution of Muslim Marriages Act, 1939 and the Muslim Women (Protection of Rights on Divorce) Act, 1986. The Shariat Act states that Muslim Personal Law will govern Muslims and that law has priority over custom. In practice, personal law is based mostly on the interpretations of the Quran. There are four schools of jurisprudence and many more legal traditions, which produce different interpretations. Women's right to property under Muslim law does have Quranic sanctions but is limited to half of what their brothers get. However, the 1937 Act categorically denies women any right to agricultural land.

The Parliament of India passed the Hindu Succession (Amendment) Act, 2005, wherein daughters and sons have been equal rights to property. According to this law, any woman, irrespective of the marital status, has full right to inherit ancestral property just like a son of the family. This law has completely abolished the Hindu Succession Act 1956 by giving equal rights to daughters in the 'Hindu Mitakshara Coparcenary property', as sons have.

But; the theoretical reforms so far have not been adequate to give all Indian women a right to property on the same footing and terms as men. It varies with region and religion. Even where law has given a right, conventions and practices do not recognise them. Women themselves relinquish their rights. Women, as daughters, wives, daughters-in-law, mothers or sisters tend to lose out and often suffer deprivation. There are numerous laws that forbid discrimination between the sexes, but in reality none are effective enough to actually bring about a revolution; a change in society. There is a need for legislation in Muslim Law to give equal share of property to the widow and daughter along with sons as done in Turkey.

Right to Maintenance. Maintenance is a right to livelihood when one is incapable of sustaining oneself. Right to maintenance forms a part of the personal law. Obligation of a husband to maintain his wife arises out of the status of the marriage. Hindu law, one of the most ancient systems of law, recognises right of any dependent person including wife, children, aged parents and widowed daughter or daughter-in-law to maintenance. The Hindu Adoptions and Maintenance Act, 1956, provides for this right. Under the Hindu law, the wife has an absolute right to claim maintenance from her husband. But, she loses her right if she deviates from the path of chastity. In assessing the amount of maintenance, the court takes into account various factors like position and liabilities of the husband. It also judges whether the wife is justified in living apart from husband. Maintenance is a right to get necessities which are reasonable from another. Maintenance includes not only food, clothes and residence, but also the things necessary for the comfort and status in which the person entitled is reasonably expected to live. Right to maintenance is not a transferable right.

Apart from the relationship of husband and wife, other relations in which there is economic dependency are also considered to be entitled to maintenance under the Hindu Adoptions and Maintenance Act, 1956. Accordingly a widowed daughter-in-law is entitled maintenance from her father-in-law to the extent of the share of her diseased husband in the said property. The minor children of a Hindu, whether legitimate or illegitimate, are entitled to claim maintenance from their parents. Similarly, the aged and infirm parents of a Hindu are entitled to claim maintenance from their children. The term parent here also includes an issueless stepmother.

Under the Muslim law, the Muslim Women Act, 1986 spells out objective of the Act as 'the protection of the rights of Muslim women who have been divorced by, or have obtained divorce from, their husbands.' The Act says that divorced woman is entitled to have a reasonable and fair provision and maintenance from her former husband, and the husband must do so within the period of idda and his obligation is not confined to the period of idda. This Act *inter alia* provides that a divorced Muslim woman is entitled to (a) reasonable and fair provision and maintenance to be made and paid to her within the iddat period by her former husband; (b) where she herself maintains children born to her, a reasonable and fair provision and maintenance to be made and paid by her former husband for a period of two years from the respective dates of birth of such children; (c) an amount equal to the sum of mehr or dower agreed to be paid to her at the time of her marriage or at any time thereafter according to the Muslim law and (d) all property given to her before or at the time of marriage or after her marriage by her relatives or friends or by husband or any relatives of the husband or his friends.

Under the Christian law a woman can claim maintenance from her spouse through criminal proceeding or/and civil proceeding. Interested parties may pursue both criminal and civil proceedings, simultaneously, as there is no legal bar to it. In criminal proceedings, the religion of the parties does not matter at all, unlike in civil proceedings. If a divorced Christian wife cannot support her in the post divorce period, she need not worry as a remedy is in store for her in law. Under the Indian Divorce Act, 1869, she can apply for alimony/maintenance in a civil court or High Court and, husband is liable to pay her alimony such sum, as the court may order, till her lifetime. The Indian Divorce Act, 1869 which is only applicable to those persons who practise Christian religion *inter alia* governs maintenance rights of a Christian wife.

Laws of maintenance are of course in place, but they are not very effective and efficient in this part of the world. Laws do not always work for the poor or helpless. The state is often found indifferent to such people. The legal process is very tortuous and torturous here. Illiterate, semi-literate and the poor woman can seldom dare to take recourse to the court of law. People often fail in their legal obligations to provide maintenance regularly and adequately to the divorced or separated wife, widows and other dependents. It is often seen that women in difficult situations are usually helped or rescued by their parents rather than by the state. Sometimes certain parents are also either not inclined or in a position to help out such needy women. Since the single women have very little to fall back upon, marriages are relatively more durable here despite all odds.

Gender Inequality. Gender inequalities refer to the obvious or hidden disparities among individuals based on sex. This problem in simple term is known as 'gender bias' which means gender stratification or drawing differences between a girl and a boy, i.e., a male or a female. In India, women were considered as an oppressed section of the society and they were neglected for centuries. Hence, the Constitution of India has incorporated provisions to guarantee equality before law and equal protection of laws for all. Similarly, there shall be no discrimination against any citizen on the ground of sex. In addition, since independence, a number of laws have been enacted in order to provide protection to women. For instance, The Dowry Prohibition Act 1961, The Equal Remuneration Act 1986, The Hindu Marriage Act 1956, The Hindu Succession Act 1956, The Muslim Women Act, 1986, The Commission of Sati (Prevention) Act 1987, the Protection of the Women from Domestic Violence Act 2005, etc. But, the laws are hardly implemented in letters and spirit. There is a massive and clinching evidence of gender bias in different walks of life. With respect to degree of prevalence of gender bias India ranks 10th out of 128 countries of the world.

The sense of insecurity, humiliation and helplessness always keep a women mum. Our whole socialisation is such that for any unsuccessful marriage which results in such violence or divorce, it is always the woman, who is held responsible. Cultural beliefs and traditions that discriminate against women may be officially discredited, but they continue to flourish at the grassroots levels. Family relations in India are governed by personal laws. The three major religious communities are—Hindu, Muslim and Christian each have their separate personal laws. They, as said before, are governed by their respective personal laws in matters of marriage, divorce, succession, adoption, guardianship and maintenance. In the laws of all the communities, women have fewer rights than that of men in corresponding situations. It is really sad that women of the minority communities in India continue to have unequal legal rights and even the women of the majority community have yet to gain complete formal equality in all aspects of family life. This is basically the problem of gender inequality.

However, inequality between men and women can take many different forms. Indeed, gender inequality is not one homogeneous phenomenon, but a collection of disparate and interlinked problems. The issue of gender inequality is one which has been publicly reverberating through society for decades. The problem of inequality in employment being one of the most pressing issues today.

The most significant factor in continued use of law to enforce patriarchal privilege is that men still control not only the legal process and the interpretation of laws, but also the subject matter and vantage point of law. It is well known that law is strictly restricted in its capacity to deliver gender justice, which in itself is contingent on the nature of law and its functioning. In this connection it is worthwhile to recall that the law itself is not a monolithic entity, which simply progresses or regresses. Historically, the development of law has been an uneven one. That is to say, more than not, what law promises on paper cannot carry through in reality. That is why law-as-legislation and law-in-practice are most of the time in contradiction with each other. To cite an example, the Indian constitution explicitly enshrines formal equality for women, but the lives and experiences of India women relentlessly continue to be characterised by substantive inequality, inequity and discrimination.

Several legal reforms have taken place since independence in India, including on equal share of daughters to property. Yet, gender equality with respect to succession or right to property remains illusive. Establishment of laws and bringing practices in conformity thereto is necessarily a long drawn out process. The government, the legislature, the judiciary, the media and civil society have to perform their roles, each in their own areas of competence and in a concerted manner for the process to be speedy and effective.

Domestic Violence. The Domestic Violence Act, 2005 has concretely dealt with the problem of domestic violence taking into consideration all the related laws and has attempted to reduce the numerous ancillary problems generally faced by such legislations. This legislation is well placed in the Indian context and social scenario, clearly reflective of the mindset of the Indian men. The Act is thus a very vital piece of legislation from the feminist point of view. The occurrence of domestic violence against women arises out of the patriarchal setup, the stereotyping of gender roles, and the distribution of power, real or perceived, in society. Following such ideology, men are believed to be stronger and more powerful than women. They control women and their lives and as a result of this power play, they may hurt women with impunity. The Domestic Violence Act was passed in furtherance of the recommendations of the United Nations Committee on the CEDAW (Convention of the Elimination of all forms of Discrimination Against Women). The

Domestic Violence Act promotes the rights of women guaranteed under Articles 14 and 15 of the Constitution of India. Domestic violence is one among several factors that hinder women in their progress, and this Act seeks to protect them from this evil. The Act deals with various forms of abuse that were either not addressed earlier, or that were addressed in ways not as broad as done here.

This piece of legislation has been long over due. It is a comprehensive law and addresses all issues related to women. It is for the first time that an Act has been passed to address women's issues in such detail. The Act is an extremely progressive one not only because it recognises women who are in a live-in-relationships but also extends protection to other women in the household, including sister and mother thus the Act includes relations of consanguinity, marriage, or through relationships in the nature of marriage, adoption, or joint family thus, 'domestic relationships' are not restricted to the marital context alone. In addition to physical violence of beating, slapping, hitting, kicking and pushing, the Act also covers sexual violence like forced intercourse, forcing his wife or mate to look at pornography or any other obscene pictures or material and child sexual abuse.

Another good thing about the Act is the fact that it deals with domestic violence regardless of the religion of the parties, as many a time wrongs are perpetrated (ab)using the protection afforded by personal laws. It is thus secular in outlook in protecting women's rights. The new law also addresses sexual abuse of children and forcing girls to marry against their wishes. This certainly proves that the new Act has been formed keeping the current relationship culture in India and the irregularities in the previous domestic violence laws in mind. It is, however, too early to predict the usefulness of this legislations to its target beneficiaries and the society as a whole.

Uniform Civil Code. In India, this term refers to the concept of an overarching Civil Law Code. A uniform civil code administers a common set of secular civil laws to govern all people, irrespective of differences in community, religion and region. This supersedes the right of citizens to be governed by different personal laws based on their religious or ethnic identity. The common areas covered by a civil code include: Personal status, rights related to acquisition and administration of property and marriage, divorce and adoption. Such codes are in place in most modern nations, but not so far in India. Here most family law is determined by the religion of the parties concerned. Hindus, Sikhs, Jains and Buddhists come under Hindu law, whereas Muslims and Christians have their own laws. Muslim law is based on the Shariat.

The passage of the Hindu Code Bills in the 1950s marked a turning point in the history of the Muslim Personal Law. Until this time, Muslim Personal Law had existed side by side with similar religious laws for Hindus and other communities. The Hindu Code Bills were a series of laws aimed at thoroughly secularising the Hindu community and bringing its laws up to modern times. The affect of the Hindu Marriage Act was to prohibit polygamy and to increase the right of the divorced wife to maintenance or alimony. The act applied to everyone in India except Muslims, Christians, Parsees, and Jews. Since Jews and Parsees were a very small minority, and since Christians were governed under an already modern or progressive law, Muslims remained the only large community with a distinct religious law that had not been amended to reflect modern concepts.

When the Indian government ratified the CEDAW (Convention of the Elimination of all forms of Discrimination Against Women) in 1993, it modified laws that were created under the colonial administration. This brought the secular-Muslim divide created after independence into sharp focus. As a matter of fact, the Constitution of India contains in it a series of contradictions that have made it difficult for the government of India to reform or dismantle Islamic personal law. India's leaders at the time of framing of constitution for republic India wanted a secular constitution on the model of a Western democracy. But, surprisingly what resulted was not secularism in the Western sense of the term, but rather a 'secular' state with religious laws for its religious groups. In India 'secular' means 'non-intervening in the matter of Islamic religion.

Those wishing to reform the Muslim Personal Law have often cited Muslim countries as examples that such reform is possible. In this regard a question is often raised that if Muslim countries can reform Muslim Personal Law, and if Western democracies have fully secular systems, then why are Indian Muslims living under laws passed in the 1930s? There are Muslims who are in favour of either doing away with the Personal Law or reforming it. Enumerable liberal Muslim intelligentsia have opined through the media that polygamy should be banned outright, women should have an easier time petitioning for a divorce, the husbands should not be able to use the triple talaq method of divorce and the maintenance be granted as it is with the non-Muslims. Yet, the old system continues to perpetuate.

In India, the experiment of personal laws for various groups has been a failure in achieving equal treatment for all citizens. The country legislated away all of the personal laws, with the exception of laws applying to Muslims who are regarded as minority. Other minorities have been brought into line along Western standards of secular and equal rights. However, out of fears of creating widespread rioting and rebellion, the government has shelved any reforms for the muslim community. It has refused to find a legal route that would enforce equal rights for over 70 million of its muslim female citizens. The vast majority of muslims led by the Jumiat-al-Ulama and other orthodox muslim groups have fought tooth and nail against any change in their Personal Law. The muslim community stubbornly rejects reform, and in essence its rejection may ensure that its privileged position is intact. Most muslims are resistant to change because they believe that any change in their personal law would result in the destruction of muslim culture in India.

Family Court. With a view to protecting possible threats to marriage, dignity of women and interests of other members in society, the Government of India introduced the system of family courts in 1984 through enactment of a legislation. The Family Courts Act 1984 was adopted as a part of the trends of legal reforms concerning women. The Act is expected to facilitate satisfactory resolution of disputes concerning the family through a forum expected to work expeditiously in a just manner and with an approach ensuring maximum welfare of society and dignity of women. Family courts are expected to deal with marriage, matrimonial dissolution, maintenance and alimony, custody, education and support of children, settlement of spousal property and guardianship and custody of child's person and property. Matters relating to will, however, are as usual dealt with by civil courts.

Every state government after the consultation with the High Court establishes a Family Court in the district. One or more judges head it and preference is given to female judges. The Family Courts Act was set up to promote conciliation and secure speedy settlement of disputes relating to marriage and family affairs, based on non-adversarial and multi-disciplinary approach. The Family Courts are expected to (i) adopt a radically different approach than that adopted in ordinary civil proceedings, and (ii) make reasonable efforts for conciliated settlement before the trial commenced, and during this stage the proceedings are to be informal. Gender sensitised personnel, including judges, social workers and other trained staff are expected to hear and resolve family related issues by eliminating the rigid rules of procedure. To preserve the informality of procedures, it was specifically laid down that the parties to a dispute were not entitled, as a matter of right, to be represented by legal practitioners. The proceedings are conducted in secret and once an agreement has been reached there would be no appeal. However, the court can seek the assistance of legal experts as amicus curiae in the interest of justice. The FCs are supposed to follow simplified rules of evidence and procedure so as to effectively deal with the family disputes, and for achieving this purpose the Code of Civil Procedure was amended. Judges responsible for bringing about conciliation are supposedly committed to the need to protect and preserve the institution of marriage and to promote the welfare of children.

CONCLUSION

The rise in the number of single member household, break-down of traditional joint family system, increase in cases of divorce, individual male migration to cities for work, erosion of authority of patriarch, the attrition of traditional family values, increase in the number of working mothers in cities and single parents, rise in domestic violence and practices of dowry, neglect of children and elderly, and poor regard for family laws are enough indications of the danger that the family and ultimately society are progressively facing in India. To combat the continuing erosion of values and the institution of family, there is a need of a set of strong, consistent policies to strengthen the Indian family system. Otherwise, India would be left with no choice, but to face the same problems which are generally faced by many families of developed countries now.

To be more specific, the family needs an increased support in the areas of child care, social services, income assistance and health services than ever before. It is, however, recognised that the formulation of a comprehensive single national policy given the large size and heterogeneity of society like that of India is quite a difficult and cumbersome task.

At the same time, it is also recognised that the formulation of new norms for a desired type of family system based on modern values is perhaps fraught with serious problems of various kinds. The state may not have the required political will to do so for some political expediency or mileage. Since ours is a soft state, law does not always prove to be so effective and hence, it may be difficult to regulate the Indian family system through a formal public policy. Increasing state intervention in an informal organisation like family may be unpalatable to many and it could be counterproductive as well. It is, however, not argued that the development of a national family policy would be an exercise in futility. In fact, in view of problems of various kinds and possible challenges of future there is a need of Family Policy Council in each state of India to conduct policy analysis, promote intergenerational solidarity, facilitate strategic leadership involvement and influence public opinion. It should be an autonomous entity with no link with the state except for financial aid and it should have a uniform purpose: helping family in responsible parenthood, serving as a voice for the family and assisting advocates for family ideals who aim to recapture the moral and intellectual high ground in the public arena.

It is recognised that under the prevailing circumstances the civil society can play a more crucial and effective role than the state. In any case, because of rising individualism, competitiveness and openness in society and ever-increasing aspirations for higher attainments in life coupled with greater autonomy of individuals in society, an ideal family life may be a distant dream. Wittingly or unwittingly the people should by and large remain prepared to pay the likely prices of modern or post-modern way of life. Traditionalism is no answer, either.

NOTES AND REFERENCES

Ahluwalia, Montek Singh, 2001, *Report of the Task Force on Employment Opportunities,* New Delhi: Planning Commission, Government of India.

Anderson, Michael R., 1993, 'Islamic law and the colonial encounter in British India', in David Arnold and Peter Robb (eds.), *Institutions and Ideologies: A SOAS South Asia Reader,* London: Curzon Press Ltd., Pp. 165-185.

Bhattacharya, Prakash, 2002, 'Old age income security: Indian perspective', *Insurance Chronicle* (July).

Chen, M., 2000, *Perpetual Mourning: Widowhood in Rural India,* Delhi: Oxford University Press.

Choudhary, J. N., 1988, *Divorce in Indian Society: A Sociological Study of Marriage Disruption and Role Adjustment,* Jaipur: Printwell Publishers.

Diwan, Paras, 1983, *Family Law: Law of Marriage and Divorce in India.* New Delhi: Sterling Publishers Private Limited.

Dreze, J., 1990, 'Widows in rural India', DEP Paper No. 26. Development Economics Research Programme, STICERD, London: London School of Economics.

Driver, E.D. and A. E. Driver,1988, 'Social and demographic correlates of consanguineous marriages of south India', *Journal of Comparative Family Studies, Vol.* 19: 229-244.

George, P.O., 2000, 'Family as focus', *The Hindu Sunday Magazine,* March 12: 42-43.

Gupta, Giri Raj, 1978, 'The joint family', in Man Singh Das and Panos D. Bardis (eds.). *The Family in Asia,* London: George Allen & Unwin, Pp. 72-87.

ILO, 1996, *Child labour: Targeting the Intolerable,* Geneva: International Labour Office.

National Human Development Report, 2001, New Delhi: Planning Commission, Government of India.

Nair, P.T., 1978, *Marriage and Dowry in India,* Calcutta: Minerva Associates.

National Family Health Survey-1 (1992-93), 1994, *India: Introductory Report,* Mumbai: IIPS and ORC Macro.

National Family Health Survey-2 (1998-99), 2000, *India: Introductory Report,* Mumbai: IIPS and ORC Macro.

Saini, Debi S., 1994, 'Children of a lesser God, child labour law and compulsory primary education', *Social Action,* July-September, Vol.44. No. 3.

Singh, J. P., 1984, 'The changing household size in India', *Journal of Asian and African Studies* (The Hague), Vol. 19 (1-2): 86-95.

Myth and Reality, New Delhi: Gyan Publishing House, Pp. 56-70.

—, 2002, 'Social and cultural aspects of gender inequality and discrimination in India', *Asian Profile,* Vol. 30(2): 163-176.

—, 2004, 'The contemporary Indian family', in Bert N. Adams and Jan Trost (Eds.), *Handbook of World Families,* California: Sage Publications Inc., Pp. 129-166.

—, 2005, 'Dowry in India: A search for new social identity', *The Eastern Anthropologist,* Vol 58 (2), April-June, 199-220.

Singh, K.S., 1997, *The Scheduled Tribes* (People of India, Vol. III), New Delhi: Oxford University Press.

Skolnick, Arlene and Skolnick, Jerome H., 1980, *Family in Transition,* Boston: Little, Brown and Company. UN, 2008, *World Population Prospects: The 2008 Revision,* Population Division of the Department of Economic and Social Affairs of the United Nations Secretariat.

UNC, 1997, *Uttar Pradesh Male Reproductive Health Survey 1995-96* (The EVALUATION Project), Chapel Hill, NC: Carolina Population Center, University of North Carolina at Chapel Hill.

WHO (Department of Health Promotion), 2002, 'Health and aging: A discussion paper,' Second United Nations Assembly on Aging, Madrid (Spain), April.

BIBLIOGRAPHY

Alwin, D. (1990), Historical changes in parental orientations to children, *Sociological Studies of Child Development*, Vol. 3, pp. 65-86.

Alwin, D.F. (1992), Attitude development in adulthood: the role of generational and life-cycle factors. Paper presented at the symposium *Dynamics of cohort and generations research*, Utrecht, The Netherlands, December 12-14, 1991.

Alwin, D.F. and R.J. McCammon (2003), Generations, Cohorts, and Social Change. In J.T. Mortimer and M.J. Shanahan (Eds.), *Handbook of the Life Course*. New York: Kluwer Academic/Plenum Publishers. pp. 23-49.

Bandura, A. (1991), *Social cognitive theory of self-regulation. Organisational Behaviour and Human Decision Processes*, Vol. 50, pp. 248-287.

Bandura, A. (1997), *Self-efficacy: The exercise of contro*l. New York: W.H. Freeman.

Coppola, L. (2003), *Education and union formation as simultaneous processes in Italy and Spain*, Max Planck Institute for Demographic Research (MPIDR), Working Paper, WP 2003-026, July 2003, Rostock, Germany.

Corijn, M. and E. Klijzing (eds.). 2001. *Transitions to adulthood in Europe. European Studies of Population*, Vol. 10, Kluwer Academic Publishers, Dordrecht.

D'Andrade, R.G. (1984), Cultural meaning systems. In: R.A.Schweder and R.A. Levine (eds.,), *Culture theory. Essays on mind, self and emotion.* Cambridge University Press. Cambridge, pp. 88-119.

D'Andrade, R.G. (1992), Schemas and motivation. In: R.G. D'Andrade and C. Strauss (eds.), *Human motives and cultural models.* Cambridge University Press, Cambridge, pp. 23-44.

D'Andrade, R.G. (1995), *The development of cognitive anthropology.* Cambridge University Press, Cambridge.

Das Gupta, M. (1996) Life Course Perspectives on Women's Autonomy and Health Outcomes. *Health Transition Review*, Supplement 6, pp. 213-231.

Elder, G.H., Jr., M.K. Johnson, and R. Crosnoe (2003), The Emergence and Development of the Life Course. In: *Handbook of the Life Course*, by J.T. Mortimer and M. J. Shanahan (eds.), Howard Kaplan, series editor, Plenum: New York.

Ember, C.R. and M. Ember (2001), *Cross-cultural research methods.* New York: Rowman & Littlefield Publishers, Inc.

Gadourek, I. (1982), *Social Change as redefinition of roles. A study of structural and causal relationships in the Netherlands of the 'seventies'*, Van Gorcum, Assen, The Netherlands.

Gauntlett, D. (2002), *Media, Gender and Identity: An Introduction*, Routledge, London and New York.

Gerson, K. (1985), *Hard Choices: How women decide about work, career and motherhood.* University of California.

Hutter, I. (1998), Reproductive health and child spacing in rural South India; contribution to a reorientation of population policies in India. A background paper to the IDPAD project. *Demographic Reports* 23, Population Research Centre, Groningen.

Hutter, I., B.M.Ramesh, K.T.Rajarama and P.Ritti (2002), Reproductive health and child spacing in rural South India; basic report of the in-depth interviews, female and male perspectives. *Demographic Reports* 27, Population Research Centre, University of Groningen.

Ingham R., I. Vanwesenbeeck, and D. Kirkland (1999), Interviewing on sensitive topics. In A. Memon and R.Bull (eds.,), *Handbook of the Psychology of Interviewing.* John Wiley and Sons Ltd.

Jejeebhoy, S.J. and S. Kulkarni (1989), Demand for children and reproductive motivation. In: S.N.Singh., M.K.Premi, P.S.Bhatia and A.Bose (ed.,), *Population transition in India*, Vol. 2. B.R. Publishing Corporation, Delhi, pp. 107-123.

Kapadia, K.M. (1965), *Marriage and Family in India*, Oxford University Press, London.

Kapur, P. (1970), *Marriage and the working women in India*. Vikas Publications, New Delhi.

Lesthaeghe, R. (2000), Europe's demographic issues: Fertility, household formation and replacement migration. Paper presented at the conference *Population studies in Britain and in the Netherlands*, Utrecht, 31st Aug and 1st Sept. 2000.

Lesthaeghe, R. (2001), Postponement and Recuperation: Recent fertility trends and forecasts in six Western European countries. Paper presented at the IUSSP Seminar, *International perspectives on low fertility: Trends, theories and policies*, Tokyo, 21-23 March 2001.

Lesthaeghe, R. and C. Vanderhoeft (2001), Ready, willing, and able: a conceptualisation of transitions to new behavioural forms. In: J.B. Casterline (ed.), *Diffusion Processes and Fertility Transition: Selected Perspectives*, Committee on Population National Research Council, Washington, DC: National Academy Press, pp.240-264.

Morgan, P.S. and R. B. King (2001), Why have children in the 21st century? Biological predisposition, social coercion, rational choice. *European Journal of Population*. 17 (1): pp. 3-20.

Mouzelis, N. (1991), Modernity: a non-European conceptualisation, *British Journal of Sociology*, Routledge, (part of Taylor and Francis Group), 1 March 1999, vol. 50, no. 1, pp. 141-159.

Mydral, A. and V. Klien. (1956), *Women's Two Roles: Home and Work*. London: Routledge and Kegan Paul.

Narayana, G. (1982), Job analysis of workload assessment of female workers in India, *ASCI Journal of Management*, 11 (2), pp. 99-109.

National Education Policy (1992), Ministry of Education, Government of India, New Delhi.

NFHS (1992-1993), *National Family Health Survey, Karnataka Report*. International Institute of Population Sciences, Bombay, India.

Runyan, W.M. (1984), The life course as a theoretical orientation. In: W.M.Runyan (ed.), *Life histories and psychobiography. Explorations in theory and method*. New York, Oxford University Press.

Ryder, N.B. (1985), The cohort concept in the study of social change, In: W.M.Mason and S.E.Fienberg, (eds.), *Cohort Analysis in Social Research*. Springer Verlag: New York. Reprinted from American Sociological Review, 30 (1965), p. 843-861.

Saberwal, Satish 1982. 'Uncertain Transplants: Anthropology and Sociology in India', in T.K. Oommen and Partha Mukherji (eds). *Indian Sociology: Reflections and Introspections.* Bombay: Popular Prakashan. 1986. pp. 214-232.

Saran, A.K. 1958. 'India'. In J.S. Roucek (ed). *Contemporary Sociology.* New York: Philosophical Library. pp.1013-34.

—, 1962. Review of '*Contributions to Indian Sociology* No. IV'. *Eastern Anthropologist.* V. 15. N.1. (Jan-Apr). pp. 53-68.

Sarkar, Benoy Kumar 1985. *The Positive Background of Hindu Sociology.* (Reprinted). Delhi: Motilal Banarasidas.

Schokkaert, E., and L. Van Ootegem. 1990. *Sen's Concept of the Living Standard Applied to the Belgian Unemployed. Recherches Economques de Louvain* 56.

Seal, Brajendranath 1985. *The Positive Sciences of the Ancient Hindus.* (Reprinted) Delhi: Motilal Banarasidas.

Sen, Amartya. 1980. *Equality of What? In Tanner Lectures on Human Values,* vol. I, edited by S. McMurrin. Cambridge: Cambridge University Press, and Salt Lake City: University of Utah Press.

Shah, Mihir 1985. 'The Kaniatchi Form of Labour'. *Economic and Political Weekly.* (Review of Political Economy). V. 20. N.30. pp. PE65-PE78.

Shils, Edward 1961. 'The Intellectual Between Tradition and Modernity: The Indian Situation'. *Comparative Studies in Society and History.* Supplement 1. pp. 1-120.

Singer, Milton 1972. *When A Great Tradition Modernises: An Anthropological Approach to Indian Civilisation.* New York: Praeger.

Singh, Yogendra 1973. *Modernisation of Indian Tradition.* (2nd printing 1977). Faridabad, Haryana: Thompson Press.

Srinivas, M.N. 1971a. *Social Change in Modern India.* Berkeley: University of California Press. (First published 1966, fifth printing).

—, 1971b. 'Modernisation: A Few Queries'. In A.R. Desai (ed). *Essays on Modernisation of Underdeveloped Societies.* Bombay: Thacker & Co..V.1. pp.149-58.

—, 1992. *On Living in a Revolution and other Essays*, Delhi: Oxford University Press.

—, 1994. *The Dominant Caste and Other Essays.* (Revised and enlarged Oxford India Paperbacks edition). Delhi: Oxford University Press.

—, 1996. 'Indian anthropologists and the study of Indian society'. *Economic and Political Weekly.* V.31. N.11. pp.656-657.

Srinivas, M.N. and M.N. Panini 1973: 'The Development of Sociology and Social Anthropology in India'. In T.K.Oommen and Partha Mukherji (eds) *Indian Sociology: Reflections and Introspections.* Bombay: Popular Prakashan.1986. pp.16-55.

Strauss, C. and N. Quinn (1997), A cognitive theory of cultural meaning. Publication of the Society for Psychological Anthropology. Cambridge University Press.

Tandon, R.K. (1998), *Women in Modern India*, Indian Publishers Distributors, Delhi. Thornton, A., W.G.Axinn and J.D. Teachman (1995), The influence of school enrollment and accumulation on cohabitation and marriage in early adulthood, *American Sociological Review.* 60(5): 762-774.

Thorner, Alice 1982. 'Semi-Feudalism or Capitalism? Contemporary Debatê on Classes and Modes of Production in India'. *Economic and Political Weekly.* V.17. N.49, pp.1961-78; N.50, pp.1993-99; and N.51, pp. 2061-66.

Thorner, Daniel 1980. *The Shaping of Modern India.* New Delhi: Sameeksha Trust and Allied Publishers.

Tinker, Irene, ed. 1990. *Persistent Deprivations.* New York: Oxford University Press.

Uberoi, Patricia (ed.) 1996. *Social Reform, Sexuality and the State.* New Delhi: Sage Publications.

Vlassoff, C. (1996), Against the odds: The changing impact of schooling on female autonomy and fertility in an Indian village, in R. Jeffery and A.M. Basu (eds.), *Girls' Schooling, Women's autonomy and fertility change in South Asia,* Sage Publications, New Delhi.

Wengraf, T. (2001), *Qualitative Research Interviewing Biographic Narrative and Semi-Structured Methods*. London: Sage Publications.

Westoff, C.F. (1992), *Age at marriage, age at birth and fertility in Africa*. World Bank Technical Paper No. 169. Washington D.C.: The World Bank.

Williams, Raymond 1983. *Keywords: A Vocabulary of Culture and Society.* (Revised edition). New York: Oxford University Press.

—, 1989. *The Politics of Modernism: Against the New Conformists.* London: Verso.

Wolfe, Marshall. 1994. *Some Paradoxes of Social Exclusion. Discussion Paper 63*. Geneva: International Institute of Labour Studies.

World Bank. 1993. *The East Asian Miracle. Oxford:* Oxford University Press.

Weiner, Myron (ed.) 1966. *Modernisation: The Dynamics of Growth.* New York: Basic Books.

Yunus, Mohammad. 1998. *Statement. Asian Development Bank Seminar on Inclusion or Exclusion: Social Development Challenges for Asia and Europe*, Geneva, 27 April.

INDEX

D

E

F

P

R

S

T

U

V

W

Y